Rethinking Intelligence

About the Authors

Ashok K. Srivastava, Ph.D., is Reader in Educational Psychology in the Department of Educational Research and Policy Perspective, National Council of Educational Research and Training (NCERT), New Delhi. After earning a doctorate in Psychology from Utkal University, he taught at North-Eastern Hill University. During his academic career spanning over two decades, he has been associated with designing courses and training teacher educators in educational psychology, research methodology and action research methodology. In addition to publishing more than 35 papers in international and national journals, he has authored or edited *Conflicts and Their Resolutions, Readings on Child and Adolescent Psychology,* and *Child Development: The Indian Perspective.* His forthcoming work is a review chapter on Dynamics of Schooling for the Fifth Survey of Psychological Research, sponsored by the Indian Council of Social Science Research. He can be contacted at ashokksrivastava@yahoo.com.

Girishwar Misra, Ph.D., is Professor and former Head, Department of Psychology, and Dean Faculty of Arts, University of Delhi. He has been Fulbright Fellow at Swarthmore College and the University of Michigan. During his academic career spanning over three decades, he has previously taught at the Universities of Bhopal, Allahabad and Gorakhpur. The Government of Madhya Pradesh conferred upon him the Radhakrishnan and Dr. Hari Singh Gaur Awards. Professor Misra has authored or edited *Psychological Consequences of Prolonged Deprivation, Deprivation: Its Social Roots and Psychological Consequences, Applied social Psychology in India, Perspectives on Indigenous Psychology, Psychological Perspectives on Stress and Health, Psychology of Poverty and Social Disadvantage, Contributions to Psychology in India and Psychology and Societal Development.* He has been President and Convener of the National Academy of Psychology, India. He is currently editing its journal *Psychological Studies.* He can be contacted at misragirishwar@gmail.com.

Rethinking Intelligence

Conceptualising Human Competence in Cultural Context

ASHOK K. SRIVASTAVA
National Council of Educational Research and Training, New Delhi

and

GIRISHWAR MISRA
University of Delhi, Delhi

CONCEPT PUBLISHING COMPANY, NEW DELHI-110059

Cataloging in Publication Data—DK
Courtesy: D.K. Agencies (P) Ltd. <docinfo@dkagencies.com>

Srivastava, Ashok K. (Ashok Kumar), 1957-
Rethinking intelligence : conceptualising human competence in cultural context / Ashok K. Srivastava and Girishwar Misra.
p. cm.
With reference to India.
Includes bibliographical references (p.)
Includes index.
ISBN 8180693392

1. Social intelligence—India. 2. Intelligence tests—India. I. Title.

DDC 153.930 954 22

ISBN 81-8069-339-2

First Published 2007

Published and Printed by
Ashok Kumar Mittal
Concept Publishing Company,
A/15-16, Commercial Block, Mohan Garden,
New Delhi-110059 (INDIA)

Phones : 25351460, 25351794
Fax : 091-11-25357103
Email : publishing@conceptpub.com

Foreword

Human competence instead of IQ as a subtitle places this book as a progressive and contemporary treatise on intelligence. Indian research of the last century on intelligence was lagging behind advancements in both theory and test construction in Euro-American literature. This book has been successful in correcting that situation. At the same time, the book is very much concerned with work on intelligence in India, work that stems from both traditional Indian philosophy and empirical research. In this sense, parapharasing one of Mahatma Gandhi's statements, the authors have allowed international research ideas blow through their doors and windows freely, but have refused to be blown off their feet. The result is highly satisfactory, a book that's not stuffy and insular to contemporary winds of change, and yet records some selected contributions that are essentially sensitive and clearly unique to the Indian context.

The first two chapters of the book review classical and contemporary views of intelligence. This is followed by a review of intelligence research in India. Next two chapters are concerned with the references to intelligence in essentially traditional Indian philosophic and religious texts. The text reports an excellent empirical study concerned with 'lay people's view of intelligence'. The last chapter, chapter 7, is entitled epilogue; it highlights the major ideas contained in the previous chapter. It reminds the reader that in the Indian context, character and personality is as much a part of an intelligent person as sheer quickness in thinking and academic knowledge. Some implications for educational practices are then discussed. The epilogue ends with comments on cross-cultural testing of intelligence.

Rather than reviewing the contents of the chapter in some detail, in my foreword, I will focus on some aspects of a theme that is so central to the book, conceptualization of intelligence beyond IQ. There are three faces of Assessment:

1. Assess performance "What can she do?"
2. Explain Processes "How did she think about it?" and
3. Intervention "Can you help her think better?"

IQ tests can provide only the first, and even that is not too satisfactory as the norms may discriminate against minority children especially such children who have a cultural disadvantage. Further IQ cannot have an explanatory value nor are the results of IQ-like tests easily interpreted mainly because they lack a theory beyond 'general ability'. This concept of general ability is not useful. It cannot reveal processes which a child uses in solving the problems in the test.

One of the most important goals of any theory such as the Planning-Attention-Simultaneous-Successive (PASS) and its measure, Cognitive Assessment System (CAS), is to merge theory and application. By doing so,

— Theory can direct test interpretation
— Theory gives a perspective to view children's successes and problems
— Theory can guide intervention

PASS is a multiple view of intelligence instead of general ability view, which is assumed in the typical IQ test. In spite of these limitations, the IQ tests are used in India, and often lack psychometric properties in standardization and norming. Most of the tests are derived from Binet and Wechsler. As is known, IQ tests have not changed since 1905 (Binet) and 1939 (Wechsler).

It is obvious that new tests driven by theory such as PASS must be widely used replacing the standard IQ tests. This will stimulate research into cognitive processes, especially difficulties in processing among special populations—some 15-20 per cent will benefit from assessment of cognitive processes followed by interventions to ameliorate the cognitive deficit.

Much has been written about administration of culturally inappropriate tests in India. However, when a test such as CAS does not contain either items from school achievement and general knowledge, the risk of culturally inappropriateness is much reduced. I fully sympathize with those who object to a simple translation of a test of intelligence with alien content. I would urge the indigenous test developers to go a step further and re-examine the theoretical assumption behind the alien test. Sometimes a search for such assumption ends in failure. That is a good reason to abandon the translation and adaptation of the test. Sometimes the theoretical assumptions have become invalid in view of contemporary psychological theories. Remember that a test can never be culture free. All higher mental activities are influenced by culture of the thinker. The socio-historical view of mental activities has become quite acceptable. Then how does one use tests developed in one culture (such as in the so-called Hindi-belt) to another cultural region (e.g., Tamil Nadu)? Further dissections of cultural practices (Adivasi and among adivasi population, further divisions are necessary) would become untenable although it may breed numerous thesis topics for Master's degree.

A partial solution may be suggested: To decrease domain-specificity of the test and at the same time enhancing its domain-generality. PASS theory, for example, originates in neuropsychology and cognitive psychology, is supported by domain-general functional divisions of the brain. It's tests (CAS) are construct validated across several countries and languages.

I will end this foreword by elaborating on the last point—construct validity and cross-cultural applications, but only briefly, before I do that, let me add that as long as a theory of human intellectual competence yields measurable norms, relates to processes behind performances on the tests, and can guide interventional programmes based on that theory, it will be useful. Four examples of the application of CAS in four different populations are given below. These include a sample of high and low achieving children in India (Mumbai), normal and epileptic children in Spain (Catalunya), normal school children in Japan (Western Japan) and Canadian aboriginal children in a reservation in Western Canada. The CAS yields four major cognitive processing scores, which are Planning, Attention, Simultaneous and Successive processing as mentioned before. In the sample from India, Jagruti Sarnath compared high and low achieving children and showed a consistently higher score in each of the 4 CAS scales for the high achieving group, which was expected. However, what is particularly interesting for cross-cultural psychology is that both groups exceeded the American norm for Sucessive processing, scoring above a standard score of 100. This is perhaps consistent with the cultural emphasis on immediate memory and working memory (Successive scale measure both) in Indian schools. The Spanish sample was slightly higher than American norms for Simultaneous processing. However, the important finding related to the contrast between normal and epileptic children; the latter group was distinctly lower in Successive processing. In terms of construct validity, the results are consistent with previous findings that epileptic children in general (we assumed that most were diagnosed as temporal lobe epilepsy) show impairment in Successive processing. The Japanese sample exceeded American norms for Simultaneous processing by one standard deviation. Consistent with the emphasis on visual-spatial processing in Japanese culture, and the way Japanese children learn to write Kanji characters, their superiority in Simultaneous processing is not a surprise. Finally, the Canadian aboriginal children usually do not grow up in a verbal and literate culture. Their traditional mode of learning is through modelling and imitation, through doing rather than learning a set of verbal rules, and reading books that promote Successive processing. They were found to be generally low in Successive processing.

The book by Srivastava and Misra contains several warnings against using culturally inappropriate tests of human competence. The studies across the four cultures introduce an interesting point to discuss—As long as we are aware of the cultural differences that might be expected, and our studies test the construct validity of the measures we are using, even obvious transgression of rules in those warnings can give us insightful results.

J.P. Das
University of Alberta
Edmonton, Canada

Acknowledgements

The research on which this monograph is based was possible with the support from Educational Research and Innovations Committee (ERIC) research grant of the National Council of Educational Research and Training (NCERT), New Delhi.

Parts of this research were presented at the annual conventions of the National Academy of Psychology (NAOP) at Bhubaneswar (1997), and also as an invited address at the 2003 convention of NAOP held at Bhubaneswar. Prof. Sudhakar Rath, the then Head of the Department of Psychology, Utkal University, extended the invitation. These presentations and discussions helped in shaping this work.

Some parts of this work were presented at the International Congress of the International Association of Cross-Cultural Psychology (IACCP), Bellingham, Seattle (1998). It was included in the subsequent volume of the conference proceedings *Merging Past, Present, and Future in Cross-Cultural Psychology* edited by Walter Lonner and his colleagues (1999, Swets & Zeitlinger). A contribution was also made to the International Congress of Psychology at Stockholm (2000) and International Association of Cross-Cultural Psychology, Warsaw (2000). It is included in the IACCP proceedings *New Directions in Cross-Cultural Psychology* (2002, WIPP) edited by Pawel Boski and his colleagues. Participation in these conferences was possible by the support from DST and ARTS. Prof. John Adair of Manitoba University was generous to extend the necessary help to facilitate attending the IACCP through ARTS grant.

Parts of this research have been earlier published in various journals including *Psychology and Developing Societies* (Sage), *Journal of Indian Psychology, Indian Psychological Review, Indian Educational Review, Indian Psychological Abstracts and Reviews*

(Sage). We are grateful to the reviewers and editors for critical comments and inputs.

The feedback from Professors Durganand Sinha (late), J.P. Das, B.N. Puhan, Janak Pandey, and G.C. Gupta has been helpful in shaping this work.

The study on lay people was a multicentric collaborative effort in which Prof. P. Prakash, Mysore University, Mysore; Prof. B.G. Singh, Pt. R.S. University, Raipur; Prof. Adesh Agarwal, Gorakhpur University, Gorakhpur; and Dr. Shah Alam, Aligarh Muslim University participated as co-researchers. We take this opportunity to express our thanks to them. It was due to the tiring efforts of Ms Kamalesh Panwar that the data collected from different centres could be given a shape.

Last but not the least we place on record our deep appreciation and sense of gratefulness to the participants who provided data and inputs to construct lay people's perspective on intelligence.

Ashok K. Srivastava
Girishwar Misra

Contents

1

Introduction

The present study grew out of authors' personal experiences, dissatisfaction with the study of human intelligence in general and the way it has been shaped in the Indian context, in particular. As a humble beginning, it took the form of critique and reconstruction of intelligence in a manner that respects the diversity in cultural experiences and is open to the contemporary scholarship in the field. In order to help readers to place the work in a proper perspective it seems worthwhile to briefly situate it in the narrative of research efforts in the field of intelligence.

The study of intelligence and the history of intelligence testing presents a strange story. Nearly a century ago, Alfred Binet was asked to understand the problems of mentally retarded children in the school setting of Paris. Entrusted with this assignment, he devised a way to distinguish such children from those who were doing well in the school and academics. The test to assess intelligence through some standardized instrument provided a handy tool to serve many purposes and it became a major impetus for research on intelligence. Without bothering much about the concept itself, the measurement efforts led to establishment of industries for this purpose. The research proliferated and a variety of accounts of 'intelligence' were put forward and different measures of intelligence gained popularity in research and professional world of psychological practice.

Basic to this entire endeavour was a model of the individual striving to excel in meeting the mental demands. It was an individualistic, functional, and pragmatic position that rendered the process of intelligence into an objective score of a person that may be treated like any other aspect of physical reality. Inherent in almost all the early theoretical models of intelligence has been the idea that intelligence is primarily something inside person, an ability largely inscribed in cortical processes that one carries as an innate gift. It was viewed, as a cognitive process, invoking the mental operations engaging abstraction, reasoning, logic, calculation and the like.

The emerging picture of intelligence, as a context free mental/intellectual functioning, gained legitimacy, and eventually got institutionalized in the academic and applied world. As an internal and centrally located process, it was thought to be primarily of neuro-physiological kind of stuff. The researchers became seriously engaged in figuring out its essential ingredients or components. While there could not be any consensus on the nature of intelligence, the professional socialization over the years was so strong that the absence of conceptual clarity could hardly deter the practices of intelligence testing and there was a boom in the related research. Perhaps, such a proliferation of research has no parallel in the history of the discipline of psychology.

The faith of these scientists was so strong that they could afford to ignore other developments in the discipline. The concept of IQ was claimed to be one of the most powerful contributions from psychology to society. Parents, employers, clinicians and trainers experienced a sense of empowerment in using intelligence tests. Intelligence, reified through the technology of intelligence tests, furnished a concrete, solid and dependable account of the potential and performance of a person. Being an objective and dependable summary representation of a person's potential of one's intellectual endowment, IQ has survived and the intelligence testing industry flourished. Considered as a predictor of success in life, the efforts have started to boost the level of IQ. Studies started about heretibility or genetic determination and environmental modifiability of intelligence. These developments had socio-political and economic overtones too.

The research efforts, however, could not succeed in clarifying the composition of intelligence nor there has been any cumulative achievement in deciphering the basic or core of intelligence during the century old saga of intelligence research. Today we have larger number of theories of intelligence than what we used to have in the past. They differ not only in the number of components of intelligence but also in defining and describing what it is. Perhaps the researchers were working with different metaphors of mind in which theories and concepts across the metaphors were incommensurate. The theories and concepts evolving in the traditions of different metaphors informed our understanding of intelligence in diverse ways.

Theoretically the discourse about intelligence could not keep itself apart from the developments ensuing in other domains of psychology. Studies of cognitive development in Piagetian, post-Piagetian, Vygotskyian and other traditions, studies in cross-cultural psychology and cultural psychology, and developments in the disciplines of cognitive science, neuroscience, artificial intelligence and consciousness studies have brought into focus the fact that the monolithic view of intelligence is not only insufficient but also undermines the shared and contextual nature of intelligence which owes a lot to the meanings and practices of diverse cultures. During the past two decades the call given by leading psychologists to map multiple intelligences, practical intelligence, successful intelligence, emotional intelligence, creative intelligence, spiritual intelligence and wisdom clearly reflects a strong urge to outgrow the classical model of intelligence and develop alternative vision of human competence.

The study of intelligence has also been extended to non-Western cultural settings. The emerging understanding tends to suggest that the technological intelligence and speed are not universally valued qualities of intelligence. In the Latin, African and Asian cultures the social dimensions too are important. Human intelligence shows diversity and various segments of population like lay people, illiterate and common masses too have many things to offer. Humanity has lived successfully for many thousand years than the discipline of psychology and as such it can certainly enrich our understanding of human competence in its various forms. As Richard Nisbett (2003) in *The Geography of Thought* persuasively argues thought is culturally structured. The Asian (Chinese) people think globally (circular/cyclical), and the Europeans analytically (linear).

Intelligence is often conceptualized and assessed according to Western standards, which do not do justice with the competencies and skills that are valued in other cultures. It may be noted that this does not mean that cultures are, static and homogeneous, and people belonging to one culture shall share one style of thinking. In fact schooling and industrialization do have certain homogenizing effects. Thus it is the experience of a particular kind that shapes intelligence rather than mere living in a cultural (geographical) setting. People may or may not be the same in their experiential content in a given culture.

In the Indian context, where psychology grew in the Western tradition of research, intelligence has a history of implantation of Western models. Many of its pioneers were trained at the Euro-American centres of excellence. They developed intelligence tests within the borrowed Western theoretical frameworks without questioning their relevance and examining the claims for universality. Perhaps, the novelty of the exercise was attractive and positivist-empiricist meta theory was dominant. This did not allow thinking beyond the given mould of thought. It is, therefore, not very surprising that adaptation of Western intelligence tests became an important component of research programmes. The mainstream research in the field of intelligence continued with the psychometric approach without any dialogue with the developments in other related areas.

The psychometric view dominated the scene and still serves the purpose of articulating the received or official view. The researchers have been vigorously pursuing the antecedents, correlates and consequences of intelligence, which for all practical purposes was reduced to an equivalent of IQ. They were relating performance on various intelligence tests for various groups. Intelligence test has become a need of researcher and society. Anything that is available is used uncritically. Other voices were marginalized and the condition continues.

The present research has far-reaching implications in the area of conceptualization and assessment of cognitive functions leading to alternate and culturally appropriate perspective on intellectual functioning and its assessment. The two broad objectives of the study were: (a) to document, analyze and present the indigenous thought, as evident in Indian scholarly and folk traditions, and (b) to examine the socio-cultural construction of intelligence through the study of people's perspectives. The study attempted to address the following two broad sets of research questions.

1. What are the salient indigenous notions of intelligence available in the Indian scholarly and folk or popular traditions? How far they enable psychologists to develop a viable concept of intelligence? In which way these notions complement, contradict and extend the prevailing view of intelligence?
2. How does the lay people in the contemporary Indian society conceptualize intelligence? What are the sub-cultural variations in the perspectives of the lay people coming from different eco-cultural backgrounds?

To answer these research questions, a systematic attempt was made to analyze Sanskrit *Suktis* and Hindi proverbs employing content analysis procedure. Also, a theoretical analysis of the discourse on wisdom as contained in *Bhagavad Gita* (or Song of the Blessed One), which consisted of 700 stanzas, was carried out. Further, empirical studies of lay people's everyday understanding and use of intelligence were conducted at five different centres in India representing various age, gender, and eco-cultural groups. The focus was on listing behaviours of intelligent persons and some other related issues, and assessing people's notion of intelligence on the basis of descriptions of pertinent situations.

The present volume is organized in eight chapters. The first chapter introduces the topic. The second chapter presents a historical overview of the classical conceptualization of intelligence. Chapter three contains an account of the contemporary approach towards understanding intelligence. The fourth chapter documents an overview of research on intelligence in India. The focus of chapter five is on the perspective of the traditional Indian notion of intelligence. It is done through an analysis of Sanskrit *Suktis* and Hindi proverbs. Chapter six is devoted to the analysis of *Bhagavad Gita,* which is essentially a *Samkhya Yoga* treatise on Wisdom. Chapter seven presents the findings of a multicentric study of lay people's understanding and use of intelligence. The last chapter summarizes the work and examines certain implications of the research. The emerging notion has been termed as integral intelligence.

2

Classical Conceptualisation of Intelligence

INTRODUCTION

In recent years, conceptualisation of intelligence and its measurement is passing through an exciting phase. The traditional approaches are facing challenges from different quarters. The major challenges include (a) the impact of information science and technology, (b) new directions in research on learning vis-à-vis educational processes, (c) expansion of the discourse on intelligence by incorporating new domains, and (d) developments in the study of culture—cognition relationships. Already there are manifest concerns about the local, cultural, and indigenous variations in the expression of intelligence. In order to create a context for appraising these developments this chapter presents an overview of some of the classical views on intelligence in the field of psychology.

Since long, understanding the intellective abilities, competencies and skills has been recognized as one of the important demands on societal systems evolved around the globe. Currently its assessment has become an integral part of the arrangements made to efficiently carry out the everyday affairs in different spheres of life in most of the modern societies. It is, therefore, not surprising to notice a close correspondence between the individual and the society in respect to the valuation of functions and activities in the domain of intellective functions. As Vygotsky (1978) has argued, the roots of intellectual processes and skills are situated in the socio-cultural matrix of the people in a society during a given socio-historical period. This view is also echoed in several recent formulations of development (Brody, 1997; Harkness & Super, 1993; Haslam & Baron, 1994; Lave & Weneger, 1991). Even cultural variations in the conceptualization of mind have been documented (Lillard, 1998). In this context, Valsiner (1989) has argued that all human psychological processes are social in nature. This indicates that human thinking shares an interdependent relationship with the social practices and folk models of mind prevailing in a given society. It is now firmly believed that mind rarely works alone. The different types of intelligence revealed through various practices are distributed—across minds, persons, and the environments, both natural and artificial. Thus intelligence is accomplished rather than possessed (Pea, 1993). These views are against the representational position on knowledge and favour a constructionist perspective. The observations of cultural construction of cognitive functions often indicate a need to study the nature and use of cognitive processes as situated in context. These developments indicate that the traditional psychometric approach to intelligence is insufficient. It is gradually being replaced by a processual approach with emphasis on intelligence as grounded in the socio-cultural context.

Notwithstanding the above observations, the study of intelligence, with few exceptions, has been preoccupied with the modes of its assessment as an entity within a positivist framework. This has generated tools and instruments for determining a person's intelligence—a summary statement of performance and/or potentials—relative to the normative groups. The scores on such psychological tests—IQs—have assumed decisive role in a variety of practical settings. This has reinforced the academic and professional practice of assessing intelligence and using its outcomes for diagnosis, prediction and modification of intellective functions. The technology of intelligence-assessment has been commercialized and market forces are playing key role in promoting the prevailing practices of intelligence assessment.

In recent years, the relationship between culture and cognition has received renewed impetus from researchers. For a long time, however, culture remained on the margin of psychological investigations. This was quite natural in view of the natural scientific and positivist ethos of the discipline. Thus, psychological functions assumed their existence independent of the context in which they emerge or manifest and develop. They were treated as abstract and context-free. The salience and primacy of biological nature of human beings was emphasized. Culture, however, could get attention of psychologists with the advent of cross-cultural psychology that, while maintaining its stand for universalism, did provide some space for cultural variation. Thus many of the western theories were tested in non-western cultural contexts. More recently, the developments in cultural and indigenous psychologies have paved the way for relating culture with psychological functioning. The two, culture and psyche, are intertwined in such a way that they make each other up (Shweder, 1990). They are mutually constituted (Miller & Goodnow, 1995). This view stresses that mind is socially co-constructed; that is, it emerges in the course of social interaction as people participate in meaningful activities (Gauvain, 1998). An underlying assumption of this view is that people understand the world indirectly, or through mediation, rather than directly (Wertsch, Rio & Alvarez, 1995). Mediation is by nature socio-cultural, occurring on two fronts. It occurs through social processes, as interaction with others leads to socially organized ways of understanding. It also occurs culturally, in that cultures provide organized practices as well as symbolic and material tools that help shape human action. Here the status of culture in psychological investigation is not confined to a mere independent variable, rather it is constitutive. From this perspective culture informs our views of intelligence, relevant behaviours, processes, outcomes and the dynamics of its development.

Early work in cross-cultural psychology stressed the ecological context and differences in adaptive demands were used to explain cultural differences in intelligence. In contrast, the cultural psychological approach assumes that objective knowledge is culture dependent, enculturation is a creative process, and contexts are culturally interpreted. These assumptions suggest that individual psychological processes are situated in a cultural context. They question the evolutionary account of intelligence. The functionality (or demand), however, is culturally determined. Thus various cultural contexts do not differ only in the types of opportunities for intellectual development but affect the form in which cognitive potentials are realized. It has been indicated that abstract thought, the hallmark of intelligence, is valued differently in diverse cultures.

The stress on socio-cultural context demands attending to the characteristics, traits, or skills that are valued in everyday life of a given society. This necessitates examination of social representations, also known as lay theories or implicit theories, which are shared by people of a culture, passed on from one generation to the next, and imposed upon each of us without our conscious ascent. In contrast to the explicit, formal, and "scientific" explanation of a behavioural phenomenon, layman's implicit, informal and "non-scientific" explanations are derived primarily from self-observation (Bem, 1967).

Furnham (1988) has noted certain characteristics of lay theories. First, lay theories are often implicit than explicit. Second, they are rarely, if ever, presented formally and, therefore, lay theories are frequently ambiguous, incoherent and inconsistent. People can hold two mutually incompatible or contradictory ideas or beliefs at the same time and not particularly troubled by that inconsistency. Third, lay theories often rely on the principle of inductivism while scientific theories usually rely on deductivism. Inductivism suggests that people must accumulate evidence (by observation or experiment) and, therefore, make inferences. Fourth, lay theories are often correlational in nature and, therefore, cause-effect relationships cannot be inferred. Fifth, lay theories are often descriptive and content oriented while scientific theories are explanatory and process-oriented. Sixth, in their attempt to explain other's social behaviour, lay people often ignore contextual factors and prefer to locate the causes of human behaviour in an individual's personality, motives, etc. Seventh, lay people formulate theories for scientific phenomena based on information that they receive but do not generalize to abstract theoretical principles.

It may be noted that lay and scientific theories are not opposed to each other. Rather, lay theories overlap with scientific theories; they function in similar ways, indeed one may be seen as an outgrowth of the other. Lay people can and do formulate theories that are explicit, coherent and falsifiable, as do scientists who are frequently far from infallible in their own model.

Lay beliefs develop as a result of induction or experience, construction or inference, and deductions from observations, analogy or extrapolation from specific encounters, and authority or acceptance of ideas from others, the media, etc. (Sarbin, Taft, & Bailey, 1960). These beliefs serve to make the world a stable, orderly and predictable place. People's beliefs not only change over time but may be expressed differently in different situations. These beliefs serve to maintain balance and consistency in one's life and thus bolster or maintain self-esteem. They help to ensure group solidarity and provide a social or moral framework through which one comprehends new facts. Thus lay theories are more psychological than logical in nature. Different methodologies have been profitably used to explore lay theories of human behaviour including self-report tests and observation of behaviour.

In the field of intelligence, more than 50 years ago, Flugel (1947) asked 300 lay people, including housewives, civil servants, and factory workers, 16 questions about intelligence and found about 10 issues where there were major differences and only four where there was agreement. Various opinion poll type studies have been conducted in many different countries at specific points of time (Fontes *et al.*, 1983). Robert Sternberg is one of the few people who has done systematic research on lay theories of intelligence (Sternberg, Conway, Ketron, & Bernstein, 1981). Sternberg argued that ordinary lay people have definite ideas as to what intelligence actually is, and how to measure it, and that, equally, academic, scientific researchers' ideas are also firmly based in the real world. Sternberg (1982) noted:

> On the whole, the informal theories of intelligence that laymen carry around in their heads—without ever realizing that their ideas constitute theories—conform fairly closely to the most widely accepted formal theories of intelligence that scientists have constructed. That is, what psychologists

> study as intelligence seems to correspond, in general, to what people untrained in psychology mean by intelligence. On the other hand, what psychologists study correspond to only *part* of what people mean by intelligence in our society, which includes a lot more than IQ tests measure. (p. 35)

Sternberg (1985) argues that lay people's theories of intelligence overlap with but also go beyond the skills measured by tests. That is, the intelligent person is believed to solve problems well, reason clearly, think logically, have a good store of information, but is also able to balance information, and shows one's intelligence in worldly as well as academic contexts. Therefore, test of a lay theory is quite different from a scientific theory. These lay theories change over time. Furthermore, they are learnt and hence culture bound.

It may be naive to assume that there are no individual, group, sub-cultural or even cultural differences in lay people's understanding of the nature of intelligence. Anthropological and psychological studies have shown remarkable cultural differences in the meaning of the notion of intelligence (for details, refer Chapter 3).

Studies in the domain of intelligence and its assessment in India point out that, owing to prolonged colonial influence, researchers became dependent on the borrowed concepts and measures and no concerted effort could be launched to analyze intellective functions rooted in the Indian socio-cultural context. This has led to a distorted view of the field and proliferation of poor quality assessment devices. While the members of academic community have constantly reiterated these limitations, not much innovation of theoretical or methodological kind is noticeable (Kulkarni & Puhan, 1988; Misra, Sahoo, & Puhan, 1997; Srivastava, Tripathi, & Misra, 1996). Mukherjee (1997) noted that "in most Indian psycho-educational literature there is a total neglect of proper conceptualization and theoretical underpinning as well as absence of riogour in methodology" (p. 678). The psychometric characteristics of the tests developed in India leave much to be desired. At many places, reviewers of the tests on various grounds have questioned the information given in the test manual. Also, test constructors have not shown their familiarity with the recent developments related to the conceptualization of intelligence throughout the globe. There is considerable lack of initiative, programmatic research, creativity, and commitment among the researchers. Although intelligence testing in India, as Sinha (1983) has remarked, remained for long one of the most popular academic pursuits for psychologists and educationists, not much has been achieved in terms of theoretical contribution and instrument development. Also, the researchers have neglected the indigenous sources of insight available in the Indian tradition. The scholarly texts and folk wisdom are rich in terms of precepts and ideas related to intelligence.

Thus contemporary Indian research on intellective functions for long has largely been atheoretical, and instrument-dependent. In recent years works of theorists like J.P. Das, Jensen, Piaget and Witkin have received some attention and several cross-cultural investigations using age, grade, SES, and residential background have been undertaken (see Misra, 1983; Misra & Tripathi, 1998). However, all these efforts are largely confirmatory in nature and oftentimes describe and reiterate certain patterns that have already been documented in earlier studies.

The Indian scholarly and folk traditions are full of references related to the notion of intelligence. Very limited attempts so far have been done to retrieve some of these concepts, examine their significance and explore the possibility of using them in developing alternative perspectives on intelligence. In preliminary works of this kind, researchers (Das, 1994; Srivastava & Misra, 1999a, b, c, 2000; Srivastava, Tripathi, & Misra, 1995) have shown that Indian accounts of intellective concepts are fresh and pregnant with many unexplored possibilities. Also, attempts to examine the relevance of these concepts in the present changing Indian context are rare (Srivastava & Misra, 2001).

The Indian tradition emphasizes a socially constituted/embedded and a relational concept of person with a context-sensitive design of human action. It views the individual as a social being with the shared and relational notion of control. It also simultaneously subscribes to temporal and atemporal existence (*nitya* and *anitya*) of a human being (Misra & Gergen, 1993). This tradition stresses such excellences as *priyamvada* (felicitous speech), *dama* (restraint), *satyavachana* (truthfulness), *dana* (charity) and *daya* (compassion) (Mahadevan, 1978). A person showing the excellence of *priyamvada* has no eye for obstinate argumentation and also has a meticulous sense of place and time (*desa-kalavit*). The concepts of *jitendriya* (ability to manage and regulate one's body and mind), *nishkama karma* (non-attached action), *sthitprajna* (one whose intellect is stable), and the yogic and religious practices including the observance of *vratas* (fasts) refer to self-chosen restraint by the individual. Truthfulness has been another highly valued ideal in the Indian tradition. *Satyam vada; Dharman Chara* (be truthful in speech; be good and right in whatever you do) has been the motto of the Indian society. Truth was, however, inclusive of the common good and welfare of society. Human excellences such as *tyaga* (sacrifice) and *seva* (service) were also stressed in the Indian tradition (Ranganathananda, 1978). There are numerous instances when people, even in extreme situations of competition and envy, were guided by the values such as chivalry, rectitude and righteousness (for details, Raina & Srivastava, 2000).

Having a predominantly agrarian form of economy, India has witnessed the development of common characteristics and outlook with loyalty to family or clan. Interdependence, sharing and harmony with the social world have continued to operate as its core values. An Indian's behaviour is characterized by reciprocity, and strong mutual caring where emotional connectedness is viewed essential with constant flow of affect between persons. As novelist Lapierre (1986:56) remarks, "every individual in India is always linked to the rest of the social body by a network of incredible diversified ties, with the result that no one in this gigantic country.... could ever be completely abandoned". The self in India has elements of individuality as well as relationship. It is defined more in terms of a relational orientation (Misra & Giri, 1994). The child-rearing practices stress the inculcation of these values. Also, Indian parents give primacy to the familial values of children (for example, extending the family tree, service to elders and material contribution received from them) (Misra, Srivastava, & Gupta, 1999).

The Indian scenario thus locates individuality in context(s) and tries to understand it as positioned with respect to the features of the context in which it is embedded. Individuals have no independent existence; rather they are always people in the social situations where the situation and the person mutually define each other (Misra & Gergen, 1993). It may be noted that the traditional Indian culture has not been static over the years. Rather, it has been undergoing transformation under the modern influences. To Srinivas (1966), some of the changes reflect *sanskritisation* in which a person low in the social hierarchy (a lower caste person) emulates and behaves like a higher (Brahman) caste person. Secularization (or less importance to religious beliefs), modernization, industrialization, urbanization (movement of a large number of persons from rural to urban centres) and Westernization (change in the behaviour patterns resulting due to Western cultural ethos) are also taking place.

Since recent conceptualization of intelligence considers it culturally variable, it becomes essential to understand the nature of intelligence in the Indian context. The emphasis of this volume is to highlight the nature of intelligence as evident in Indian scholarly and folk literature. Also, it examines the ways this complements, contradicts and extends the prevailing view of intelligence. It further presents the results of a exploration examining the socio-cultural construction of intelligence through the exploration of people's perspective. Against this backdrop this chapter analyses the psychometric tradition of intelligence that dominated most part of the twentieth century. The trends in the use of tests in cultures other than the cultures of their origin have been discussed in the second section. Third section presents an account of the alternatives to psychological testing. Finally, the report of the APA Task Force on the status of intelligence research has been summarized.

EARLY PERSPECTIVES ON INTELLIGENCE

A perusal of the *Great Books of the Western World* (1987) indicates that at least some concept of intelligence goes back to the ancient Greeks (Sternberg, 1990a). Beginning with Homer, a sixth century B.C. writer, to John Locke, an empiricist philosopher of the nineteenth century, the dominant view about intelligence in the Western world has been that there are different *kinds* or aspects of intelligence and that people *differ* in these aspects. In general, intelligence was taken as an important natural human disposition. For example, Homer saw intelligence as "an entity", Plato as the "ability to learn", Aristotle as "quick wit", Augustine as "good qualities", Aquinas as "universal deeper understanding", Montaigne as "ability to seek out knowledge and truth", Pascal as "precise intellect and mathematical intellect", and Locke distinguished between wit and judgement. It was only Adam Smith, an economic philosopher of the nineteenth century, who traced an economic origin of the differences in talent. Immanuel Kant believed that intelligence comprised of *understanding, judgement* and *reason*. J.S. Mill was particularly interested in one facet of intellect, *i.e.*, originality. William James remarked that humans and non-humans differ in their ability to associate ideas by similarity.

The work of Esquirol (1838), a Frenchman, on mental disorders is considered to be the beginning of the modern era of mental testing. However, the term *mental test* first appeared in the work of J.M. Cattell (1890) who proposed a set of physical and mental measurements. Work on human inheritance by Darwin (1859, 1872) and Galton (1869), as well as Quetelet's (1842) applications of probability to the sphere of measurement are also landmarks in the history of human intelligence. A pre-Darwinian writer, Abercrombie (1839), foreshadowed more recent portrayals of the active, adaptive functions of "intellectual power" or reason. Porter (1891) argued that knowing is a pre-eminently active operation of the intellect, that in "knowing, we are not so much recipients as actors" (p. 61). It was argued that intelligence functioned so as to adapt a complex organism to complex environments; it acts as a "selecting agency", an efficacious instrument of survival. In this way researchers' attention came to be focused on the *modus operandi* of the phenomenon and on the process of intelligence, called cognition or intellection (Stout & Baldwin, 1901). Greater consideration was given to the practical operations of intelligence than to the analysis and comparison of its content (Dixon, Kramer & Baltes, 1985). Furthermore, this conceptualization of intelligence as an active form of "consciousness" was combined with a "genetic" (or developmental) approach (Angell, 1907; Baldwin, 1902) to psychological ontogenesis. Interestingly enough many recent writers have voiced the significance of an active, functional, and pragmatic view of intelligence (Baltes, Dittmann – Kohli, & Dixon, 1984).

The most notable advances in the early twentieth century were made in the design and production of objective methods of assessment under the influence of natural sciences which necessitated creation of concrete, objective and quantifiable reality. The first systematic attempt to develop a test of intelligence was made by Alfred Binet, a Frenchman. At the request of the French Ministry of Education, in 1904, Binet attempted to devise a method to identify children who did not benefit from regular classroom teaching and needed to be placed in special schools. Binet, with his student T. Simon, developed the first test of intelligence in 1905. The test consisted of 30 items ranging from the ability to touch one's nose or ear when asked, to the ability to draw designs from memory and define abstract concepts. Unlike Galton who reduced intelligence to sensory, perceptual, and motor processes, Binet argued that the core of intelligence consisted of more complex mental processes such as memory, imagery, comprehension, and judgment. Binet and Simon (1911) developed practical means of identifying children academically at risk. Although Binet had devised a rudimentary form of scaling, it was Stern (1912) who proposed *Intelligence Quotient (IQ)* as an indication of a person's overall mental calibre. Binet's more immediate legacy, however, was in his methods, which contributed to the growth of psychometric formulations and procedures, such as those of Spearman (1927). According to Guilford (1967), these psychometric procedures emphasized "the need for a multiple-aptitude view of intelligence" (p. 23).

Definitions of Intelligence

A functional definition, given by Boring in 1923, states that intelligence is *"what the tests test"*. Broadly, it is viewed in terms of a capacity to profit from experience and to go beyond the given to the possible. Table 2.1 contains some of the early definitions of intelligence.

Table 2.1: Definitions of Intelligence

Psychologist	*Definition*
Binet and Simon (1905)	The ability to judge well, to comprehend well, to reason well.
Spearman (1923)	General intelligence which involves mainly the education of relations and correlates.
Terman (1916)	The capacity to form concepts and to group their significance.
Thurstone (1921)	The capacity to inhibit instinctive adjustments, flexibly imagine different responses, and realize modified instinctive adjustments into overt behaviour.
Wechsler (1939)	The aggregate or global capacity of the individual to act purposefully, to think rationally, and to deal effectively with the environment.
Piaget (1972)	Adaptation to the physical and social environment.

An analysis of these definitions may indicate that intelligence consists of three general classes of skills or abilities:

- Adapting to new situations and changing task demands,
- Learning or profiting optimally from experience or training, and
- Thinking abstractly using symbols and concepts.

A further analysis will indicate that the skills mentioned in the first category also encompass the last two. For successful adaptation one needs to have the ability to learn (the complex features of the environment) and get benefit of one's past experience as well as higher-level mental abilities requiring the use of symbols and concepts (such as reasoning, problem solving, etc.).

The Computation of Intelligence Quotient or "IQ"

Ever since Binet's great success in devising tests to distinguish mentally retarded children from those with behaviour problems, intelligence testing occupied a central place in the theory and practice of the disciplines of psychology, education and human development. The tests of intelligence have been used extensively in selection, training, evaluation, and diagnosis in clinical, industrial, defence, and educational settings. These tests are based on psychometric approach and come in many forms. Some may use only verbal items, others may employ non-verbal items, still others may use a combination of verbal and non-verbal items. Some tests generate a composite score while others may also describe an individual's performance on a number of dimensions, in addition to generating a composite score. The test scores are usually converted to a scale, known as IQ scores, in which the mean is 100 and standard deviation is 15. For this a mental age equivalent to the test score is obtained which is further divided by the chronological age. It is assumed that approximately 95 per cent of the population scores within two standard deviations of the mean *i.e.*, between 70 and 130. This type of assessment obviously is based upon the assumption that human intellect is quantifiable (Brown, 1992).

The concept of mental age (MA), as proposed by Binet, has for several reasons (*e.g., equivocality, non-linearity,* and *unidimensionality*), proved to be of a weak link in the psychometric analysis of intelligence. Intelligence Quotient (IQ) has tended to be computed on the basis of relative performance within a given group (Deviation IQ), as is done in Wechsler Adult Intelligence Scale (WAIS) (Wechsler, 1958) and Wechsler Intelligence Scale for Children (WISC) (Wechsler, 1974).

The quantification of intellective functions had its roots in the theory of psychological measurement, which posited that a test score consisted of true and error components. The true score represents actual ability of the person, a quantity that is supposed to be relatively stable across equivalent tests as long as they measure the same ability. The error score may be due to various factors that may enable a person to sometimes answer correctly an item that he does not know, and sometimes to answer incorrectly an item that he knows. In other words, a true score is different from the observed score (Gulliksen, 1950). Thus, the measurement of intellective capacity, guided by this postulate, makes the observed score less dependable to a certain extent.

THEORIES OF INTELLIGENCE

A number of psychometric theories of intelligence such as the Two Factor Theory (Spearman, 1927), the Theory of Primary Mental Abilities (Thurstone, 1938), Hierarchical Theories (Vernon, 1971), the Structure of Intellect Model (Guilford, 1967, 1982), and Human Cognition Abilities (Carroll, 1993) have been proposed (Table 2.2). These theories are based upon the statistical method of factor analysis and consider IQ as an indicator of intelligence. The tests based on these theories prescribe a single score of performance.

IQ scores are aggregate indices of performance on a variety of tasks demanding intellectual operations. The choice of an aggregate score rather than a profile of individual test scores is justified by the observation that the individual scores are positively related to all of the other scores in the battery (Carroll, 1993). The commonality among all possible measures of cognitive ability that form a positive manifold is called '*g*' or general intelligence. Thus Brody (1997) states, "an IQ score is an aggregate index of scores on subtests that belong to the matrix of tests that are part of the positive manifold of intellectual tasks. Therefore, an IQ may be thought of as a measure of "g" (p. 1046).

Table 2.2: Psychometric Theories of Intelligence

Theory	*Assumptions*
1. Two Factor Theory (Spearman, 1927)	Intelligence consists of **General** ('g') and **Specific** ('s') factors. All intellectual activities share a single common factor, called 'g', which is characterized as mental energy. There are a number of specific factors 's', each being strictly specific to a single activity. Psychological tests measure 'g' factor only.

(*Contd.*)

Table 2.2 (*Contd.*)

Theory	*Assumptions*
2. Theory of Primary Mental Abilities (Thurstone, 1938)	Intelligence consists of seven major factors: **Verbal Comprehension, Verbal Fluency, Inductive Reasoning, Spatial Visualization, Number, Memory, and Perceptual Speed.**
3. Hierarchical Theories (Vernon, 1971)	At the top of the hierarchy is **factor**. At the next level are two broad group factors, corresponding to **verbal-educational** (v:ed) and **practical-mechanical** (k:m) aptitudes. These major factors may be further subdivided. The verbal-educational factor, for example, yields verbal and numerical factors among others. Similarly the practical-mechanical factor may split into sub-factors as mechanical-information, spatial, and psychomotor abilities. Still narrower sub-factors can be identified by further analysis.
4. Structure of Intellect Model (Guilford, 1967, 1982)	This theory organizes intellectual traits along three dimensions: **Operation**—what the respondent does, **Contents**—the nature of the materials or information on which operations are performed, and **Product**—the form in which information is processed by the respondents. Guilford's classification includes **6×5×6 categories**, resulting into 180 cells in the model. In each cell at least one factor or ability is expected; some cells may contain more than one factor.
5. Fluid and Crystallized Intelligence (Cattel, 1971)	There is two *'g'* factors; *'gf'* (for fluid intelligence) and *'ge'* (for crystallized intelligence). Fluid intelligence includes the ability to think creatively, to reason abstractly, to make inferences from data, and to understand relationships. It is strongly influnced by heredity. In contrast, crystallized intelligence includes what a person learns and retains from experience; so, it is strongly influence by environment.
6. Level Land Level II Abilities (Jensen, 1972)	Level I denotes **associative learning** (such as rote learning and memory). Level II refers to a general class of abilities involving effective

(*Contd.*)

Table 2.2 *(Contd.)*

Theory	*Assumptions*
	transformation or manipulation of stimuli, as evinced in **higher order learning**, such as reasoning and problem-solving.
7. Human Cognitive Abilities (Carrol, 1993)	Three tired hierarchical model, the apex of the hierarchy is the **"general factor"** or "g", which has a substantial genetic component (at least 50 per cent). The second level includes **"broad abilities"**, like learning, memory, verbal fluency, perceptual abilities, and fluid and crystallized intelligence. Broad abilities appear to be influenced by the interaction of heredity and environment. The final level includes **"narrow abilities"**, which refer to the specific skills required in response to different environmental demands. For example, the ability to drive a car is a specific ability. They are primarily learnt.

IQ as the Predictor and the Criterion Variable

The IQ notion of intelligence has not only inspired the most research and attracted the maximum attention but is by far the most widely used concept in practical settings. A large number of tests measuring IQ have been developed employing a factorial approach and are used to predict school performance (Cronback & Snow, 1977), years of education (Rehberg & Rosenthal, 1978), social status and income (Ceći & Williams, 1997; Jencks, 1979; White, 1982), job performance (Hunters, 1983), social outcomes (Moffitt, Gabrielli, Mednick, & Schulsinger, 1981), as well as non-academic knowledge (Lubinski & Humphreys, 1997). Alfred Binet originally developed intelligence tests to measure children's ability to succeed in school. They predict school performance fairly well: the correlation between IQ scores and grade is about 0.50 (accounting for about 25% of the overall variance). They also predict scores on school achievement tests. Correlations between IQ scores and total years of education are about 0.55, implying that differences in psychometric intelligence account for about 30 per cent of the outcome variance. IQ scores are found to predict various measures of job performance including supervisor's ratings, work samples, etc. to some extent. Psychometric intelligence is negatively correlated with certain socially undesirable outcomes such as juvenile delinquency. Also, many recent studies show that the speed with which people perform very simple perceptual and cognitive tasks is positively correlated with psychometric intelligence (for reviews see Ceci, 1990; Deary, 1995; Vernon, 1987).

How does staying in school influences IQ scores? Ceci and Williams (1997) cite seven types of evidence to support the argument that staying in school elevates IQ. They include the effect of intermittent school attendance, delayed school start-up, remaining in school longer, discontinued schooling, summer vacations, early-year birth dates, and cross-sequential trends, etc.

Studies have reported relationship between intelligence and background variables (*e.g.*, caste, race, ethnicity, and region) and personal attributes (*e.g.*, age, sex, behaviour styles and dispositions). Intelligence tests are constructed in a manner to nullify the score differences between males and females. However, studies have reported gender differences depending upon the type of task employed in the study. Differences favouring males appear on visual-spatial tasks like mental rotation and spatio-temporal tasks like tracing a moving object through space (Masters & Sanders, 1993), mathematical performance (Halpern, 1992), and mechanical reasoning (Stanley, Benbow, Brody, Dauber, & Lupkowsky, 1990). Females, on the other hand, have clear advantage on quantitative tasks in the early school years (Hyde, Fennema, & Lamon, 1990) and verbal tasks (Hines, 1990). Many males than females are diagnosed with dyslexia and other reading disabilities and there are many more male stutterers (Yairi & Ambrose, 1992). After meta-analyzing 152 researches on sex differences, Born, Bleichrodt, and Flier (1987) concluded that females score significantly higher on the Verbal factor, Memory and Perceptual speed. Males score significantly higher on General Intelligence, Reasoning, Number, Closure, Space General, Space Orientation, and Space Visualization. Finally, no significant differences were noted on fluency or on Verbal abilities.

Examining the relationship between birth order, family size and intelligence, Rodgers, Cleveland, Ooord, and Rowe (2000) concluded that the belief that birth order influences intelligence and children born later in a given family are less intelligent appears to be wrong. Also, the earlier belief that larger the size of the family the lower the IQ level of children does not seem tenable. It is probably the low IQ parents who have been making large families but the reverse is not true. There are also studies indicating increase in intelligence by intervention (Campbell & Ramey, 1994).

Cross-Cultural Differences in IQ and the Rising Curve

Researchers have attempted to compare the mean IQs of children in the Western countries with those of Asian children. The results uniformly show superior performance of Asian children over their Western counterparts. Rushton (1997) reported that Asian sub-samples (Chinese, Korean, Japanese and Filipino) averaged a higher IQ at age 7 than did White or Black sub-samples. Also, Asians have larger cranial capacity than Whites or Blacks.

Richard Lynn and his colleagues, in a series of studies, have examined IQs of children from China, Hong Kong, Korea, Britain and the United States. Chan and Lynn (1989) reported higher mean IQs of Orientals in the US and in the Pacific Basin on Raven's Coloured Progressive Matrices than those of Whites in the US and UK. A cross-generational decline in the computational and reasoning abilities in the US and cross-generational improvement in China has been reported (Geary *et al.*, 1997). The Chinese in Taiwan scored about 5 IQ points higher than British children (Lynn, 1997). Koreans scored significantly higher on the test of general intelligence and visuo-spatial abilities but were relatively weaker on the verbal test, relative to the British children (Lynn & Song, 1992). The IQ of children in Hong Kong in the mid 1980s was approximately 108 in relation to mean IQ of 100 for the US and UK children (Lynn, Pagliari, & Chan, 1988). In another study, Lynn, Chan and Eysenck (1991) reported higher mean IQ and faster reaction time on simple choice and odd-man out tasks for Hong Kong children than British children.

The mean IQ in Japan was higher than that in the US by 2-15 IQ points (Lynn, 1982). In particular, Japanese children scored lower on measures of verbal comprehension and perceptual speed, and were superior on measures of memory span, number and spatial ability (Lynn & Hampson, 1986, 1987; Lynn, Hampson & Binghan, 1987). Japanese children scored significantly higher on Columbia Mental Maturity Scale than that of American children, although this difference tended to decrease with the start of compulsory education (Misawa, Motegi, Fijita, & Hattori, 1984). Further evidence suggests that Japanese are more efficient information processors, show faster movement times (RTs) and have greater variation than British children (Lynn & Shigehisa, 1991). The simultaneous processing abilities of Japanese were significantly greater than sequential processing, relative to US children (Kaufman, McLean, Ishikumo, & Moon, 1989).

In general, the results indicate superior performance of Asian children as compared to British and American children. Also, greater variability in IQ among Asian countries than European countries has been reported (Naglieri & Bardos, 1988). In majority of these studies, Raven's Coloured Progressive Matrices and Weschler Intelligence Scale for Children have been employed.

The Flynn Effect

James Flynn has shown that IQ has been rising in many countries over the period of twentieth century and even before (Flynn, 1984, 1987, 1994, 1999). Lynn and Hampson (1986) reported that national mean IQ has been rising in Britain by 1.71 IQ points per decade since 1932. In Japan, this rise has been 7.70 IQ points per decade since 1950. There has been 3.0 IQ points rise per decade in the US since 1932. Also, this rise has been in the area of nonverbal or performance IQ and indeed there has been a drop in the Verbal Scholastic Aptitude Test scores. This rise has been explained in terms of "increases in environmental complexity" (Schooler, 1998, p. 67). Greenfield

(1998) has related this rise with historical changes in the ecocultural niche, particularly in technology, urbanization and formal education. Daily life and occupational experience both seem more complex today than in the earlier times. The population is increasingly urbanized, television exposes us to more information and presents different perspectives, and schooling facilities have largely improved. She concludes that, "the Flynn effect is an example of the historical evolution of culturally phenotypic intelligence. It is not the evolution of 'general intelligence'. However, the fact is that general intelligence must always be instantiated in a specific cultural form. Culture takes general intelligence and makes it specific" (Greenfield, 1998, p. 119).

The Limitations of "IQ" Measures

During the last two decades researchers have become increasingly dissatisfied with the study and use of IQ measures for several reasons. First, although a positive manifold exists for an indefinitely large number of measures that are related to cognitive abilities, there may be abilities that are included in the domain of intelligence that might not be included among the tests that form a positive manifold (Gardner, 1983). Also, '*g*' accounts for approximately 50 per cent of the covariance of measures of ability. Therefore, there are many cognitive ability measures in addition to *g* that might contribute to performance in many situations (Brody, 1997).

Second, psychometricians have constructed myriad intelligence test items that have little if anything to do with the kinds of thinking people do in their everyday lives. These test items are more concerned with reasoning involving artificial concepts than about reasoning with real ones. Neisser (1976) has described academic intelligence tasks (common in the classroom and on intelligence tests) as (a) formulated by others, (b) often of little or no intrinsic interest, (c) having all needed information available from the beginning and, (d) disembedded from an individual's ordinary experience. In addition, these tasks (e) usually are well defined, (f) have but one correct answer, and (g) often have just one method of obtaining the correct solution. Needless to say, the real life events are completely different from the imaginary ones and are located in specific contexts. The real world problems often are (a) formulated or in need of reformulation, (b) of personal interest, (c) lacking in information necessary for solution, (d) related to everyday experience, (e) poorly defined, (f) characterized by multiple "correct" solutions, each with liabilities as well as assets, and (g) characterized by multiple methods for picking a problem solution (Sternberg, Wagner, Williams, & Horvath, 1995).

Third, the study of tests tended to shift the focus of intelligence research away from theoretical issues to measurement issues. In almost all sciences first a theory is developed which is followed by the development of assessment procedures. The reverse was, however, true in the case of intelligence. Binet first attempted to develop a measurement procedure which was followed by different theoretical advances. Although measurement issues are of interest in their own right, they can be studied more effectively when the research on testing is theoretically based.

Fourth, adopting an unitary perspective, intelligence tests are based on the notion that a single test score – the IQ – reveals the single basic fact about people's intelligence. It may, however, be noted that ranking given along a certain dimension using IQ does not tell anything about the underlying processes. If one person is a wonderful visualizer but can rarely compose a sentence, and another person can write glowing prose but cannot begin to visualize the simplest spatial images, what do we really learn about these two persons if they are reported to have same IQ? Similarly, if one student is a math whiz but is unable to learn foreign languages, and another student has easily absorbed three foreign languages but cannot get through elementary algebra, does it mean anything to say that they have the "same" level of intelligence? Thus, while computing IQ by averaging the scores, we often lose more than we gain (Sternberg, 1988). Gregory (1994) thus observed, "the IQ notion of intelligence as a single dimension along which to judge children and adults is among the most personally and socially damaging notions of this century" (p. 17).

Fifth, the psychometric approach conceptualizes intelligence as a fixed entity. It remains stable over time and place. Test manuals praise the high "reliability" of their tests, meaning that the test scores do not tend to change much with time or place. But is intelligence really a fixed entity? The evidence suggests that it is not. Intelligence can be increased, and there now exists a variety of programmes designed to do just that (*e.g.*, Feuerstein, 1980).

Sixth, the psychometric approach relies on factor analytic models. The factor structures of intelligence tests are often times found to be too complex and vary considerably across cultures (Lonner, 1990). Puhan (1982) has shown that the factor structures of Raven's Progressive Matrices and Wechsler Adult Intelligence Scale vary in different age groups as well as across different cultural groups. Actually the factors that emerge depend on the nature of test items and do not necessarily reveal inherent characteristics, and processes of intelligence.

Seventh, it is not clear what is the duration for which any assessment of intelligence will remain valid. For instance, the validity of a pathological test is limited to a certain time period. But no such limitation is prescribed in case of intelligence test scores.

Eighth, success or failure on an intelligence test depends to a great extent on relevant prior experience as well as the capacity of a test to elicit the relevant skills. Majority of the intelligence tests tap skills required for successful living in the technologically advanced countries, which have been rightly termed by Mundy-Castle (1974) as "technological intelligence". Many of the cognitive behaviours that are assessed with the help of IQ measures do not have adaptive value in other countries (Goodnow, 1976). The items of an IQ test show bias toward western constructs (Chan, 1991; Livingston, 1995). They are based on certain assumptions that hold true only in developed countries. Some of these assumptions are: To be quick is to be smart, the high verbal reads everything with great care and comprehension, you can tell how smart a person is by the size of his vocabulary, intelligent people solve problems in the same way as less intelligent people but better, and so on. In this context, Ogbu (1986) has remarked that IQ is a special and a circumscribed form of intelligence sampled to reflect and predict the cognitive requirements for middle class jobs and education in industrialized western societies. Its origin lies in the cognitive requirements of the macro-environment of western middle class people. Individuals acquire these pre-existing adaptive or functional skills because they need them to become competent adults in the middle class world. Thus IQ tests standardized on a representative sample assess knowledge and skills deemed intelligent within that group (Cummins, 1988). On the basis of their studies on Blacks and Whites, Grubb and Ollendick (1986) argued that a sub-culture's score on an intelligence test depends on its distance from the culture on which the questions of a test are based and validated. The performance on an IQ test depends upon the differences in the culture, including linguistic differences (Berliner, 1988) and test motivation (Brescia & Fortune, 1989). Exposure to particular environmental stimuli can also facilitate performance on IQ test (Church & Katigback, 1987). In a study by Serpell (1979), Zambian and English children were required to reproduce patterns in three different media: wire models, pencil and paper, and clay. The Zambian children excelled in the wire medium to which they were most accustomed, while the English children were best with paper and pencil. Both groups performed equally well with clay. This example shows that difference in familiarity with test materials can produce marked differences in performance on tests. Chan (1991), thus, concludes that item types in western-type intelligence tests are culture-bound or at most culture-fair and not culture free.

As a critique of 'g' or psychometric theory, Sternberg (2003) argues that psychologists have confined themselves for one century to their '*g*' house. If they come out of their house, they will find that there is much more to the world than '*g*'.

The conceptualization of intelligence in terms of IQ is thus facing serious challenges. Many different theoretical perspectives have emerged in recent years which emphasize on the interface between intelligence and personality and the role of culture in understanding intellective functions. In recent years, intelligence is viewed in terms of "the mental abilities necessary for adaptation to, as well as shaping and selection of, any environmental context" (Sternberg, 1997; p. 1030).

CONDITIONS FOR THE USE OF TESTS IN OTHER CULTURES

Test Adaptation

Tests developed in other cultures are adapted to a particular context for use in that culture. Technically, the process of test adaptation is similar to that of test construction. Since test items are rooted in one's experience and cultural context, a test developed in a particular context cannot be borrowed to another cultural context and used in its available form. Patricia Greenfield (1997) argues that tests are "cultural genres". The term culture implies sharing or agreement, that is, social convention. In a culture what is shared are values, knowledge and communication. If the tests are cultural genres, then they require for use shared values, shared knowledge and shared communication. It implies that a test can be used in other cultures only if it shares values, knowledge and the process of communication of the culture of its origin. Let us discuss these three aspects of a culture in some detail.

Values and Meaning

For a test to travel freely in another culture, two things are essential – (i) the two cultures should have agreement on the value or merit of a particular response, and (ii) the items must mean the same things in different cultures.

In a study (Col, Gay, Glick, & Sharp, 1971) 20 objects divided evenly into the linguistic categories of foods, implements, food containers, and clothing were presented to Kpelle (a Liberian tribe people) participants with the instruction to sort out these objects into different categories. The results were quite revealing. Instead of sorting the objects in linguistic categories as expected by the researchers, participants made functional sorting. That is, rather than sorting the objects in groups of tools and foods, participants put a potato and a knife together because one uses the knife to cut the potato. Participants often justified their pairings by stating that a wise man could only do such and such things. When the researchers asked how would a fool classify these objects, the participants classified them in linguistic categories. In short, the researchers' criterion for intelligent behaviour was the participants' criterion for foolish; the participants' criterion for wise behaviour was the researcher's criterion for stupid. It thus emerges out that local definition of the construct to be measured need to be ascertained before using a test developed in another culture.

Certain characteristics of the stimuli also need careful attention. For example, having a boy or girl friend and dating is considered normal in the American society. If there is a question in the test relating them, Americans will have no problem. But similar kinds of behaviour are not common in the Indian society. A question seeking such type of information in a test for use with Indian people will not be acceptable.

Modes of Knowing

Many societies think that 'knowing' is a group process, not an individual one. For example, Greenfield (1997) wanted to interview Maya girls and their mothers in Mexico. She desired each girl and each mother to include in the interview and have a separate interview protocol. But this was not how the girls and their mothers saw it. The notion that a girl would have an independent viewpoint, an independent piece of knowledge, or an independent perspective was not within their worldview. Instead, they expected more knowledgeable mothers to answer for young girls and for members of the family grouping to answer cooperatively. The assumption in this process is that knowledge is product of group efforts. The partitioning of this information individual by individual was at odds with their worldview. Additionally, the ways questions are worded determine the type of response you may get in an interview situation or in a questionnaire. For example, in one of the conservation of liquid (Piaget's task) studies on rural Wolof children, Greenfield (1966), after transferring water from a shorter, fatter beaker in a longer, thinner one, asked them: "Why do you think it is the same?" or "Why do you say it is the same?" This is the standard question asked in this type of study. This question, however, elicited no response till she changed the question to "Why is the water the same (or more or less)?" At this point the unschooled children gave reasons for their judgments. Probably these children could not distinguish between their own thought and the object of thought. To them both were same. This makes a point that use of exact copy (literal translation) of the experimental procedure may lead to erroneous results.

Conventions of Communication

In many Asian and African societies including that of the Indian, children are not expected to speak before elders. When an interviewer (stranger?) asks questions, children either remain silent or give short answers and do not like to explain their responses.

It is thus evident that when a given instrument is used beyond the culture in which it was developed, it is necessary to find out the meaning or meanings that participants in the new culture attach to the instrument and to its procedure. Tests are not universal instruments. They are culture specific genres.

Bias in Test Construction/Adaptation

When a test developed in one culture is adapted for use in another culture, different kinds of biases become operative. Three types of biases have been discussed in this section. These are: construct bias, method bias and administration bias.

Construct Bias

It occurs when the construct measured is not identical across cultural groups. For example, intelligence is defined in the West in terms of reasoning, acquired knowledge and memory. Western intelligence tests were developed keeping these components in view. However, research has shown that Asian and African people give more weightage to the "Social" aspect of intelligence than the above-mentioned cognitive attributes. For example, intelligent people are reported to be more Conforming, Obedient, and Slow (in contrast to the Western view that intelligent people are fast in all activities). In Africa, "Willingness to do chores for the family", "respect for elders", "wisdom", "doing more listening than talking" are considered some of the characteristics of intelligent people.

Method Bias

It is related to the methodology of research. Two types of method bias have been envisaged: sample bias, instrument bias. The Sample bias occurs when the characteristics of the sample on which test is likely to be administered is different from the standardization sample. The samples may differ in terms of their educational level and motivation to take the test. The participants who have been frequently exposed to testing will show less motivation than participants to whom the instrument and/or the test situation has high novelty.

Another type of method bias is related to the characteristics of the instrument (*i.e.* **instrument bias**). A well-known example is **Stimulus Familiarity**. If the items (verbal or non-verbal) used in the test are familiar to the participants (*i.e.*, related to the daily life situation), they will certainly perform better than other groups who are not familiar with the type of activities included in the test. In a study, Scottish and Zambian children were asked to sort models of animals and motor vehicle in one condition, and in other condition photographs of these models. Scottish children did better when photographs were sorted, while Zambian children were better when models were used.

Administration Bias

It refers to the communication problems between interviewers and interviewees. This problem occurs more when both of them have different first languages and cultural backgrounds. Interviewee's insufficient knowledge of the testing language and inappropriate modes of address or cultural norm violations on the part of the interviewer can seriously endanger the collection of appropriate data.

MULTILINGUAL STUDIES: TRANSLATION OF TESTS

It is possible that you plan to conduct studies on samples having different languages. You construct a test in one language and want to develop equivalent version in another language. It may be noted that translation of tests involves more than rewriting the text in another language. An appropriate translation requires a balanced treatment of psychological, linguistic and cultural considerations.

There are two common procedures to develop a translation. First, there is the **Translation-back translation** procedure. A test is translated into the target language; a second person independently translates back the test in target language to the source language. For example, a test in English is first translated into Hindi and then the second person retranslates it from Hindi to English. The accuracy of translation is evaluated by comparing the original and back translated versions.

The second procedure is the **Committee Approach**, in which a group of people, often with different areas of expertise (such as cultural, linguistic and psychological) prepare a translation. It is a cooperative effort that can improve the quality of translations.

Method for Developing Culturally Appropriate Tests

For developing a test that can appropriately be used in a particular cultural setting, one needs to follow the following steps.

The Conceptual Parameters

Tests are developed to measure some hypothetical constructs. For example, one may develop a test to measure the construct of intelligence. Intelligence has been defined in different ways in the Western world. How is it conceptualized in the target culture? Thus one has to develop a local definition and identify dimensions of the construct which she/he purports to measure.

Language Parameter

This is concerned with the language of the test. In which language a test should be developed? For measuring in a local specific context should you develop a test in English even for those who don't know English? The use of local language presents an insider's view of the social reality and faithfully reflects the worldview of the respondent. On the contrary, the use of a foreign language is likely to distort social reality.

Item Parameter

The components of the tests, materials and stimuli should have cultural salience. A number of items in the Western tests are useful in the Western context. They are not applicable in other cultures, particularly collectivist societies, because of differences in emphasis on self in individualistic (*e.g.* Western countries) and on others in collectivistic (*e.g.* Asian and African) societies. It may be noted that this is not only applicable in case of verbal tests. Performance tests such as Raven's Progressive Matrices in which patterns/designs are used, are also susceptible to cultural variations.

Context Parameter

The contextual parameter is also an important consideration in the development and validation of culture specific tests. The population parameters must not be slighted. While developing a test, a careful selection of a representative sample is a primary consideration. It does not imply that only esoteric tribes or samples are to be selected. The appropriateness of sample characteristics depends upon the primary objective of test development. The process of validating a test is also a cultural experience and expression. Therefore, establishing validity of such tests requires finding out culturally relevant criteria.

ALTERNATIVES TO PSYCHOMETRIC TESTING

The growing concern about the limitations of IQ tests, especially in relation to their use on culturally diverse groups, has inspired several researchers to examine alternative methods of assessment. Some of these methods are described below.

Biological Tests of Intelligence

Matarazzo (1992) argued that biological measures such as average evoked potential (AEP) index obtained from electro-encephalogram recordings, durations of reaction times (RTs) (*e.g.*, discrimination and choice RTs), inspection times, as well as trial-to-trial intraindividual oscillations and variabilities (*i.e.*, standard deviation) in such person-specific RTs and physiological measures are more valid indices of intelligence and would be used more frequently in the twenty-first century. Chan (1991) considered the measurement of auditory reaction time as a promising alternative to intelligence. It is argued that biological tests represent a potential for objectivity, typically not achieved in the field of intelligence and cognitive testing. Also, such biological tests represent strong potential advances in social welfare, identifying deficits and special needs early, with a greater opportunity for remedial, medical, and psychiatric intervention (Davis, 1993).

The validity of RT, a measure of individual differences in intellective functioning, has recently been documented in many studies (Bates & Stough, 1997; Bowling & Mackenzie, 1996; Guo, Lei, & Luo, 1995; Lynn, Cooper & Topping, 1990). It has been reported that the speed of information processing is a key element in people's ability to think, reason and remember. Summarizing the research on links between processing speed and intelligence, Kail (2000) has shown that processing speed is (a) slower in persons with mental retardation, (b) associated conveniently with more efficient memory and reasoning, and (c) associated longitudinally with traditional IQ scores. The speed and consistency with which people perform on RT tasks discriminates between groups of individuals expected to differ in cognitive ability. For example, individuals with mental retardation have slower and less consistent reaction times than the normative population (Davis, Sparrow, & Ward, 1991). Similarly, gifted students have faster and more consistent reaction times than average students (Kranzler, Whang, & Jensen, 1994). Also, the RT is related to higher-level mental abilities. However, the relationship between speed and consistency of processing on RT with psychometric intelligence is observed only in industrialized countries. In developing countries, the correlation is very low (Choudhury & Gorman, 1999).

Dynamic Testing

Conventional measures of cognitive skills quantify developed abilities and are thus static in nature. Deriving its roots from

Vygotsky's theory of zone of potential development (ZPD), the dynamic testing, in contrast, focuses on quantifying the learning potential of the child, *i.e.*, the difference between latent capacity and developed abiiities (Grigorenko & Sternberg, 1998). The goal of dynamic testing is to evaluate, to intervene, and to enhance the developed abilities and bring it to the level of latent capacity. A number of synonymous concepts have been suggested for this paradigm: **interactive testing/assessment, process testing/assessment, measuring the zone of proximal development, assisted testing/assessment, and tests of learning potential**. Feuerstein, Rand, and Hoffman's (1979) Learning Potential Assessment Device (LPAD), Budoff's (1987) Measures of Learning Potential (MLP), and Campione and Brown's (1987) Graduated Prompts Approach (GPA) fall under this category. Let us examine them in some detail.

The LPAD is characterized as a method for assessing the potential of children, adolescents, and adults, for growth in specific cognitive processes, first by guided exposure to problems and processes of thought and subsequently by their own independent efforts. In contrast to static testing measures, the LPAD changes the practice of testing in four major areas: the structure of the instruments, the nature of the test situation, the orientation to process, and the interpretation of results. The specific instruments constituting the LPAD battery include verbal and non-verbal tasks targeted at specific skills such as analogical and numerical reasoning, categorization, and memory strategies. The 15 instruments in the battery are designed to challenge a testee to use (or to form and use) different cognitive operations (*e.g.*, serialization, classification) in different cognitive domains (*i.e.*, numeric, verbal, logico-deductive, figural). Most of the tests are based on (or are) standardized psychometric instruments, which are used in dynamic, mediational modes. For example, the LPAD directly uses the Raven's Coloured and Standard Progressive Matrices, and the Rey-Osterreith Complex Figure Test. Other instruments (*e.g.*, Set Variations I and II, the Organizer, the Representational Stencil Design Test) were developed for the LPAD specifically but either are based on or are modifications of older existing instruments. Testee's time is not limited, but tempo of their responses is registered. A limited selection of the total battery of the test is usually administered.

The MLP is designed for population of disadvantaged and low IQ students, which includes underachievers, learning disabled, recent immigrants, and other children. Budoff and his colleagues have developed dynamic version of about a dozen well known standardized tests, which include Kohs Learning Potential Task, Raven Learning Potential Test, and Picture Word Game. These instruments can be administered individually or in combination to an individual or to groups.

The key concept of Campione and Brown's GPA is transfer, or an individual's ability to use learned information flexibly and in a variety of contexts. The ratio of learning (how much instruction is needed) to transfer (how far from the original example an individual can apply the mastered knowledge) is viewed as a measure of individual difference. In this measure, the typical sequence of testing consists of several sessions that include (a) collection of static, level-of-performance information (pre-test); (b) initial learning (hinted stage); (c) static, unmediated maintenance and transfer testing (post-test); and (d) Mediated maintenance and transfer testing (hinted post-test). The training procedure is considered successful if (a) performance on the task improves as a consequence of the instruction, (b) the benefit of the training is durable, and (c) the outcome of the training is generalizable. Mediation in this approach is delivered by predetermined hints that range from general to specific. The outcome variables are viewed as measures of the child's efficiency of learning. They are operationalized by the number of prompts and by breadth of transfer.

REPORT OF THE TASK FORCE ON INTELLIGENCE

After the publication of the Herrnstein and Murray's (1994) book *The Bell Curve*, the Board of Scientific Affairs of the American Psychological Association (APA) had set up a task force under the chairmanship of Ulrich Neisser for an authoritative report on the complex and unresolved issues related to intelligence. The task force focused on finding answers to the following questions:

1 What are the significant conceptualizations of intelligence at this time?
2. What do intelligence test scores mean, what do they predict, and how well do they predict it?
3. Why do individuals differ in intelligence, and especially in their scores on intelligence tests? Do various ethnic groups display different patterns of performance on intelligence tests, and if so what might explain those differences?
4. What significant scientific issues are presently unresolved?
5. What significant scientific issues are presently involved?

The following is a summary of the report of the Task Force (Neisser, Boodoo, Bouchard Jr., Boykin, Brody, Ceci, Halpern, Lochlin, Perleff, Sternberg, & Urbina, 1996).

As regards conceptualization of intelligence, the psychometric testing has produced a substantial body of research. However, it tells us little about the forms of intelligence such as wisdom, creativity, practical knowledge, social skill, and the like. Some psychometricians focus on the common variance among abilities (which Spearman termed as '*g*' or general intelligence), others prefer to describe it with a set of independent factors, still others opt for a multifactorial description with factors hierarchically arranged and something like *g* at the top. IQs are computed on the basis of tests that tap a number of different abilities and also show correlation with information processing speed, however, the meaning of these correlations is far from clear.

The IQ accounts for 25 per cent variance of school achievement and 27 per cent of the number of years of education that individuals complete. The difference in achievement throughout the globe is explained in terms of differences in culture and schooling, rather than abilities measured by intelligence tests. Test scores also correlate with measures of accomplishment outside of school. There are also modest correlations (negative) between IQ scores and certain undesirable behaviours such as juvenile crime.

Like every trait, intelligence is the joint product of genetic and environmental variables. Gene action necessarily involves a (biochemical or social) environment; environments always act via structures to which genes have contributed. In case of intelligence, heritability is markedly lower for children (about 0.45), than for adults (about 0.75). This shows that as children grow up, differences in test scores tend increasingly to reflect differences in genotype and in individual life experience rather than differences among the families in which they are raised. It is, therefore, not known how genetic and environmental factors exert their effects. Schooling affects intelligence in many ways, not only by transmitting specific information but by developing certain intellectual skills and attributes.

There has been worldwide rise in intelligence test scores (Flynn effect), with the rise of 15 points in the last 50 years due to improved nutrition, cultural changes, experience with testing, shifts in schooling or child-rearing practice, or some other factors as yet unknown. As regards sex difference in intelligence, males typically score higher on visual-spatial and mathematical skills, females excel on a number of verbal measures. Sex hormone levels are clearly related to some of these differences, but social factors persumably play a role as well. No generalization about ethnic differences is possible.

Despite a century of research on intelligence, there are many questions that remain unanswered. The exact nature of genetic and environmental differences is not yet known. The role of nutrition in intelligence remains obscure. The relationship between information processing speed and psychometric intelligence yields no easy theoretical interpretation. It is not clear why intelligence test scores are rising over the years. It is agreed that standardized tests do not sample all forms of intelligence. To find answers to these questions, the task force recommended the need for a shared and sustained effort as well as commitment of substantial scientific resources.

CONCLUDING COMMENTS

The systematic attempt to study the concept of intelligence began with the work of Binet in early twentieth century. The concept of IQ proved to be a handy tool and a large number of theories and tools of different kinds were developed for the assessment of IQ. Tests developed in one culture were/are frequently used in other cultures without examining their psychometric properties, different kinds of biases and other procedural details. Evidence accumulated during the last two decades of the twentieth century, however, did not favour the cognitively biased, decontextualized notion of intelligence. In recent years, various alternative approaches have emerged which emphasize (a) multiplicity in intelligence, and (b) connection between cognitive, affective, and conative aspects of human mind.

3

Contemporary Approaches towards Understanding Intelligence

In the scholarly tradition of psychology derived from Aristotle, the use of term intelligence implied a preference for the two-fold classification of the mental characteristics into *intellectual* or *cognitive* (*e.g.*, discriminative and directive) characteristics, as contrasted with *dynamic* or *orectic* (*i.e.*, affective and conative) ones. This had to replace the three-fold scheme preferred by Plato. Interestingly recent developments have increasingly blurred the distinction between cognition and affect. With growing interest in concepts such as *wisdom, prudence, social intelligence, emotional intelligence* and *successful intelligence,* attention is being paid to many neglected aspects of intelligence. This chapter tries to present an overview of these concepts. It is divided into five sections. It begins with an appraisal of the changing definitions of intelligence. The second section describes theories emphasizing multiplicity in intelligence (*e.g.*, Theory of Multiple Intelligences, Triarchic Theory, and PASS Model). The developmental theories of intelligence (*e.g.*, Piaget and Vygotsky) are presented in the third section. The fourth section delineates theories emphasizing interface between cognition and emotion (*e.g.*, emotional intelligence, practical intelligence, successful intelligence, spiritual intelligence, and wisdom). Finally, the cultural construal of intelligence has been delineated in the last section.

CHANGING DEFINITIONS OF INTELLIGENCE

In 1921, in a symposium on *Intelligence and Its Measurement,* various scholars in the field of intelligence were asked to define the concept of intelligence. The most common elements in their proposed definitions were:

(a) Higher level abilities (such as abstract reasoning, mental representation, problem solving, and decision making),
(b) Ability to learn, and
(c) Ability to meet the demands of the environment effectively.

In 1986, Sternberg and Detterman asked the scholars about their viewpoints on nature and definition of intelligence. The common elements in these definitions were:

(a) Higher level abilities
(b) That which is valued by culture, and
(c) Executive processes.

An analysis of definitions of intelligence over decades indicates that *adaptation* has been a major theme all the times. As Greenfield (1998) rightly observes, since adaptation to one's own cultural "niche" makes one intelligent, intelligence is a "cultural genre". This has been clearly reflected in the latter definitions. Further, Sternberg (1997) proposes that "human beings do not just adapt to the environment: They shape their environment and, at times, select a new environment" (p. 1030). On the basis of this assumption, he (Sternberg, 1997) has proposed the following definition of intelligence:

Intelligence comprises the mental abilities necessary for adaptation to, as well as shaping and selection of, any environmental context. (p. 1030)

The definition proposed by Sternberg goes beyond the adaptive nature of intelligence. According to this definition, intelligence is not just reacting (in the form of adaptation) to the demands of the environment, but also actively shaping and selecting the environment. When a person is not able to adapt to an environment, he/she may try to bring changes in the environmental context (shaping) according to his or her own likings. For example, when you visit a relative on holidays, first of all you try to behave according to their expectations. Slowly you begin to suggest them changes according to your taste. However, bringing out change in the environmental context may not always be possible due to various reasons. In that case an intelligent person tries to find another suitable environment (selection). For example, when you find it difficult to adapt or bring about changes in the relative's house, you may go to another relative's house or go back to your home. It should be noted that intelligence does not simply mean possessing certain abilities *per se*; rather the use of these abilities in real life situations is important.

The second important point, according to Sternberg's definition, is that the environmental context has physical, biological, and cultural aspects, which may interact. The landscape of an environmental context changes over time. Thus, adequate adaptation, shaping, and selection involve a process of life-long learning, one that starts in infancy and continues throughout the life span. The processes of intelligence may be common in different environmental contexts; not the behaviours judged to be intelligent that would depend on the contexts, tasks, and specific situations.

Sternberg (1997, p. 1031) has listed certain core mental processes that may be relevant to any culture or environmental context. These are: (a) recognizing the existence of the problem, (b) defining the nature of the problem, (c) constructing a strategy to solve the problem, (d) mentally representing information about the problem, (e) allocating mental resources in solving the problem, (f) monitoring one's solution to the problem, and (g) evaluating one's solution to the problem. Although the mental processes are common across environmental contexts, people's ability, motivation, or decision to apply these processes across contexts may not be equal. Thus, people may not appear equally intelligent behaviourally in all settings.

Laypersons' and Experts' Conceptions of Intelligence

The meaning of a concept can be studied in two ways—the manner in which the experts in the field define the concept, and second is to study its popular meaning, *i.e.* the manner in which laypersons use the term in day-to-day transactions. The experts' view has been described in the preceding pages. In the second approach, laypersons (*i.e.*, persons in the street) are asked, "What does intelligence mean to you?" (refer Sternberg, Conway, Ketron, & Bernstein, 1981). The way these people define intelligence in Western countries is very similar to the experts' definitions. It may be mentioned here that one would observe cultural variations in the laypersons' conception of intelligence, which has been discussed later in this chapter. The components of intelligence and representative descriptors as given by experts and laypersons in the West are given in Table 3.1.

Table 3.1: Conception of Laypersons and Experts

Lay Persons	*Experts*
Practical Problem-solving ability	**Verbal Intelligence**
Reasons logically	Displays a good vocabulary
Identifies connections among ideas	Reads with high comprehension
Sees all aspects of a problem	Displays curiosity
Keeps an open mind	Has intellectual curiosity
Verbal Ability	**Problem-Solving Ability**
Is verbally fluent	Able to apply knowledge to problems at hand
Converses well	Makes quick and valid decisions
Is knowledgeable about a particular field of knowledge	
	Poses problems in an optimum way
	Demonstrates common sense
Social Competence	**Practical Intelligence**
Accepts others for what they are	Sizes up situations well
Admits mistakes	Evolves efficient strategies to achieve goals
Displays interest in the world at large	Awareness about the surroundings
Is on time for appointments	

It may be mentioned that while both experts and laypersons consider verbal ability and problem solving to be essential aspects of intelligence, experts placed more emphasis on verbal ability than problem solving, whereas laypersons reversed these priorities. Some disagreement between experts and laypersons is also evident. Experts consider practical intelligence an essential constituent of intelligence, whereas laypersons identify social competence as a third component. The contemporary intelligence tests do not include either the component of practical intelligence or social competence. This is considered a major limitation of intelligence tests.

INTELLIGENCE: A CONSTRUCT BASED ON METAPHORS

Psychologists have proposed numerous theories to articulate and explore the notion of intelligence. These theories, as Sternberg (1990a) has proposed, are rooted in the different *'metaphors of mind'*. A metaphor is a commitment to view a phenomenon as a specific case of a particular class of phenomenon representing the prevailing world-view. These metaphors can be grouped into classes to build taxonomy. The top branch of the taxonomy distinguishes between *inward-looking* metaphors that focus on the mental capabilities within the individual without much concern for what this means for social interaction (*e.g.*, psychometric, computational, biological and epistemological) and the *outward looking* metaphors that view intelligence as a set of behaviours to be evaluated within the context of individual's society (*e.g.* anthropological and sociological). Finally, the *systems* metaphor looks both inward and outward. A brief description of these metaphors seems pertinent (See Table 3.2).

Table 3.2: Important Theories of Intelligence and their Underlying Assumptions

Theories	*Assumptions*
1. **Computational**	
* Verbal Efficacy Theory (Hurt, 1980)	Understanding organization and model(s) of information processing underlying intelligent thought
* Componential Theory (Sternberg, 1977)	
* PASS Model (Das *et al.*, 1994)	
2. **Biological**	
* Neuropsychological Theories (Hebb, 1949; Luria, 1980; Springer & Deutsch, 1985)	Understanding intelligence in terms of role and size of the brain.
* Electrophysiological and Blood flow approaches. (Eysenck & Barrett, 1985)	Understanding intelligence either in terms of electroencephalographic measurement or cerebral blood flow in different regions of cerebrum.

(*Contd.*)

	Theories	*Assumptions*
3.	**Epistemological**	
*	Theory of Genetic Epistemology (Piaget, 1960, 1972)	Understanding of the mind through which knowledge and mental processes are organized.
4.	**Anthropological**	
*	Radical Cultural Relativism (Berry, 1974)	Emphasis on cultural differences in intelligent thought.
*	Conditional Comparativism (Cole & Means, 1981)	
*	Ethological Theory (Charlesworth, 1979)	
5.	**Sociological**	
*	Theory of Internalization (Vygotsky, 1978)	Understanding the role of social processes in development of intelligence.
*	Theory of Mediated Learning Experience (Feuerstein, 1980)	
*	Ethnographic Approach to Socialization (Heath, 1983)	
6.	**Systems**	
*	Theory of Multiple Intelligences (Gardner, 1983, 1993)	Understanding the mind in a way that cross-cuts metaphors.
*	Triarchic Theory of Intelligence (Sternberg, 1985, 1988)	
*	Bioecological Theory (Ceci, 1990)	

The psychometric theories have been briefly described in chapter 1. The computational theories seek to understand intelligence in terms of mode(s) of information processing that people deploy while they think intelligently. The main limitation of these theories lies in the fact that it is not clear how similar computer programs and human intelligence are. They also do not take into account the diverse meanings attached to intelligence in various parts of the world. Tikhomirov and Znakov (1989) have argued that the model fails to explain the processes of human understanding and does not reproduce human psychological mechanisms.

To have an understanding of the nature of intelligence, biological theories examine aspects of brain anatomy and physiology: the arborization of cortical neurons, cerebral glucose metabolism, evoked potentials, nerve conduction velocity, sex hormones, etc. Piaget's Theory of Genetic Epistemology assumes that intelligence develops in all children through a continually shifting balance between the assimilation of new information and the accommodation of those structures themselves to new information. According to Piaget, intelligence develops through four stages from sensory-motor through preoperational and concrete operational to formal operational stages. The anthropological theories seek culture specific definitions of intelligence. It is based on the notion that "cultural factors prescribe what shall be learned and at what age. As a result, different cultural environments lead to development of different patterns of ability" (Ferguson, 1954, p. 121). Thus sociological theories view intelligence as the product of social development of the individual. These theories are more concerned with how socialization in culture affects the development of intelligence. In recent years, increasingly greater attention has been paid to the importance of social context for understanding the emergence of cognitive skills. As Borkowski (1994) has noted, "the context-centered approach is more 'warm-blooded', continually rooting cognitions in specific physical and social environments"(p. 156). Finally, systems metaphor tries to understand the mind in a way that cross-cuts metaphor.

Measures based on these metaphors offer different indices of intellective functioning. Thus computationally based tests tell us quite a bit about a person's mode and quality of information processing. Biologically based tests map onto brain functioning. Measures based upon the epistemological metaphor reveal specific competencies which are useful from criterion-referenced point of view. The tests based upon anthropological metaphor need to be tailored to the culture in which the testing is taking place. In sociological metaphor the role of the examiner, as opposed to the geographic metaphor, is to help the child in the course of testing. In the systems metaphor, the actual testing depends on the way the system of the mind is conceived. *Thus these metaphors are different answers to different questions, not different answers to the same question*

(Sternberg, 1990). Further, the computational, sociological and systems metaphors subscribe to the view that intelligence can be taught. Except computational metaphor, all other metaphors emphasize on group differences. However, the roots of these differences lie in different aspects of human's transactions with culture and environment. A detailed description of all the above-mentioned theories is beyond the scope of this chapter.

New Intelligence Batteries

In 1990s, many new tests as well as revisions of earlier tests were attempted with a view to incorporate strong theoretical and research foundations into intellectual assessment. All these batteries measure general intelligence or 'g'. This section presents a brief description of the recent revisions of Wechsler, Stanford-Binet and Kaufman assessment batteries.

The Wechsler Scales

The Wechsler intelligence scales are a family of individually administered instruments for assessing the intellectual functioning of children and adults. Three scales are most popular : Wechsler Adult Intelligence Scale (WAIS), Wechsler Intelligence Scale for Children (WISC), and Wechsler Preschool and Primary Scale of Intelligence (WPPSI). The WAIS third edition appeared in 1997, WISC fourth edition in 2003, and WPPSI third edition in 2002. Table 3.3 contains the sub-tests included in these scales.

Table 3.3: Sub-Tests in Wechsler Scales (after Zhu & Weiss, 2005)

WISC-IV (2003)	WAIS-III (1997)	WPPSI-III (2002)
Vocabulary	Vocabulary	Vocabulary
Similarities	Similarities	Information
Comprehension	Information	Word Reasoning
Information	Comprehension	Similarities
Word Reasoning	Arithmetic	Comprehension
Letter-Number Sequencing	Digit Span	Block Design
Digit Span	Letter-Number Sequencing	Matrix Reasoning

(Contd.)

WISC-IV (2003)	WAIS-III (1997)	WPPSI-III (2002)
Arithmetic	Block Design	Picture Concepts
Block Design	Matrix Reasoning	Picture Completion
Matrix Reasoning	Picture Completion	Object Assembly
Picture Concepts	Picture Arrangement	Coding
Picture Completion	Digit Symbol Coding	Symbol Search
Coding	Symbol Search	Receptive Vocabulary
Symbol Search	Object Assembly (Optional)	Picture Naming
Cancellation		

The reliability of Wechsler has been found to be in 90s. The exploratory and confirmatory factor-analytic studies provide strong evidence of construct validity. These studies clearly demonstrate that in addition to measuring an overall general intellectual ability, the Wechsler scales measure four cognitive domains: Verbal Comprehension, Perceptual Organisation/Perceptual Reasoning, Working Memory, and Processing Speed. The correlations between Wechsler Scales and other measures have been found to be quite high. They have also high predictive validity. Their correlation with academic achievement ranges from .65 to .75.

Stanford-Binet Intelligence Scales

The Stanford-Binet Intelligence Scales, fifth edition (SB5), was constructed by G. H. Roid (2003). It assesses intelligence in five cognitive domains: Fluid Reasoning, Knowledge, Quantitative Reasoning, Visual-Spatial Processing, and Working Memory. Definitions of each of the factors are as follows :

- *Fluid Reasoning* is the ability to solve novel problems, whether with visual material in the Non-verbal domain or with words and print material in the Verbal domain.
- *Knowledge* is the fund of general information that is accumulated over time by individual from experiences at home, in school at work, or in the environment.
- *Quantitative Reasoning* is the ability to solve numerical problems, deal with fundamental number concepts, and solve word problems. The emphasis is on general

logic, numerical thinking, with reduced dependency on academic mathematical knowledge (such as ability to solve specific algebraic equations).

- *Visual-Spatial Processing* is the ability to see relationships among figural objects, describe or recognize spatial orientation, identify the "whole" among a diverse set of parts, and generally see patterns in visual material.
- *Working Memory* is the ability to hold both visual and verbal information in short term memory and then transform it or "sort it out".

Table 3.4 shows the contents of SB5.

Table 3.4: The Contents of SB5

The Activities that compose the 10 Subtests (5 Non-verbal and 5 Verbal Subtests) (after Roid & Pomplun, 2005)

Cognitive Factor	*Non-verbal Subtest Activities*	*Verbal Subset Activities*
Fluid Reasoning	Object-Series/Matrices	Early Reasoning Verbal Absurdities Verbal Analogies
Knowledge	Procedural Knowledge Picture Absurdities	Vocabulary
Quantitative Reasoning	Non-verbal Quantitative Reasoning	Verbal Quantitative Reasoning
Visual-Spatial Processing	Form Board Form Patterns	Position and Direction
Working Memory	Delayed Response Block Span	Memory for Sentences Last Word

The SB5 was standardized on a large sample (n=4800), aged 2-96. The internal-consistency reliability ranged between .95 to .98 for IQ scores and from .90 to .92 for the five factor index scores. Extensive studies have been conducted to find out content, criterion, and construct-related validity of SB5.

Kaufman's Tests of Cognitive Ability

Two Tests of cognitive ability developed by Kaufman have been quite popular : The Kaufman Assessment Battery for Children—Second Edition (KABCII, 2004), and the Kaufman Adolescent and Adult Intelligence Test (KAIT, 1993). Administered individually, the KABC-II measures the processing and cognitive abilities of childern and adolescents between the ages 3 years and 18 years 11 months. It consists of five sub-tests: (1) Sequential (such as word order, number recall, hand movements), (2) Simultaneous (such as Face Recognition, Conceptual Thinking, Block Counting, etc.), (3) Planning (e.g., Pattern Reasoning and Story Completion), (4) Learning (e.g., Atlantis, Rebus), (5) Knowledge (e.g., Expressive Vocabulary, Verbal Knowledge, etc.). The battery has been standardized on 3025 children and adolescents and its reliability coefficients are higher than .90. Construct validity was given support by the results of confirmatory factor analysis.

The KAIT assesses adolescents and adults from ages 11 to more than 85 years old with Fluid, Crystallized and Composite IQs, each with a mean of 100 and SD of 15. It consists of 10 subsets: Definitions, auditory Comprehension, Double Meaning, and Famous Faces (Crystallized Scale), Rebus Learning, Logical Steps, Mystery Codes, Memory for Block Designs (Fluid Scale), Rebus Delayed Recall, and Auditory Delayed Recall (Additional Subtests). Standardized on 2000 adolescents and adults, split half reliabilities are higher than .95, and retest reliability after a month was higher than .87. Exploratory and confirmatory factor analysis gave strong construct validity support.

MULTIPLICITY IN INTELLIGENCE

This section examines Gardner's Theory of Multiple Intelligences, Sternberg's Triarchic Theory, and J.P. Das PASS theory.

Theory of Multiple Intelligences

The Theory of Multiple Intelligences was developed by Howard Gardner in 1983 and published in *Frames of Mind: The Theory of Multiple Intelligences*. This book challenged the traditional psychological view of intelligence as a single capacity that drives logical and mathematical thought. Instead, it proposed that all individuals possess seven independent intelligences. Later on, he added the eighth intelligence to this list (Gardner, 1997).

Gardner identified these intelligences by synthesizing findings from disparate sources, including research at Project Zero on the development of various cognitive skills in normal children; studies of the breakdown of cognitive abilities in stroke patients and other brain damaged individuals; work with prodigies, idiot savants, autistic children, and other special populations; and a review of the literature on psychological testing and the relationship between test scores and performance on different tasks.

Gardner (1983, 1993) proposed three fundamental principles. First, intelligence is not a single entity; rather, there exists multiple intelligences, each distinct from the others. The second principle is that these intelligences are independent of each other. In other words, if a person is good in one type of intelligence, it does not give any indication about how good or bad the person may be on other intelligences. The third principle is that different types of intelligences interact. That is, different intelligences work together to provide a solution of the problem.

The eight intelligences as proposed by Gardner are described below (also refer Table 3.5):

1. **Linguistic** intelligence ("**word smart**"): Sensitivity to the meaning and order of words. Poets and writers exhibit this type of intelligence.
2. **Logical-mathematical** intelligence ("**number/ reasoning smart**"): Ability in mathematics and other complex logical systems. This type of intelligence is exhibited in scientific work.
3. **Spatial** intelligence ("**picture smart**"): The ability to "think in pictures", to perceive the visual world accurately, and recreate (or alter) it in the mind or on paper. Sailors, engineers, surgeons, pilots, car drivers, sculptors, and painters have highly developed spatial intelligence.
4. **Musical** intelligence ("**music smart**"): The ability to understand and create music. Musicians, composers and dancers show a heightened musical intelligence.

5. **Bodily-kinesthetic** intelligence ("**body smart**"): The ability to use one's body in a skilled way for self expression or toward a goal, such as those required for dancing, athletics, surgery, craft making, and the like.
6. **Interpersonal** intelligence ("**people smart**"): An ability to perceive and understand other individuals—their moods, desires, and motivations. Salespeople, politicians, teachers, clinicians, and religious leaders have high degree of interpersonal intelligence.
7. **Intrapersonal** intelligence ("**self smart**"): An ability to understand one's self, developing a sense of identity. Some novelists or counsellors use their own experience to guide others.
8. **Naturalistic** intelligence ("**nature smart**"): An ability to recognize flora and fauna and making distinction in the natural world. It is more possessed by hunters, farmers, tourists, students of biological sciences, and the like.

Hunt (2001), while reviewing Gardner's (1999) book, "*Intelligence Reframed: Multiple Intelligences in the 21st Century*" categorized the first seven intelligences in three categories: (1) Classic psychometric set (verbal, logical-mathematical, and visual-spatial intelligences), (2) social duo (interpersonal and intrapersonal intelligences), and (3) controversial ones (musical and bodily-kinesthetic intelligences).

Table 3.5: Core Capacities Associated with Eight Intelligences

Verbal Intelligence
- Understanding the order and meaning of words (Semantics and syntax)
- Explaining, teaching, and learning
- Linguistically – based humour
- Convincing others of a course of action (pervasive speaking and writing)
- Memory and recall
- Meta-linguistic analysis (language investing itself)

Logical Mathematical
- Abstract pattern recognition
- Inductive reasoning
- Deductive reasoning

(Contd.)

Table 3.5 (*Contd.*)

- Discerning relationships and connections
- Performing complex calculations
- Scientific thinking and investigation

Visual Spatial

- Active imagination
- Forming mental images (visualizing)
- Finding your way in space
- Graphic representation (painting, drawing, sculpting, etc.)
- Recognizing relationships of objects in space
- Mental manipulation of objects
- Accurate perception from different angles

Bodily – Kinesthetic

- Control of "Voluntary" body movements
- "Pre-programmed" body movements
- Expanding awareness through the body
- Mind-body connection
- Mimetic abilities
- Improved body functions

Musical

- Appreciation for the structure of music and rhythm
- "Schemes" or "frames" for hearing music
- Sensibility to sounds and vibrational patterns
- Recognition, creation and reproduction of sound, rhythm, music, tones, and vibration
- Appreciating characteristic qualities of tones and rhythms

Interpersonal

- Effective verbal-non verbal communication
- Sensibility to others' moods, feelings, temperaments, and motivations
- Working cooperatively in a group
- Deep listening to and understanding the perspective of another
- "Passing over" into the life of another
- Creating and maintaining "Synergy"

Intrapersonal

- Concentration of the mind
- Mindfulness
- Metacognition (thinking about thinking)
- Awareness and expression of different feelings

(*Contd.*)

Table 3.5 (*Contd.*)

- Transpersonal sense of the self
- Higher order thinking and reasoning

Naturalists

- Communion with nature
- Caring for, taming and interacting with living creatures
- Sensibility to nature's flora
- Recognizing and classifying members of a species
- Growing things
- Appreciating the impact of nature on the self

This theory has several implications for teachers. First, this theory states that students possess an array of skills and can be highly talented in some of the above areas of mental activity. Further, all these intelligences are needed to productively function in the society. Teachers, therefore, should think of all these intelligences of equal importance. In other words, educators should recognize and teach to a broader range of talents and skills. Second, teachers should structure the presentation of material in a manner which engages most or all of the intelligences. For example, while teaching about freedom movement, a teacher can show students maps, play freedom songs, organize a role play of what different freedom fighters said at that time, and have the students read books on freedom struggle. This kind of presentation not only excites students about learning, but also allows teachers to reinforce the same material in a variety of ways. By activating a wide assortment of intelligences, teachers can facilitate a deeper understanding of the subject material. Third, though all children are born with these intelligences, they come to the classroom with different sets of developed intelligences. This means that each child will have his unique set of intellectual strengths and weaknesses. These sets determine how easy or difficult it would be for the particular child to learn information when it is presented in a particular manner. Finally, Gardner's theory has implications for adult learning and development as well. Many adults find themselves in jobs that do not make optimal use of their most highly developed intelligences. The theory gives them a whole new way to look at their lives, examining potentials that they left behind in their childhood but now have the opportunity to develop through courses, hobbies, or other programmes of self development.

Triarchic Theory of Intelligence

Sternberg's (1985) triarchic theory consists of three categories or types of intelligences: **Analytic or componential intelligence, creative intelligence or the experiential dimension of intelligence,** and **practical or contextual intelligence.**

TRIARCHIC THEORY

Componential Subtheory	Experiential Subtheory	Contextual subtheory
Metacomponents	Novelty	Adaptation
Performance	Automation	Selection
Knowledge Acquisition		Shaping

Analytic or Componential Intelligence

This consists of internal mental mechanisms that people use to analyze, judge, compare and contrast, and evaluate information. This aspect of intelligence has been further divided into Metacomponents, Performance Components, and Knowledge Acquisition components. **Metacomponents** are the higher order or executive processes that are involved in planning strategies, monitoring progress, and allocating internal and external resources to problem solving. **Performance components** are concerned with the execution of plans and strategies developed by the metacomponents, and plays a role in relating new information to novel situations through previously inferred concepts. This component is the one that is measured best by existing intelligence tests. **Knowledge acquisition** components are the processes used in learning. It consists of selective coding (separating relevant information from irrelevant), selective combination (organizing new and old information), and selective comparison (comparing new information with the previous cognitive constructs).

Creative or Experiential Intelligence

It focuses on the relationship between the person's inner, mental world and the outer, external world. This aspect is concerned with the effect of intelligence on one's experiences as well as the effect of person's interaction with the environment on intelligence. Considered as the insightful dimension to a person's intelligence, it examines how people approach new and unfamiliar tasks. Thus, this view adds **creativity** (or novelty and originality) to the overall conception of intelligence. A creatively intelligent person may not particularly perform well on a test of intelligence but is able to combine different experiences in uniquely original ways. Creative abilities are involved in creating, inventing, discovering, and innovating. A second aspect of experiential intelligence is the ability to **automatise** or "make routine" tasks that are encountered repeatedly. An example of automatising is reading, which is carried out largely without conscious thought. Playing music is another example of this type of activity.

Practical or Contextual Intelligence

This refers to the individual's intelligence as it relates to his/her environment or socio-cultural context. It is particularly concerned with the ways people effectively shape their environments, adapt to different contexts, and make the most of their available resources. Contextual intelligence refers to "**street smarts**" or "situationally smart". Practical abilities are involved in applying, using, implementing, and putting things into practice (Sternberg, 1999). People high on contextual intelligence remain practical or down-to-earth in life. Such people remain involved in activities such as implementing, using, applying, and seeking relevance.

Based on Triarchic theory, Sternberg (1993) has developed the Sternberg Triarchic Abilities Test (STAT). It is a multidimensional instrument that is currently being used at two levels, upper elementary school and high school. It consists of 12 subtests to separately assess analytical, creative, and practical intelligences, with 4 items per subtest of multiple and essay types (see Table 3.6). It must be mentioned that Sternberg (1999) does not claim that the test is culture-fair. In fact, "no test can be culture-faire because intelligence is always embedded in a cultural context" (p. 150).

Table 3.6: Sternberg Triarchic Abilities Test (STAT) (adapted from Sternberg, 1999)

	Multiple Type	
1.	Analytical-Verbal (artificial words)	Students see a novel word embedded in a paragraph, and have to infer its meaning from the context.
2.	Analytical-Quantitative (number series)	Students have to say what number should come next in a series of numbers.
3.	Analytical-Figural (Matrices)	Students see a figural matrix with the lower right entry missing, and have to say which of the options fits the missing space.
4.	Practical-Verbal (Everyday reasoning)	Students have to solve a set of everyday problems in the life of an adolescent (e.g., what to do about a friend who seems to have a substance-abuse problem).
5.	Practical-Quantitative (Everyday math)	Students have to solve math problems based on scenarios requiring the use of math in everyday life (e.g., buying tickets for a ballgame or making chocolate chip cookies).
6.	Practical-Figural (route planning)	Students are presented with the map of an area (e.g., entertainment park), and have to answer questions about navigating effectively through the area depicted by the map.
7.	Creative-Verbal (novel analogies)	Students are presented with verbal analogies preceded by counterfactual premises (e.g., money falls off tree), and must solve the analogies as though the counterfactual premises were true.

(*Contd.*)

Table 3.6 (*Contd.*)

8.	Creative Quantitative (novel number operations)	Students are presented with rules for novel number operations (*e.g., flix*, for which numerical manipulations differ depending upon whether the first of two operands is greater then, equal to, or less than the second). Students have to use the novel number operations to solve presented math problems.
9.	Creative-Figural (novel series completion)	Students are first presented with a figural series that involves one or more transformations; then they must apply the rule of the original series to a new figure with a different appearance, to complete a new series.
10.	Analytical Essay	Students have to analyze the advantages and disadvantages of having police or security guards in a school building.
11.	Creative Essay	Students have to describe how they would reform their school to create an ideal school
12.	Practical Essay	Students have to specify a problem in their life, and to state three practical solutions for solving it.

Sternberg (1999) reported that the test was administered to 326 students from around the United States and from South Africa. The interesting finding was that the students scoring high on analytical intelligence looked like a typical "bright" group of students—mostly White, upper-middle class, and from well known high schools. In contrast, the students scoring high on creative and practical intelligence looked quite different. They were more minority students, more students from diverse socio-economic backgrounds, and more students from less well-known high schools.

Consistent with Triarchic theory, Sternberg, Dennis, and Beaty (1996) have developed the Cognitive Abilities Survey (CAS) for use with adolescents and adults. It has nine subtests: Arithmetic Correction, Anomalous Pictures, Embedded Words, Map Reading, Mystery Words, Newspaper Arguments, Practical Math, Proverbs, and Verbal Correction (for details, Sternberg, 1999).

Studies (e.g., Sternberg, Torff, & Grigorenko, 1998) were conducted to examine the efficacy of the triarchic theory as applied to classroom learning and performance. Students of third and eighth grades were given traditional instruction (primarily memory based), critical thinking instruction (primarily analytically based), and triarchically based instruction (involving infusion of analytical, creative, and practical instruction). Results established the superiority of triarchic instruction over memory-based and analytically based instruction at both the grade levels.

The triarchic theory is a general theory of human intelligence. Much of Sternberg's early research focused on analogies and syllogistic reasoning. Sternberg has used this theory to explain exceptional intelligence (gifted and retardation) in children and also to critique existing intelligence tests. Based on Triarchic theory, Sternberg outlined certain training principles. These are as follows:

- Training of intellectual performance must be socioculturally relevant to the individual.
- A training programme should provide links between the training and real-world behaviour.
- A training programme should provide explicit instruction in strategies for coping with novel tasks/situations.
- A training programme should provide explicit instruction in both executive and non-executive information processing and interactions between the two.
- Training programmes should actively encourage individuals to manifest their differences in strategies and styles.

PASS Theory of Intelligence

Based on information processing approach, J.P. Das, Naglieri, and Kirby (1994) proposed four main cognitive functions: **Planning, Attention, Simultaneous**, and **Successive** processing (hence the name PASS). Das has used A.R. Luria's, neuropsychological conceptualization of human cognitive processes as a base for developing this model. The basic statement of the model is that intelligence can be understood as a result of the interdependent functioning of three neurological systems: those responsible for arousal (and **attention**), coding (or **processing**), and **planning.** The two coding processes are **simultaneous and successive.** Thus the theory is known as PASS (Planning, Attention, Simultaneous and Successive) Theory (Fig. 3.1).

The first component in PASS theory is arousal and attention. The arousal system is located in the brain stem and lower cortex, and includes the reticular activating system. Arousal is involved in the maintenance of attention as well as in selective attention. This is a basic function that influences a person's competence in coding of information and in planning, and which, in turn, is influenced by coding and planning.

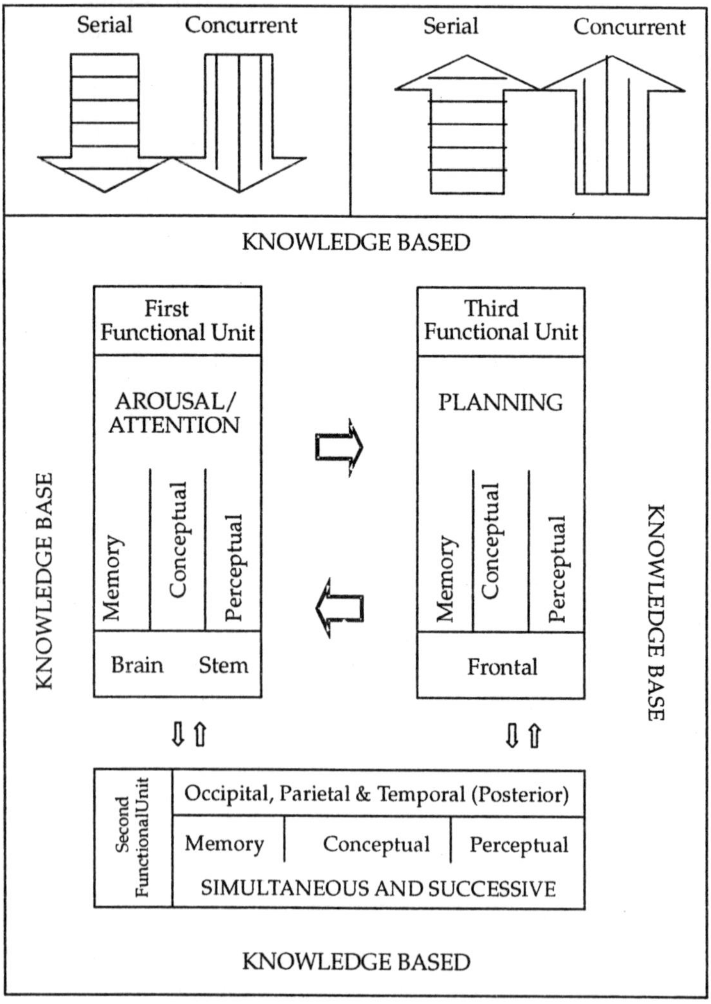

Fig. 3.1: PASS model of ability (after J P Das, 2001)

Coding or processing of information includes reception, interpretation, transformation, and storage of information through simultaneous and successive cognitive processes. Simultaneous processing involves the integration of stimuli into groups (each element of a task is related to every other in a quasi-spatial form). Successive processing involves the integration of stimuli into a specific linear series (each element is related only to the next). Simultaneous and successive processes can be applied to tasks of various modalities (auditory, visual, kinesthetic), involving different types of stimuli (verbal or nonverbal), and may take place during direct perception, retention of information, and at higher conceptual levels.

Planning refers to generation of plans or problems as well as to goal setting, strategy selection, and performance monitoring. It is located in the prefrontal areas of the brain. Sample tests from the Cognitive Assessment System developed by Das and his colleagues are given in Table 3.7.

Das believes that the relationship among the PASS processes is dynamic. It means that they respond to the experiences of the individual, are subject to developmental changes, and form an interrelated system. The three components are related and at the same time maintain independence by having distinct functions.

In sum, the Unitarian perspective of IQ has been rejected by the contemporary theories of intelligence. The theories of Gardner, Sternberg and Das clearly endorse that intelligence is not one; rather there is multiplicity in intelligence. Further, these multiple dimensions do not work in isolation. Instead, they interact with each other and form a meaningful whole.

DEVELOPMENTAL THEORIES

This section contains summary of two prominent developmental theories of intelligence. These are the theories of Piaget and Vygotsky.

Table 3.7: Sample Tests for the Assessment of Planning, Attention, Simultaneous, and Successive Processes

---

Planned Connections (for Planning): This test requires children to develop some effective way of connecting sequential stimuli (*e.g.*, the numbers 1-2-3-4-5) which appears in a diverse manner on a page. For the first five trials a child is required to connect the series of numbers in their proper numerical sequence (1 to 2, 2 to 3, etc.). On the last two trials the child is required to alternatively connect numbers and letters in their proper sequence (1 to A, A to 2, 2 to B, B to 3, and so on). The test score is the time in seconds taken by the child in each trial separately as well as on all the trials.

Expressive Attention (for Attention): This task consists of three pages, although only the last page is used as a measure of attention. The first and second pages contain the words RED, BLUE, and GREEN written in the respective colours (page 1) or coloured rectangle of these colours in varying orders (page 2) arranged in eight rows and five columns. The task before the child is to read all the words on page 1 or say the names of the colours on page 2 as fast as possible. The selective attention component of this task is apparent on page 3 through the use of an interference paradigm. Page 3 contains the words red, blue, and green printed in colours different than the words (*e.g.* word GREEN printed in red colour). The child's task is to name the colour used to print the word, rather than read the word, as fast as possible. Time needed to complete is recorded.

Raven's Progressive Matrices (for Simultaneous Processes): These matrices are used to assess the simultaneous processes. In this test, the task involves the completion of figural analogies using a progressive matrix format. The child is required to choose one of the six options that best completes the abstract analogy. The requirement that each component of the matrix must be interrelated to the others makes this task congruent with the simultaneous paradigm. The scores for this test are the total number of correct choices and the time taken by the child to complete the task

Digit Span (for Successive Processes): You present, for example, the following series of digits to the child

4-7-9

2-5-8-9

3-5-6-9-11

After each presentation the child is required to recall the digits. In this case, the items are related to each other in a series.

Piaget's Theory

The best-known developmentally based conception of intelligence is certainly that of the Swiss psychologist Jean Piaget (1972). Piaget described intelligence in terms of continually shifting balance between assimilation of new information and accommodation of existing structures to the new information. Thus, assimilation refers to the process by which new objects/events/information are grasped, and accommodation refers to the process by which existing structure is modified to meet the resistance to straightforward grasping of the new objects/events/information. Piaget conceived that intelligence develops through four irreversible stages: Sensory-motor (0-2 years of age), pre-operational (2-7 years), concrete operational (7-11 years), and formal-operational (approximately 11-15 years). It may be mentioned that these ages are approximations and one finds cultural differences in the onset or termination of these stages. There are certain characteristics of each stage. The sensory-motor stage makes a transition from a biological to a psychological being. During this stage, the child remains egocentric, shows understanding about the concept of object permanence, and develops the ability to think using symbols and signs. A pre-operational child is egocentric, is not capable of reversible thought, is unable to attend to more than one aspect of a task simultaneously, considers inanimate objects as living beings, is unable to conserve, and perceives states rather than transformations. These abilities are acquired during concrete operational stage. However, children during concrete operational stage can think of only those objects or events that are physically present before them. It is only during the formal operational stage that children achieve the capacity of logical adult thinking and reasoning. The ability to do abstract thinking also emerges during this stage.

Piaget's theory and work inspired tremendous amount of work throughout the globe. Recent research has, however, shown that children's development is more gradual than stage-like. It is unlikely that children will first acquire the characteristics of one stage and then move to the next stage. Rather, it is possible that children may exhibit the characteristics of pre-operational stage on one task and be at concrete operational at another. The age ranges corresponding to each stage are not similar in all cultures. It has also been reported that in many traditional societies the stage of formal operations does not exist.

Vygotsky's Theory

Lev Vygotsky (1978), unlike Piaget, argued that all intellectual abilities are primarily social in origin. The child sees people doing different things, which she internalizes or directs itself toward inwards. In early interaction with parents, language and thought first appear and continue to develop through contact with teachers and others.

Vygotsky's most important contribution was his concept of "**Zone of Proximal Development**" (ZPD). It represented the distance between the actual level of development as determined by independent problem solving (without guided instruction) and the level of potential development as determined by problem solving under adult guidance or in collaboration with more capable peers. Suppose two students have chronological ages of 10 years, and mental ages of 8 years and you give them some coaching on type of material being used for testing and how to solve those questions, etc. After this coaching one child may solve questions meant for 8 years old children, while other one can solve questions meant for 11-year-old students. It is this difference (11 minus 8), which indicates ZPD.

The ZPD reflects what one can become. It is the grey area between the things the learner can do alone and the things the learner can with the help from a more knowledgeable person or peer group (see Fig. 2.2). This grey encompasses the functions in a child that have not matured yet, but are in the process of developing and maturing. It is concerned with functions and processes that will mature tomorrow and are currently in embryonic stage. These functions could be termed the 'buds' or 'flowers' of development rather than fruits of development. The actual level of development characterizes development retrospectively., while ZPD characterizes development prospectively. Thus it is a forward-looking approach. This provides a hint to psychologists and educationists that with the help what an individual can become. It refers to the learning potential of a child: what he or she can become with guided support from parents and teachers. The methodology of Dynamic testing is used for the assessment of ZPD. It is done in two phases. In the first phase, also called interactional phase, when an assessment task is presented to the child, an adult (usually parents or teachers) mediates between the task (by adjusting frequency, order, complexity, etc.) and the child (by arousing him or her to a higher level of curiosity). In other words, the adult acts as a catalyst. In the second phase, the child is given the task or the test to solve them independently.

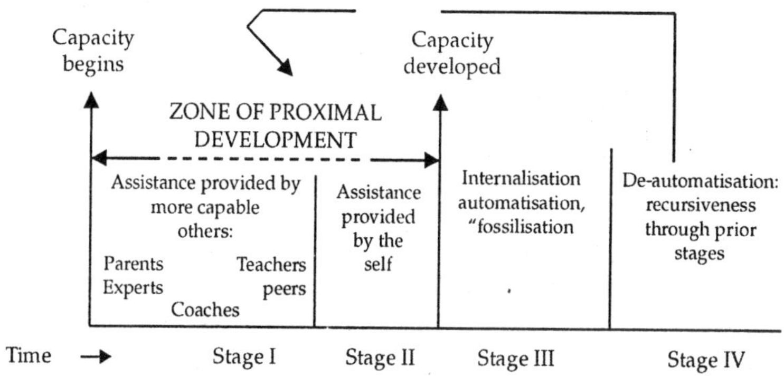

Fig. 3.2: Four-Stage Model of ZPD (after Tharp and Gallimore, 1988)

It may be noted that Vygotsky theory does not contradict Piaget's theory; rather it reflects their different cultural backgrounds. While Piaget's theory reflects his biology background, the socialist background of Vygotsky is reflected in his theory. Vygotsky stressed the sociability of interaction and implied that the child is not egocentric if he or she can interpret the social clues of others. Theory of Mediated Learning Experience of Feuerstein (1980) is based upon Vygotsky's theory. A special type of instruction programme, called scaffolding, has been derived from Vygotsky's theory where the amount and form of guidance given to the child is adjusted according to his or her level of development. The scaffolding from adults provides a temporary support for the child which can be removed once the child is able to work at higher level without support. It is more useful when the child attempts to learn new skills, offering more support early and gradually withdrawing as the child withdraws.

INTERFACE BETWEEN COGNITION AND EMOTION

This section delineates the concepts of emotional intelligence, practical intelligence, successful intelligence, spiritual intelligence, wisdom, and prudence.

Emotional Intelligence

It was the failure of the IQ notion to predict real life experiences (not more than 20% of the total variance, Sternberg, Wagner, Williams, & Hovarth, 1995) that ignited the attempts to understand intelligence from a broader perspective. Since the eighteenth century, mind has been considered to consist of three parts: cognition (or thought), affect (including emotion), and motivation (or conation) (see Hilgard, 1980). The conceptualization of intelligence has so far largely remained confined to the cognitive domain alone. The emotional dimension includes the emotion themselves, moods, evaluations, and other feeling states, including fatigue or energy. Literally, emotional intelligence is something which connects emotions with intelligence. However, not everything that connects emotions with intelligence is emotional intelligence (*e.g.*, mood, congruent judgement).

The first academic work on emotional intelligence appeared in 1990 when Salovey and Mayor published an article in *Imagination, Cognition, and Personality*. Shortly after this, Goleman (1995) popularized this concept by publishing a book titled "*Emotional Intelligence*". It became more popular for the claims that (a) people with high emotional intelligence are more socially effective than others in certain respects, and (b) emotional intelligence has the potential to contribute substantially to the individual and the society. This claim attracted extensive media coverage, culminating, perhaps, when *Time* magazine on October 2, 1995, asked the question

"What is your EQ?" on its cover, and stated, "It's not your IQ. It's not even a number. But emotional intelligence may be the best predictor of success in life, redefining what it means to be smart" (cited in Mayer, Salovey, & Caruso, 2000, p. 396). Thereafter the concept became very popular and appeared in many magazines, and newspapers in India and abroad.

Mayer & Salovey (1997, p. 10) defined emotional intelligence as follows:

> Emotional intelligence involves the ability to perceive accurately, appraise, and express emotion; the ability to access and/or generate feelings when they facilitate thought; the ability to understand emotion and emotional knowledge; and the ability to regulate emotions to promote emotional and intellectual growth.

The domain of emotional intelligence describes several discrete emotional abilities, which are presented in Table 3.8. These abilities can be divided into four classes. The most basic of these abilities is perception and appraisal of emotions in oneself and others and also being in position to express these emotions accurately. The second set of skills involves understanding of emotions, including weighing emotions against one another as well against other thoughts and using them for problem solving. At the third level, understanding and reasoning about emotions take place. "Emotional intelligence involves the ability to recognize emotions, to know how they unfold, and to reason about them accordingly" (Mayer, Salovey, & Caruso, 2000, p. 400). The fourth and highest level of emotional intelligence involves the management and regulation of emotion in oneself and others such as knowing how to calm down after feeling angry.

Mayer, Caruso, and Salovey (1999) have argued that the above ability model meets several standard criteria and, thus, can be scientifically considered intelligence. First, it is capable of being operationalized as a set of abilities. Second, it meets certain correlational criteria. The abilities defined by emotional intelligence are interrelated and also are related to pre-existing intelligences, while also showing some unique variations. It relates to verbal intelligence at a low-to-moderate level and reliably with self reported empathy (Mayer & Geher, 1996). The existence of emotional intelligence indicates the type of person emotional, romantic, thinker-with-a-heart, engaged in sophisticated information processing, and contributes to our lives and culture. Third, the abilities of emotional intelligence develop with age and experience.

Table 3.8: The Emotional Intelligence Framework (adapted from Mayer & Salovey, 1999)

Perception, Appraisal, and Expression of Emotion
Identifying emotions in one's own subjective states
Identifying emotion in other people
Expressing emotions accurately
Discriminating between feelings; between honest and dishonest expressions of feelings
Emotional Facilitation of Cognitive Activities
Redirecting and prioritizing thinking based on feelings
Using emotions to facilitate judgements
Capitalizing on feelings to take advantage of the perspectives they offer
Using emotional states to facilitate problem-solving and creativity
Understanding and Analyzing Emotional Information and Employing Emotional Knowledge
Understanding how different emotions are related
Understanding the causes and consequences of various emotions
Interpreting complex feelings, such as blends and contradictory states
Understanding transitions between emotions
Regulation of Emotion
Being open to feelings that are pleasant and unpleasant
Monitoring and reflecting on emotions
Engaging with or detaching from emotional state
Managing emotions in self
Managing emotions

Mayer, Salovey, and Caruso (2000, p. 400) have listed certain characteristics of emotionally intelligent persons. Such persons are more likely to (a) have grown up in biosocially adaptive homes (*i.e.*, have had emotionally sensitive parenting), (b) be non-defensive, (c) be able to reframe emotions effectively (*i.e.*, be realistically optimistic and appreciative), (d) choose good emotional role models, (e) be able to communicate and discuss feelings, and (f) develop expert knowledge in a particular emotional area such as aesthetic, moral or ethical feeling, social problem solving, leadership, or spiritual feeling.

There are certain other models of emotional intelligence that are called mixed models as they combine abilities and personality in their definitions. For example, Bar-On's (1997) model mixes abilities such as emotional self-awareness with personal independence, self-regard, and mood. Goleman (1995) defined emotional intelligence in terms of (a) knowing one's emotions, (b) managing emotions, (c) motivating oneself, (d) recognizing emotions in others, and (e) handling relationships. This model is also considered a mixed model as it combines motivation with abilities.

Presently a number of assessment devices for the measurement of emotional intelligence are available. Under ability model, the most comprehensive method is the Multifactor Emotional Intelligence Scale (MEIS) developed by Mayer, Salovey, and Caruso (1997). It consists of 12 ability measures of emotional intelligence divided into 4 classes or "branches" of abilities: Perceiving, Facilitating, Understanding, and Managing emotion. Under perceiving, Emotional Perception in Faces, Music, Designs, and Stories has been included. Facilitation contains two tests that measure Synthesia Judgements and Feeling Biases. Understanding is assessed through four tests. The last one measures Emotional Management in the Self and Others. V.K. Shanwal (2002), as a part of his doctoral work, developed an Indian adaptation of the MEIS for use with primary school children. There are many self-report and other measures of emotional intelligence (for details, Srivastava, Sibia, & Misra, in press).

The above description of emotional intelligence seems more appropriate in the Western context where self is considered an independent, self-contained, and autonomous entity (Markus & Kitayama, 1991). In contrast to this, self in non-Western societies, particularly India, is defined in relation to others. Here the person is not considered separate from the social context but as more connected and less differentiated from others. In particular, Marriott (1976) argued that Hindu conceptions assume that the self is an open entity that is given shape by the social context. The work of other scholars (*e.g.*, Kakar, 1978; Miller, Bersoff, & Horwood, 1990; Misra, 1994; Ramanujan, 1990) also endorses this view. Sibia, Srivastava and Misra (2003, 2004, 2005) have proposed a model of emotional intelligence in the Indian cultural context. It has five dimensions: (a) Social Sensitivity (*e.g.*, showing respect for significant others, pro-social activities, expressing and experiencing affection, building social support for oneself, and expression and control of negative emotions), (b) Time orientation (preparedness to meet future contingencies, and ability to monitor progress in one's life course), (c) Pro-social values (values related to the welfare of the society such as patience, affect, tolerance, kindness, endurance, etc.), (d) Action tendencies (competencies such as persistence, dedication, discipline, punctuality, etc.), and (e) Affective states (quality of emotional life such as being happy, contended, creative, open to exposure, optimism, etc.). However, this model needs to be empirically examined.

Practical Intelligence

In view of the controversy about the relationship between intelligence test scores and job performance, a distinction between academic intelligence and practical intelligence has also been proposed (Sternberg & Wagner, 1986). It is argued that the tasks required for two kinds of intelligences are quite different (refer Chapter 1 for distinction). While academically intelligent persons are characterized as *book smarts*, practically intelligents are *street smarts*. Studies (*e.g.*, Williams, Denney, & Schadler, 1983) have shown that older adults commonly report growth in practical abilities over the years, even though their academic abilities decline. Also, evidence supports the idea that practical and academic abilities follow different courses in adult development (*e.g.*, Cornelius & Caspi, 1987; Denney & Palmer, 1981).

The hallmark of the practically intelligent individuals is their facile acquisition and use of *tacit knowledge*. Tacit knowledge refers to action-oriented knowledge, acquired without any direct help from others, that allows individuals to achieve goals they personally value. The acquisition and use of such knowledge appears to be uniquely important to competent performance in real-world endeavours, as it is procedural, intimately related to action, and takes the form of "knowing how" rather than "knowing what". Tacit knowledge is usually acquired on its own. It is the knowledge that is unspoken, underemphasized, or poorly conveyed, but is more important for life-long learning and success (Sternberg, 1997; Sternberg, Wagner, Williams, & Horvath, 1995). This kind of knowledge (knowing how) is also called *procedural knowledge* and is different from *declarative knowledge* (knowing that). Tacit knowledge is always situation or context specific. It is practically useful and is instrumental to the attainment of goals people value.

Successful Intelligence

In his recent book titled '*Successful Intelligence: How Practical and Creative Intelligence Determine Success in Life*' Sternberg (2000) has advanced the notion of successful intelligence. According to him, intelligence tests normally assess inert intelligence that does not lead to a goal directed movement. Persons scoring high on these tests can recall facts, may even be able to reason with these facts, but don't necessarily know how to use them to make a difference, either to themselves or to anyone else. Successful intelligence, on the other hand, is the kind of intelligence used to achieve important goals. People who succeed are those who have managed to acquire, develop, and apply a full range of intellectual skills. These individuals may or may not succeed on conventional tests. However, they know their strengths; they know their weaknesses. They capitalize on their strengths; they compensate for or correct their weaknesses.

There are three components of successful intelligence: The **analytical aspect** that is used to solve problems; the **creative part** to decide what problems to solve; and the **practical aspect** to make solutions effective. Analytical intelligence refers to the higher order mental processes involved in problem solving. Problem solving requires six basic steps: Problem recognition, Problem definition, Formulation of strategy, Representing information,

Allocating resources, and Monitoring and evaluation. Successfully intelligent people recognize a problem, define them correctly and thereby solve those problems that really confront them, rather than extraneous ones. While formulating their strategy for problem solving, successfully intelligent people focus on long-range planning rather than rushing in and later having to rethink their strategy. Such persons represent information about a problem as accurately as possible, with a focus on how they can use that information effectively. Successfully intelligent people carefully allocate their resources for both short-term and long-term plans. They do not always make the correct decisions, but they monitor and evaluate their decisions and then correct their errors as they discover them.

Successfully intelligent people have many things in common. Some of the attributes/characteristics of successfully intelligent people are as follows:

- Ability to motivate themselves
- Ability to control impulses
- Perseverance
- Ability to translate thought into action
- Focus on product than processes
- Completing tasks and following through
- Ability to initiate actions
- Ability to take risks and accept fair blame
- Ability to surmount personal difficulties, and show independence and reasonable amount of self-confidence
- Goal-directed behaviour
- Moderation in behaviour
- Ability to delay gratification

Spiritual Intelligence

For better part of the twentieth century IQ has been benchmark for measuring intelligence. The past decade saw growing interest in emotional intelligence, which was considered prerequisite for the most effective use of IQ. Now we have Spiritual Intelligence (SQ), which is supposed to integrate IQ and EQ in an entirely new paradigm of human thought. Danah Zohar and Ian Marshall in their book on "*Spiritual Intelligence: The Ultimate Intelligence*" (2001) explain that SQ underlies our beliefs and values, our sense of vision, and consequently our daily actions. Vaughan (2002) defines spiritual intelligence as follows:

> Spiritual intelligence is concerned with the inner life of mind and spirit and its relationship to being in the world. Spiritual intelligence implies a capacity for deep understanding of existential questions and insights into multiple levels of consciousness. Spiritual intelligence also implies awareness of spirit as the ground of being or as the creative life force of evolution. (p. 19)

She (Vaughan, 2002, p. 19) further explains that spiritual intelligence opens the heart, illuminates the mind, and inspires the soul, connecting the individual human psyche to the underlying ground of being. Increasing awareness to the inner spiritual life includes paying attention to subjective thoughts and feelings and cultivating empathy. It also includes the capacity to see things from more than one perspective, and to recognize the relationships between perception, beliefs, and behaviour. Spiritual intelligence helps in providing meaning to self and situations, asking new questions, and defining boundaries. It is very important for innovation and creative leadership. Spiritual intelligence brings in integrity, morality, and sense of ethics.

Spirituality is found in the hearts and minds of people. Thus, it is not necessarily connected to religion. Vaughan (2002) explains:

> Spiritual maturity implies exercising wisdom and compassion in relationship to other people, regardless of gender, creed, age, or ethnic origin, as well as reverence and respect for all forms of life. Spiritual maturity also suggests a subjective sense of insight and understanding based on the willingness to recognize illusions, to love in the face of impermanence, and to come to terms with existential freedom

> and mortality. It implies a depth and width of vision that encompasses a whole spectrum of perspectives and multiple modes of knowing. Furthermore, spiritual maturity implies connecting the inner life of mind and spirit with the outer life of action and service in the world. (p.21)

The development of spiritual intelligence involves enlightenment, awakening, inner peace or self-realization. The process of development of spiritual intelligence involves a transformation of consciousness. The integral yoga of the Indian sage, Sri Aurobindo, considered the attainment of transcendental freedom (*i.e.*, ascent of the divine) as only the first step. A further goal is descent of the new consciousness for world transformation.

There are a few practices common to the world religions that foster opening heart and mind, and help people cultivate some of these qualities. These are: motivation for spiritual growth and the universal desire for happiness, emotional transformation for healing old wounds and cultivating love and gratitude, ethical living for peace of mind, attentional training for concentration, the awakening of spiritual vision, wisdom and service (Walsh, 1999). Enhancing awareness and cultivating sensitivity to inner realms of experience, and practices such as yoga, meditation, psychotherapy, vision quests, journaling, music, and movement contribute to the development of spiritual intelligence (Vaughan, 2002).

Wisdom

Since the beginning of civilization, wisdom has been considered a rare and super human quality, and a wise person has always been admired in almost all societies. It has been more associated with God. The internal structure of wisdom comprises a unique blend of cognitive, interpersonal, social and personality attributes (Sternberg, 1990b). In the developmental theory of Erikson (1959) wisdom is an outcome or result of successfully negotiating the conflict between integrity versus despair. This happens in the course of progressively deeper confrontation with all aspects of the self (Jung, 1953), or as a result of transcending the narcissistic preoccupation with self (Kohut,

1978). Wisdom is also thought as a form of post formal and dialectic thought, a kind of integrative thought process that embraces paradox and transformation, awareness of the limits of personal knowledge, integration of emotional and cognitive components, and expert knowledge about fundamental pragmatics of life (Baltes & Smith, 1991). Maciel, Staudinger, Smith and Baltes (1992) argue that wisdom related performance is more than an intellectual capacity or personality characteristic, and not necessarily related to age. Aspects of intelligence and personality may contribute to wisdom, but they do not define wisdom. It appears that factors such as being open towards aesthetics, feelings, values and ideas, being reflective, affectionate in interpersonal contexts, and moderately intelligent might demonstrate higher levels of wisdom related performance.

Wisdom in the West was conceptualized as something that only concerned to the God but also various aspects of conscious daily experiences. A broad knowledge data base was considered to be a core ingredient for attaining wisdom (Csikszentmihalyi & Rathunde, 1990). In contrast, the Eastern interpretations of wisdom stress on integration of multiple aspects of human consciousness. While in the West, the word "understanding" refers to the psychological processes that involve cognitive representational structures and their vehicles (*e.g.*, words), the Eastern tradition emphasizes the mental faculty that is more direct and intuitive without overt intellectualization but a great deal of emotional involvement. Words are thought to be neither necessary nor sufficient but an obstruction of one's path to wisdom. In a recent study, Takahashi and Bordia (2000) examined the meaning of the concept of wisdom among American, Australian, Indian, and Japanese undergraduate students. While the Americans and Australians (the West) considered a wise person to be "experienced" and "knowledgeable", the Indian and Japanese (the East) associated wisdom with "discrete" followed by "aged" and "experienced", whereas "knowledgeable" was clustered at the last step of the analysis.

Considerable effort has been made to identify laypersons or common views of wisdom. Studies (*e.g.*, Clayton & Birren, 1980; Orwoll & Perlmutter, 1990) indicate that wisdom is associated with cognitive, affective, and reflective components, which get more differentiated with age. A wise person is characterized as experienced, intuitive, introspective, pragmatic, understanding, gentle, empathetic, intelligent, peaceful, knowledgeable, and observant.

Analysing the characteristics of a wise person, Maciel, Sowarka, Smith and Baltes (1992) noted that the wisdom related knowledge consists of the following dimensions: *Procedural knowledge* (a wise person knows when to give/withhold advice), *factual knowledge* (Comprehension of the nature of human existence), *relativism* (the role of particular life situations for an optimal decision), *uncertainty* (recognising the limits of his/her knowledge), and *life-span contextualism*. Other wisdom-related domains are *intelligence, social intelligence* (*e.g.*, empathy) and *personality* (*e.g.* good listener). Thus a wise person is one whose advice is solicited for solving difficult life problems.

Prudence

Haslam's (1991) notion of prudence or "practical reason" or "practical wisdom", emphasizes on the practical achievement of personal goals, plans, and intentions. It is involved in achieving harmony among personal goals, and in their successful "co-satisfiability" (Charles, 1984). It reflects thinking in practical contexts, rather than in intellectual domain only. The kind of intelligence implicit in prudence is characterized by a flexible and applied concern for the practical contingencies of behaviour, especially in the face of uncertainty. A prudent person adopts a cautious attitude to risk and is moderate in aspirations. Prudence refers to some sort of rule-governed behaviour, but still has the provision of flexibility between rules and particularities of cases. In this way prudence primarily refers to the faculty of good judgement (Haslam & Baron, 1994).

Social Intelligence

This facet of intelligence represents the efforts of individuals to solve problems of daily life and work toward desired goals (Cantor & Harlow, 1994). A socially intelligent person interprets normative tasks in personal terms by construing particular kinds of context as relevant to task pursuit, and endorsing particular kinds of strategies to work on those tasks in respective contexts.

Consciousness

Smirnov (1994) has discussed the construct of intelligence as rooted in the Russian *theory of activity*. Among its several characteristics, an activity is object oriented (be it natural or cultural); is of social, historical-cultural nature; is always mediated by objects, signs, symbols and interaction with other people; is goal directed, and is productive. Thus the Russian notion of *consciousness* stands for shared knowledge. As consciousness arises in an individual, it contains the image of the world including the image of the individual also. This image gives rise to an activity because an activity is directed by conscious image of an expected result. As the results of the activity are incorporated into the image, the image changes. The image of the world present in the consciousness consists of three components *i.e., sensation, meanings* and *personal sense.* The most basic level of consciousness, *i.e.,* sensory essence includes the impressions experienced through each of the senses and is not received by the individual in its pure form. The meaning develops in social interaction. The personal sense of events, the third component of consciousness, may differ not only from individual to individual, but also from the objective meaning, although the individual may fully understand the objective meaning of the situation.

This section described various kinds of intelligence such as emotional intelligence, practical intelligence, successful intelligence, spiritual intelligence, wisdom, prudence, etc. In all of them, attempts have been made to establish a linkage between the cognitive and affective domains as well as with real life experiences.

CULTURE AND INTELLIGENCE

> "Intelligence cannot be fully or even meaningfully understood outside its cultural context. Work that seeks to study intelligence acontextually risks the imposition of an

> investigator's view of the world on the rest of the world. Moreover, work on intelligence within a single culture may fail to do justice to the range of skills and knowledge that may constitute intelligence broadly defined and risks drawing false and hasty generalization."
> (Sternberg, 2004, p. 325)

The cultural view assumes that the roots of cognitive intellectual processes and skills are situated in the socio-cultural matrix of the people during a given socio-historical period (*e.g.*, Cole, 1990; Laboratory of Comparative Human Cognition, 1983; Lave & Wenger, 1991; Ochs, 1988; Rogoff & Chavajay, 1995; Valsiner, 1994; Wertsch, 1991). Culture is seen as influencing behaviours which are considered intelligent, the processes underlying intelligent behaviour, and the direction of intellectual development (Miller, 1996). Hayman (1998) recognized the decisive role of culture in defining intelligence and creating intelligent differences. Butterworth (1994) argued that understanding intelligence requires referring to the internal representation of knowledge, external or contextual factors, and the behavioural expression of intelligence. Since successful adaptation to one's own niche makes one intelligent (Scheibel, 1996), Greenfield (1998) argued that intelligence is a cultural genre: "Cultures define intelligence by what is adaptive in their particular eco-cultural niche" (p. 83). In the words of Cole and Cole (1993, p. 502), "intelligence cannot be tested independently of the culture that gives rise to the test."

The cultural perspective assumes that different modes of cognition are valued in different contexts. The abstract modes of thought are treated as prototypical in modern Western cultures while traditional cultures value concrete modes (Geertz, 1973). Ramanujan (1990) observes that Hindu Indian culture contrasts with Western culture in its valuing of what he characterises *context-sensitive* (as compared with *context-free*) cognitive orientations. Also, among the Thai as well as the Kpelle of North Africa contextualisation rather than universalisation is accorded greater cultural value (Goodnow, 1976). The work of Nisbett (2001) has shown global vs. analytical thinking as a major cultural variation in cognition. The highly individualistic cultural view of the self in Western countries leads them to emphasize on abstract psychological dispositions and to describe others in a more impersonal way. In contrast, the relational cultural views of the self among Hindu Indians tend to place greater stress on aspects of social context and to describe others in a more self-involved way (Bond & Cheung, 1983; Mischel, 1968; Shweder & Bourne, 1982). These cultural and sub-cultural groups in non-Western cultures promote the development of different competencies and the behaviours that constitute intelligence (Charlesworth, 1979; Ruzgis & Grigorenko, 1994; Sternberg, 1988). Thus, the cultural psychological perspective is concerned with the role of cultural meanings and practices in defining what is adaptive and promoted in a given cultural settings.

Pea (1993) has advanced the notion of distributed intelligence. In sharp contrast to the common focus on intelligence as an attribute of individuals, carried primarily in internal transformation of mental representations of symbols for goals, objects, and relations, the concept of distributed intelligence refers to the idea that the resources that shape and enable activity are distributed in configuration across people, environments, and situations. In other words, intelligence is accomplished and crafted rather than possessed. There are both social and material dimensions of this distribution. The social distribution of intelligence comes from its construction in activities such as guided participation in joint action common in parent-child interaction or apprenticeship, or through people's collaborative effort to achieve shared goals. The material distribution of intelligence originates in the situated invention of uses for aspects of the environment or the exploitation of the affordances of designated artifacts, either of which may contribute to supporting the achievement of an activity's goal.

The cultural perspective recognizes the role of social representation of various aspects of understanding. These representations are constructions of the people, collective in character and are mixtures of percepts, images and concepts (Carugati, 1990). They are shared by a large number of persons, passed on from one generation to the next, and imposed upon each of us without our conscious assent (Moscovici, 1984). In conceptualizing intelligence researchers have shown interest in everyday ideas (Goodnow, 1988), lay concepts or implicit theories (Sternberg, Conway, Ketron & Bernstein, 1981), parental belief systems (Sigel, 1985) and folk model of mind (D'Andrade, 1987). In contrast to data driven theories, the data in social representation or implicit theories of intelligence do not consist of scores on cognitive tests, rather people's notions of intelligence, often in the form of definitions, lists of characteristics typical of an intelligent person, synonyms of intelligence, and so on (Ruzgis & Grigorenko, 1994).

In studying people's conceptions of intelligence several methods have been used including collecting people's description of an intelligent person (Neisser, 1979), analysing attributes displayed in local proverbs (Irvine, 1969), rating behaviours which describe characteristics of an intelligent person (Sternberg *et al.*, 1981), rating on relevance of various aspects of intellectual competence (Gill & Keats, 1980), and rating on the relevance of traditional intelligence test items measuring intelligence (Chen, Braithwaite & Huang, 1982). The methods of collecting people's spontaneous responses to define intelligence (*e.g.*, Neisser, 1979) yield valuable information but exert little or no control over what people do or say. In contrast, the rating method (*e.g.*, Chen *et al.*, 1982; Gill & Keats, 1980) requires people to do or say by setting a pool of attributes, behaviours or problems as targets for people to rate in relation to the concept of intelligence (M.J. Chen & H.C. Chen, 1988).

The Western culture, characterized by urbanization, high technology, and formal schooling as the major modes of socialization for young adulthood (Greenfield, 1998), emphasizes on factors such as *generalization* (or going beyond the information given), *speed* (faster performance is superior), *minimal moves* (the best performance calls for reaching the solution in fewest steps), *no hands* (a preference for mental rather than physical manipulations), and *something of one's own* (a preference for originality or creativity) (Goodnow, 1976). The presuppositions about intelligence in the Western world are: more understanding of the physical world than the social world, being able to think for yourself rather than compliance, and emphasis on speed than slowness. To the Western culture, silence means lack of knowledge (Irvine, 1978). Therefore, expression, verbal or otherwise, is highly valued.

Cross-cultural research is increasingly showing greater

diversity in what is valued in terms of 'intelligence'. For instance, Gill and Keats (1980) found that Australian University students valued academic skills and the ability to adapt to new events, whereas Malay students valued practical skills, speed and creativity. The Malay students emphasize social and cognitive attributes (Dasen, 1984). The Chinese view of intelligence consists of *non-verbal reasoning ability, verbal reasoning ability* and *rote memory* (M.J. Chen, 1994). The Chinese and Australians share similar underlying structure of the concept of intelligence and also value non-verbal reasoning skills very highly. However, Australians rate memory skills as most difficult whereas Chinese see it as the most easy one. In an earlier study, M.J. Chen, Braithwaite and Huang (1982) noted that Chinese students regard memory for facts as important whereas Australians see memory skills as trivial. M.J. Chen and H.C. Chen (1988) compared the concepts of intelligence of Chinese graduates from Chinese and English schools in Hong Kong. These groups considered non-verbal reasoning skill as the most important skill relevant to intelligence. Verbal reasoning and social skills were next, followed by the numerical skill with the retrieval skill being the least relevant. However, the Chinese school group tended to rate the verbal reasoning skill as less relevant than did the English school group. In general, the Chinese conception gives more emphasis to reflection and self-efficacy and sees a much closer link between intelligence and morality (Yang & Sternberg, 1997).

The findings from South African research also present a contrast to the views of intelligence held in the Western world. For example, in Africa, in the 1970s, it was found that there was an emphasis on social (rather than technological) intelligence (Mundy-Castle, 1974), on behaviour that leads to respect for and compliance with society's approved ways (Wober, 1975), and on slowness, that is, deliberation (Wober, 1974). The Africans (Serpell, 1982), in contrast to middle class Americans, emphasize on capability in specific situations and social responsibility (*e.g.*, cooperativeness, obedience). Chewa adults in Central Africa rated village children on intelligence with reference to attributes such as obedience, cooperation, respectfulness, and willingness (Serpell, 1974, 1977). Kenyan parents' notion of intelligence includes responsible participation in family and social life (Super & Harkness, 1983). They defined intelligence as "the ability to do what is needed to be done around the homestead *without being asked*" (Harkness, Super & Keefer, 1992, p. 105). The conception of intelligence among rural Kenyans constitutes of the following four terms : *rieko* (knowledge and skills), *luoro* (respect), *winjo* (comprehension of how to handle real-life problems), and *paro* (initiative) (Grigorenko, Geissler, Prince, Okatcha, Nokes & Kenny, 2001). S.H. Irvine (1970) found that the Shona (in Zimbabwe) word for intelligence, *ngware*, refers to be prudent and cautious, particularly in social relationships, because misfortunes are conceived of part of a gestalt of human relationships. A similar emphasis on social aspect of intelligence emerged in two other African groups, the Songhay of Mali and the Samia of Kenya (Putnam & Kilbride, 1980). The Zambian Chi-Chewas' concept of *nzelu*, in addition to the cognitive components, also includes dimensions of wisdom, cleverness, and responsibility within the Zambian cultural context. Thus, as compared to Western children, the Zambian children learn a broader notion of intelligence.

Durojaiye (1993) has noted that among the Yoruba in Africa the concept of intelligence is multifaceted. First, there is admiration for the individual who in a discussion on any important issue does more listening than talking – the "still waters run deep" type of person. Second, there is the respect given by the Yoruba to the person who, having all sides of an issue, can respond by placing the issue in its proper cultural context. Third, the Yoruba admire constructive intelligence and despise destructive intelligence or skill in deception or cunningness. Schiele (1991) noted that African-American epistemology of intelligence includes the spiritual, the rhythmic, and the affective dimensions of life. Thus the salient features of intelligence in the African populations are those that facilitate and maintain harmonious and stable intergroup relations (Ruzgis & Grigorenko, 1994).

Dasen (1984) has noted that in Boule an intelligent person shows the following characteristics in order of importance: *serviceableness* (service of the family and community, which requires the individual to show initiative, responsibility, knowhow, obedience and honesty), showing *politeness* and *respect for elders* and to *speak well in public.* An intelligent child is one who can retell a story or an event with precision, to speak in socially appropriate ways and to act like adult. A study of Baoule (Dasen, Dembele, Ettien, Kabran, Kamagate, Koffi, L.N'guessan, 1985) confirmed the predominance of social components (such as the willingness to do chores for the family, respect for elders and wisdom) over technological components (such as attention, observation, speed of learning, school intelligence and manual dexterity).

The Pacific ethnopsychologies are quite social in nature. Some of them view intellectual behaviour as essentially interpersonal in nature. A person with 'knowledge' is able to win out in argumentation and influence others (White, 1985). The Bimin-Kuskusmin's concept of intellect encompasses a wide range of the notions including will, desire, intention, consciousness, understanding, motivation, concentration and social competence, all of them have a distinctively social force and scope in the context and possess more or less masculine connotations (Poole, 1985). Lutz (1985) has noted that Ifaluk people distinguish between unsocialized, unmanipulable or idiosyncratic mental events and socially generated mental events. To them there are two halves of the brain, one good and one bad. People are advised to separate the good from the bad and throw away disruptive thoughts/emotions. Verbalizing one's thought or emotion is treated as a sign of intelligence. Intelligent persons are expected to show calmness. The Tobians equate intelligence with learning or cognitive skills (Black, 1985).

Azuma and Kashiwagi (1987) have indicated that the Japanese concept of social intelligence has five factors *i.e.*, positive social competence (*e.g.*, sociable, humorous, effective speaker), receptive social competence (*e.g.*, ability to take another's point of view, sympathetic, modest, admits mistakes, knows one's place), task efficiency (*e.g.*, works efficiently, good insights, plans ahead, clear decisions), originality (*e.g.*, original and sharp), reading and writing (*e.g.*, good writer, writes letters often, good reader). There is a clear overlap in the notion of intelligence held by Malay, Chinese, Japanese, African, and Pacific people. All of them include an emphasis on harmonious group functioning. This view differs from the Western perspective of intelligence where the emphasis is on cognitive abilities and individual attainments. Interestingly, the emerging socio-cultural approach to cognitive development envisions intellectual development of children as one rooted in participation in socio-cultural activities (Rogoff & Chavajay, 1995).

Some studies in the Western cultural set-up have indicated developmental changes in the social representation of intelligence. Yussen and Kane (1983) have noted that younger children's conceptions of intelligence were less differentiated. They believed that a person's level of intelligence can be assessed by his/her overt behaviour. In contrast, older children were more likely to characterize intelligence as an internalized quality of an individual. It was also found that children characterized intelligence in terms of protecting oneself from physical informities and quantum of knowledge. Adults emphasized on wisdom, or reasoned judgement based on experience, including both its cumulative nature and sharing with others. In a subsequent study, Alexander (1985) found gifted children (aged 12-17 years) were more close to the adults' conception of intelligence.

Working on children's implicit theories of intelligence, Dweck and Elliot (1983) have identified two broad categories *i.e., incremental* and *entity theories*. The incremental view tends to emphasize on learning and increasing competence through learning, while the entity view emphasizes performance and judgement of competence through performance. The incremental theory considers a task optimal if it maximizes learning, thus making people smarter. This view tends to focus less on broad traits and, instead, tends to understand outcomes and actions in terms of more specific behavioural or psychological mediators. For the entity view, the optimal task is one that maximizes 'looking smart'.

As Sternberg and Grigorenko (2005) have observed taking cultural contexts into account helps individuals, schools, and societies in important ways. It will help recognizing individuals with talent and facilitate use of their talents. The schools will be able to teach and assess children better, and society uses rather than wastes the talent of its members. They warn that "we can pretend to measure intelligence across cultures simply by translating Western tests and giving them to individuals in a variety of cultures. But such measurement is only a pretence. Individuals in other cultures often do not do well on our tests, nor would we do well on theirs. The processes of intelligence are universal, but their manifestations are not" (Sternberg & Grigorenko, 2005, p. 374).

LEGAL CHALLENGES TO THE NEW CONCEPTS OF INTELLIGENCE

The road is not smooth for the newly proposed concepts of intelligence, such as tacit knowledge, practical intelligence, multiple intelligence, emotional intelligence, etc. Barrett, Kramen, and Lucke (2003) have argued that despite all theorists' claim of validity, if challenged in court, they would fail. The authors argue that majority of the new theories do not meet the Daubert Standards for scientific tests, a set of guidelines for admissibility of scientific evidence into court.

The first of the Daubert criteria states that the theory must have been tested, or is at least able to be tested, Gardner admits that he is not going to develop tests and attempt to empirically prove his theory. Goleman's theory is so diffuse that it can never be tested. Mayer and Salovey have a theory but negative results. Tacit knowledge has been criticized due to its lack of a coherent definition.

The second criteria is that the theory must have been published in peer reviewed publications. This has also not been met by these new concepts. These concepts have primarily been published in trade books and book chapters without adequate peer review.

The third criteria is that there must be a known or potential error rate. Within selection contexts, either insufficient data exist or the data show that the instruments are not valid. It is impossible to determine the number of true positives, true negatives, false positives and false negatives to be expected in using the technique.

The fourth of the criteria says that the theory must be generally accepted in the relevant scientific community. All of the conceptualizations have been critiqued by practitioners and professionals in the area of Industrial/Organizational psychology. It is doubtful that there is any acceptance of the concept in the relevant field.

The fifth of the Daubert criteria asserts that the methods for testing the theory must meet scientific standards. All of the attempts to validate the instruments discussed here use non-standard procedures. They confuse predictors and criteria, make unwarranted statistical adjustments to the data, try schemes of using experts to develop prototypes, and manipulate data to get desired results when all else fail. Finally, none of the studies have ever used a predictive validation design (for further details, Barrett, Kramen, & Lucke, 2003).

CONCLUDING COMMENTS

The recent conceptualization of intelligence is certainly at variance from the earlier ones in many respects. First, intelligence is not considered simply in terms of adaptation to the environment; rather an intelligent person also selects and gives shape to the environment according to his or her preference. Thus, an intelligent person plays a more active role. Second, the recent view does not believe in the unitary nature of intelligence. The theories of Gardner and Sternberg demonstrate multiplicity in intelligence. Third, it is believed that the socio-cultural and historical factors play important roles in development of intelligence. Also, the assessment of intelligence should not be restricted to what has been developed; rather it should aim at the potential for development. Fourth, it has strongly emerged that intelligence is not limited to the cognitive domain alone. The concepts of emotional intelligence, successful intelligence, wisdom, spiritual intelligence, etc., demonstrate that it involves interface between cognition and affect. Lastly, the notion of intelligence as understood in the West is not universal. People in non-Western societies, including African and Asian, view intelligence more in terms of social competence and maintaining harmony and stability within in-groups. In these societies, an intelligent person is perceived as one who shows greater willingness to cooperate with in-group members, has many role-related obligations, and places in-group goals ahead of individual goals. It is in this context that latter chapters report results of the effort made to understand the nature of intelligence in the Indian cultural context. More specifically, attempts were made to examine the nature of intelligence as reflected in ancient scholarly (*e.g.*, Sanskrit *suktis*, and *Bhagavad Gita*), and folk (*e.g.*, Hindi proverbs) traditions. Also, lay people's conception of intelligence were analyzed in a multicentric study to have an understanding about the contemporary notion of intelligence.

4

Research on Intelligence in India: An Overview

The study of intelligence has assumed a significant place in the disciplines of psychology, education and human development in India. It has proved as one of the strongest claims of practical and applied initiatives on the part of psychology. Intelligence tests have been used extensively for selection, training, evaluation, and diagnosis in clinical, industrial, defence, and educational settings. The disciplines of psychology and education are now more than eight decades old in India. The first Department of psychology was established at Calcutta University in 1916 followed by Universities of Mysore (1924), Aligarh (1932), and Patna (1946). The departments of education were also established about the same time (Panda, 1991). With this long history of academic work in Psychology and education in India and in view of the fact that the study of intelligence has occupied a central place in these departments, it seems appropriate to examine the developments in this field over the years.

Beginning with 1970, a number of surveys of research in India have appeared. Prominent among them are four surveys of research in psychology (Mitra, 1972; Pareek, 1980; Pandey, 1988, 2000) and five surveys of research in education (Buch, 1974, 1979, 1987, 1991; NCERT, 1997). Research related to intelligence has been covered under various heads in these surveys such as methodology and research technique (Mitra, 1972), theory and methods (Mukherjee, 1980), psychological assessment (Kulkarni & Puhan, 1988; Mukherjee, 1997), tests and measurement (Mitra & Kumar, 1974; Kumar & Mitra, 1979; Kulkarni & Kumar, 1987; Kumar, 1991), developmental psychology (Parmeswaran, 1972; Anandlakshmy, 1980; Saraswathi & Dutta, 1988), cognitive processes (Gupta, 1980; Broota, 1988; Mishra, 1997, Tripathi, 1988), intelligence and cognitive processes (Das & Thapa, 2000), social psychology of education (Panda, 1991; Nayar, 1997), and correlates of achievement (Dave, 1974; Anand & Dave, 1979; Anand & Padma, 1987; Padma, 1991). Thus, these surveys cover majority of the studies in psychology up to 1995 and in education up to 1993. Researches completed after these periods are available in *Indian Psychological Abstracts, Indian Psychological Abstracts and Reviews*, and to some extent in *Indian Educational Abstracts* and in a chapter by Misra and Tripathi (1998).

This chapter presents an overview of the trends of research in the field of intelligence. In particular, it has two goals. First, it analyzes the tradition of intelligence testing in the Indian context. Second, it examines the studies investigating the relationship of intelligence with other processes and variables.

THE TRADITION OF INTELLIGENCE TESTING IN MODERN INDIA

Historically, it was the Christian missionaries who first began to use psychological tests in India. Up to 1921 the missionaries engaged in educational work displayed interest in the construction and validation of some well-known psychological tests. Mitra (1968) noted that it was Dr. Rice who first attempted the standardization of Binet-Simon test in India in Urdu and Punjabi. Kamat, in the thirties, adapted the 1917 version of Binet test in Marathi and Kannada. Shukla, in the 1940s, developed its Gujarati version. Mahalonobis was the pioneer who developed a group intelligence test in Bengali. Subsequently, Sohan Lal, S.S. Jalota, and S.M. Mohsin in Hindi and K.G. Desai in Gujarati developed intelligence tests. Utilizing some existing Western tests like Alexander Pass-a-long, Kohs Block Design, and a few others, Bhatia (1955) standardized for the first time in India a battery of performance tests for the school-going children. The first doctorate in test construction was awarded to K.G. Desai in 1954 for group test of intelligence in Gujarati. Subsequently, a number of intelligence tests were developed either originally or were adaptations of tests developed in the West. Menzel (1956) published the first book on test and measurement in India.

Intelligence testing for long has remained the most popular pursuit amongst psychologists. Harper (1960) observed that in 1956, about 40 per cent of the test development work in India was related to intelligence. Ganguli (1971) noted that during 1920 to 1967, 13 per cent studies in psychology were related to mental testing. Kumar (1991) reported that up to 1988 about 43 per cent doctoral dissertations and institutional studies on test development were related to intelligence and about 2 per cent to social intelligence. A decade-wise classification of Ph.D. and institutional studies on intelligence tests in India (Kumar, 1991) revealed that the development of intelligence test was at its peak during the 1960s and 1970s, with the result that almost 70 per cent tests were developed during these two decades. However, it was only during the later years that the psychological processes related to intelligence drew the attention of researchers.

Efforts have been made to document the details of these tests in a number of volumes. The first mental measurement handbook for India (Long & Mehta, 1966) listed 103 tests of intelligence in various Indian languages. In addition to the first and second handbooks, Pestonjee (1997) has recently brought out *Third Handbook of Psychological and Social Instruments*. The National Library of Educational and Psychological Tests (NLEPT) at the National Council of Educational Research and Training (NCERT), New Delhi brings out reviews of published tests in its bulletins and has published *Indian Mental Measurement Handbook: Intelligence and Aptitude Tests* (Jain, 1991). The NLEPT has information about 43 published intelligence tests and 5 unpublished tests. Two experts have reviewed each of these tests and their reviews are available either in the bulletins or in the handbook. A summary of these tests is presented below (for details, Srivastava, Tripathi, & Misra, 1996).

A decade-wise classification of the tests showed that 49 per cent of the tests were published during 1971-80, followed by the period 1951-55 (19 per cent). Almost equal number of them (16 per cent) were constructed during the subsequent decades, *i.e.* 1961-70 and 1981-90. The year of publication for 6 tests could not be ascertained. Out of these tests, maximum number of tests (51 per cent) were available in Hindi, followed by non-verbal

(19 per cent) and English language (14 per cent) tests. Only 5 per cent tests were available in Gujarati and 2 per cent each in Bengali, Marathi and Tamil languages. No information were available at NLEPT with regard to intelligence tests in other Indian languages. Further, majority of the tests (81 per cent) were administrable in group setting.

An analysis of the applicability of these tests to various age-groups revealed that maximum number (30 tests or 70 per cent) of them were meant for the age-group 13-17 years (secondary and senior secondary levels), followed by 10-13 years (elementary level, 58 per cent), 5-10 years (primary level, 28 per cent) and university/college (17+ years, 26 per cent). Only 6 tests (14 per cent) were available for use with pre-school children (up to 5 years). The age ranges for 4 tests (9 per cent) were not available. On the dimension of time requirement, it was observed that no time limit was specified in the manuals for 11 tests (26 per cent). Ten tests (23 per cent) required 31 to 40 minutes and the same number demanded 11-20 minutes for test administration. Likewise, 4 tests (9 per cent) required 21-30 minutes, 2 tests (5 per cent) 51-60 minutes, one test (2 per cent) 41-50 minutes and another test 120 minutes. The details of time requirement for 4 tests (9 per cent) were not specified in the test manuals.

As regards standardization sample, it was surprising to note that this information was not available for 11 (almost 25 per cent) tests. For the remaining tests, the sample size ranged between 35 to more than 5000. About 5 per cent tests were standardized on samples ranging between 100 to 200, 9 per cent on 200-500, 7 per cent on 500-1000, 23 per cent on 1000-2000, and 16 per cent on 2000-5000 individuals. The split-half reliability was estimated for as many as 53 per cent of the tests, followed by retest reliability (49 per cent) and Kuder-Richardson reliability (23 per cent). The criterion validity was reported for maximum number of tests (59 per cent). Other types of validities reported include concurrent (9 per cent), factorial (7 per cent), intrinsic, predictive and construct (5 per cent each). In 53 per cent cases more than one type of validity were reported. The information about reliability and validity were not available for 26 per cent and 30 per cent tests, respectively.

Tests available at NLEPT were reviewed by scholars with a

view to help researchers "to the use the tests with better discrimination" (Muralidharan, 1991, p.v.). It is interesting to note that reviewers have cautioned against the use of more than half (23 tests or 55 per cent) of the intelligence tests. About 26 per cent of the tests are considered useful but their norms are not adequate. Only four tests (10 per cent) are categorized as excellent on the criteria of language, adequacy of norms, and the psychometric properties.

Intelligence in Relation to Other Processes and Variables: An Analysis of Published Studies

The frequency of the use of intelligence tests in psychological research during one decade, *i.e.*, 1980-89 is shown in Table 3.1. In this analysis only those studies were taken into account the abstracts of which were published in the *Indian Psychological Abstracts* (year 1980-89). Of the 114 studies analyzed, Jalota's General Mental Ability Test was used most frequently (21.93 per cent), followed by Cattell's Culture Fair Intelligence Test (10.53 per cent), and Bhatia's Performance Battery (8.77 per cent). Joshi's Intelligence Test and Wechsler Adult Intelligence Scale were used each in 5.26 per cent researches, followed by Stanford-Binet Test (4.38 per cent).

USE OF INTELLIGENCE TESTS BY SCHOOL COUNSELLORS

With a view to understand the use of intelligence tests in professional practice, an attempt was made to know the experiences of school counsellors. A majority of senior secondary schools run by Delhi Administration have provision for an Educational and Vocational Guidance Counsellor. About 140 counsellors are working in 200 schools of Delhi (Bhatnagar, 1994). Providing educational and vocational guidance to the students, individual's appraisal and counselling, and collection and dissemination of occupational information are some of the duties that the counsellors are expected to perform in schools. The counsellors have their monthly meeting at Educational Vocational Guidance Bureau, Karol Bagh, New Delhi. On two such meetings, the participating counsellors (n = 45) filled up specially designed 11-item open-ended questionnaire regarding the status, use and satisfaction with the available intelligence tests. The analysis of responses revealed the trends (see Srivastava, et al. 1996) that are presented below.

Table 4.1: Frequency of Usage of Intelligence Tests in Psychological Researches in India (1980-89)

S.No.	*Test*	*Frequency*
1.	Jalota's Group Test of Mental Ability	25
2.	Culture Fair Intelligence Test	12
3.	Bhatia's Performance Test of Intelligence	10
4.	Standard Progressive Matrices	10
5.	Joshi's Test of General Mental Ability	6
6.	Wechsler Adult Performance Scale	6
7.	Stanford-Binet (Indian adaptation)	5
8.	Intelligence Test (author not specified)	4
9.	Nafde's Non-verbal Test of Intelligence	3
10.	Malen's Intelligence Test	3
11.	Tandon's Group Test of Intelligence	3
12.	Mehrotra's Mixed Type Group Test of Intelligence	2
13.	Bender Gestalt Test	2
14.	Alexander's Pass-a-long Test	2
15.	Desai and Bhatt's Group Test of Intelligence	2
16.	Desai's Intelligence Test (verbal)	2
17.	Mohsin's the Bihar Test of General Intelligence	2
18.	Mehta's Group Intelligence Test	2
19.	Ahuja's Group Test of Intelligence	1
20.	NCERT General Ability Test	1
21.	Hebb-Williams' Closed Field Intelligence Test	1
22.	Otis Quick Scoring Mental Ability Test	1
23.	Ojha and Chowdhry's Verbal Intelligence Test	1
24.	Thorndike Intelligence Test (non-verbal form A)	1
25.	Hundal's General Mental Ability Test	1
26.	Vernon's Non-verbal Group Test	1
27.	McCarthy Scale of Children's Abilities	1
28.	Kerala University Verbal Group Test of Intelligence	1
29.	Joshi's Algebraic Concepts Test	1
30.	The P.S.M. General Intelligence Test	1
31.	New Test of Intelligence	1
	Total	Studies 114

The counsellors agreed that their profession demanded the use of intelligence tests for different purposes, such as guidance (96 per cent), counselling (89 per cent), diagnosis (69 per cent), testing (60 per cent), personnel selection (29 per cent) and placement (16 per cent). Also, majority of them reported multiple uses of tests (*i.e.* 45 per cent reported three or less than three), one-third (33 per cent) four, and 22 per cent more than four uses of intelligence test).

When asked about the particulars of intelligence test(s) that they use in their counselling work, the counsellors mentioned only four tests, *i.e.* Raven's Standard Progressive Matrices (SPM) (96%), Test of General Mental Ability by Jalota (27%), Bhatia's Performance Battery (22%), and Indian adaptation of Stanford-Binet test by Kulshrestha (4%). When asked to rate their overall satisfaction with the test on a five-point scale, about 11 per cent indicated very high level of satisfaction, 24 per cent were satisfied, about half (49%) reported moderate degree of satisfaction, 9 per cent low degree of satisfaction, and 4 per cent were not satisfied. The responses to the question about additional efforts made by them to achieve a dependable measure of intelligence were quite varied. These included use of more than one intelligence test (42 per cent), scholastic achievement (27%), teachers' rating (11%), students interview (9%), observation of students' behaviour (7 per cent), and parental interview (7%).

Despite limitations of the available intelligence tests, school counsellors do use these tests for different reasons, such as easy handling (60%), easy availability (60%), being the best among the available ones (60%) and time requirement (58%). Majority of them (27%) were unhappy about the limitations of available intelligence tests as they did not explain the social intelligence of children. About 31 per cent wanted to have a comprehensive test of intelligence which could inform subjects' multi-dimensional intelligence with local norms.

Asked to state their preferred notion of intelligence, about one-third school counsellors conceptualized intelligence as "ability" which enables them to adjust with the environment. Some considered it a "global single capacity" (15%), and others as a "composite of different mental abilities" (15%).

The analysis of the available tests shows that the tradition of intelligence testing in India is in trouble. The tests are not only old in terms of norms and contents but are also inadequate on other psychometric criteria. Instead of using multivariate methods for assessing psychometric properties, test constructors have generally remained content with one or two types of reliabilities and validities (Kumar, 1991; Mukherjee, 1993). Also, most of the tests have been virtually developed on the basis of a 'one-shot' study (Mukherjee, 1997). As regards theoretical preference, most of the tests adopt a factorial approach and include the categories of reasoning of various sorts. In fact, the theoretical developments in intelligence testing after 1950 or so have not received attention from them.

It is needless to say that some form of assessment of individuals will always be needed in the society. The demand for tools assessing individual differences will continue and increase for selection, placement, training, counselling and diagnostic purposes. However, analysis of the available tests reflects their inappropriateness on several grounds. Test items are often alien to the particular socio-cultural milieu. To meet the demand of appraisal, test users seldom examine the psychometric properties of the test. They choose a test which is easy to handle, easily available and consumes less time. The requirements for sound administration of a psychological test are seldom met.

It is interesting to note that the intelligence testing industry has grown with greater concern for developing certain instruments for practical purposes rather than facilitating understanding of the concept of intelligence. Ability testing even in the case of bodily functions and capacities (*e.g.*, visual acuity, lung functioning, hand grip, etc.) is person, object and context-dependent and generalizations are constrained by them. The psychometric technology has, however, obviously been struggling with these constraints but has affirmed the faith of psychologists in their power to tap intelligence in reliable and valid manner. The new developments in this area demand that the concepts and tools both be examined critically.

So far as the conceptualization of intelligence is concerned, there is a perceptible move towards multiple processes of knowledge acquisition and utilization rather than treating intelligence as a disposition. Also, what will be included in these processes cannot be divorced from the socio-cultural milieu or ecology within which behaviours take place (Carugati, 1990). Intelligence cannot be treated merely as a summary statement about a person's potential and behaviour on intelligence tests. Taking the socio-cultural context in view adds one more dimension to the whole debate as it requires attending to the characteristics, traits, or skills which are valued in a given society. Therefore, the social representation of intelligence also needs research attention. The insights from anthropological and ethnopsychological studies suggest that there are variations in the use of the notion of intelligence and support the case for developing indigenous measures.

RELATIONSHIP OF INTELLIGENCE WITH OTHER VARIABLES AND PROCESSES

By the end of the 1970s, the stress on the development of tests of intelligence took a back seat. As Gupta (1980), in his ICSSR sponsored review on cognitive processes, observed, "intelligence test era seems to be over. Attempts are being made to understand the intellectual processes underlying different aspects of behaviour" (p. 234). Such attempts have been diverse in nature and have mostly employed psychometric technique for the assessment of intelligence. The following is a summary of these attempts.

Nutritional Status

Researchers agree that nutritional status affects the development of intelligence among children (Padmavati, Devdas, & Indira, 1968; Patel, 1983; Werner & Muralidharan, 1970) and malnutrition hinders mental development (Das & Singha, 1974; Srikantaiah & Sastry, 1969). Amanda (1991) noted significant relationship between breast feeding (at least for 4 months) and level of intelligence.

Developmental Changes

Phatak (1970) examined the motor and mental growth of Indian babies on Bayley scales using both longitudinal and cross-sectional methods. Growth was faster up to six months after which the rate decreased. A close perusal of the norms given in the manuals of the tests developed in India does evince age-related increment in test scores. There have been some efforts to see age-related changes in the structure of intelligence. While some studies (Banu, 1998; Bhakoo, Kaur, Narang & Verma, 1977) show increase in intelligence with age, a factor analysis of scores on Binet-Kamath test did not evince any substantial change in the composition of general intelligence between 4 to 7 years (Chattopadhyaya & Bhattacharya, 1981). Puhan (1982) has demonstrated that the factor structure of RPM does not remain the same over different age and cultural groups.

Jensen's Level I and Level II theory of mental ability has also received some attention. Jachuck and J. Das (1982) found that growth of Level II was influenced by caste, economic background and age while Level I was not influenced by these variables. Jachuck and Khandai (1983) demonstrated the dependence of Level II ability on Level I and significant effect of environmental variables on the development of these abilities.

Sex Differences

Sex differences in intelligence have been reported in a number of studies. Evidence (Deshpande, 1971; Faroqui, 1974) suggests that boys are more intelligent than girls. In contrast, Hundal (1969) found girls to be more intelligent than boys. Pal and Misra (1992) observed that boys performed better in mathematical reasoning, while girls excelled boys in non-verbal intelligence, classification, verbal facility, analytical thinking, similarity exploration, fluency and flexibility. Desai (1971, 1974) noted that third born boys excel all others (first, second and later born) while first and second born girls tend to be high on intelligence among the girls. Gupta (1991) examined the effect of the time of day on intelligence. The results indicate that intelligence test performance of female college going students was better in the evening than in the morning or in the afternoon.

Home Environment

Tiwari and Srivastava (1998) found that family environment was a significant predictor of intelligence. Parental education, occupation, and income positively affect the IQ of children (Sangwan, 2001). Rai and Pandey (1994) studied the relationship between parental rearing style and intelligence and found that non-rejected group of students was better than the rejected group in intellectual ability. Based on the results of his studies Joshi (2001) concluded that socialization plays an important role in cognitive development of children.

Deprivation

In view of prevailing poverty conditions, a large majority of Indian homes are considered disadvantaged, be it economic, social, cultural, or educational. Included in this category is the population belonging to backward and low castes (SC/ST), low socio-economic status, large family sizes etc. The children belonging to this category are denied the opportunity to satisfy their psychological needs and to develop mentally at their natural, inherent rates because of lack of proper stimulation in the home. Studies conducted to examine the intellectual functioning of such children suggest that "in general, the deprived people perform on majority of the cognitive/and intellective tasks at a lower level than their privileged counterparts" (Misra & Mohanty, 2000; p. 270).

The research findings however, show different trends. Tripathi and Misra (1975) noted a positive relationship between affluence and intelligence. Mohanty (1980) observed that socio-culturally advantaged children performed better than disadvantaged children on the RPM (coloured form). Intelligence test scores of children from low castes are lower than their high caste counterparts (Basavanna & Rani, 1984; Das & Mona, 1990; Murthy & S.C. Panda, 1987). On the basis of a series of studies Das (1974) reported that high caste and economic status enhance cognitive competence. High caste children were found better on numerical and non-verbal ability (Sharma, 1981). Das and Singha (1974) reported detrimental influence of low caste and poverty on intelligence test scores. Gupta, Mukherjee, and

Chatterjee (1993) found that urban boys scored highest on Standard Progressive Matrices and lowest score was for rural girls. Many other studies (*e.g.*, S. Gupta, 1991; R. Gupta, 2000; Mukherjee, Chatterjee & Gupta, 1992; Puttabuddi, 1983) lend support to it. In contrast, there are studies that do not reveal differences between performance of low and high caste children (Rangari, 1987). Rath (1974) found no difference in children of Brahmans and SC/ST in basic intelligence. Rangari and Palsane (1982) investigated the intelligence of SC and non-SC students at different SES levels. They found that SC and non-SC students of first, second and fifth SES levels did not differ in their intelligence. It follows that caste difference is more pronounced for the middle social class groups.

Singh and Sinha (1983) found that non-Santal students had higher IQ scores than Santal students on WAIS. Sinha (1980) compared tribal (Oraons) and non-tribal students on non-verbal intelligence. The two groups did not differ in scores on different sub-scales, *i.e.*, Passalong Test, Block Design Test, and Cube Construction Test. Using Jensen's theory, Jachuck and her associates (Jachuck, 1984; Jachuck & Khandai, 1983) have shown negative effects of deprivational factors (*e.g.*, SES, Caste) and cumulative deficit on intellective measures. The differences have been explained in terms of environmental factors. In her later study, Jachuck (1993) reported significant positive effect of high SES and preschool experience on intelligence test performance. Recently, Nigam (2001) reported significant differences in cognitive development between rural and urban boys of high SES; but the same was not true for low SES boys.

Intelligence test scores are adversely affected by parental deprivation (Pathak, Saxena & Mishra, 1983). Children reared in orphanages suffering from familial deprivation were low on intelligence (Khetri, 1965a, b; Singh, 2001). Studies (Chatterjee, Mukherjee & Banerjee, 1972; Mehta, 1960) have shown positive relationship between family size and intelligence. Incidence of mental retardation has been reported to be higher among lower class groups (48%) (Mata Prasad *et al.*, 1988).

Research relating caste with intellectual performance does not suggest that intellectual deficiencies of low caste groups have any genetic basis. Even if it is assumed that *Brahmans* and *Harijans* have retained their genetic pools (Das & Singha, 1975), it is difficult to prove differences in their innate abilities (Das & Khurana, 1988). On the other hand, the available studies generally suggest little or no difference between the intellectual performance of children of high and low caste groups in the early years. The differences tend to become evident somewhat around the age of 8 or 9 years. Beyond that, we have two kinds of evidence. One suggests that the differences between the two caste groups become greater, representing a phenomenon called "cumulative deficit" for the low caste children (Whiteman & Deutsch, 1968) or "broomstick effect" for the SC children (Sinha, 1977). Another trend suggests that differences between the intellectual performance of two caste groups are levelled off around the age of 12 or 13 years (Shukla, 1991; Tripathi, 1991). These trends clearly refute the notion of genetic or in born differences between low and high caste groups. On the other hand, we can think of certain biological (associated with pervasive malnutrition and childhood diseases) and experiential factors which are largely associated with the conditions of poverty and deprivation, underlying differences between the two groups (Singh, 2000). The attempts have been made to examine the impact of enriched environment on intellectual performance of children belonging to the disadvantaged groups. The results of these efforts have been encouraging (see Dwivedi & Dubey, 1989; Misra, 1990; Muralidharan, 1970; Rath, Dash & Das, 1979; Sinha, Tripathi & Misra, 1982; Tripathi, 1988).

Academic Achievement

There is ample evidence to support the view that intelligent children do better on school achievement (*e.g.*, Joshi & Passi, 1968; Kakar, 1970; Pathak, 1962; Rao, 1971; Rastogi, 1974; Sinha, 1970). While reviewing studies related to correlates of achievement, Balasubramaniyam (1997) observed that there is "corroborative evidence to prove that intelligence is a correlate of achievement" (p. 724). Several other studies have reported the relationship of high SES and high IQ with achievement in science (*e.g.*, Sudhir & Muraleedharan-Pillai, 1987; Singh & Dwivedi, 1983). Aswal (2001) found significant correlation between intelligence and achievement in mathematics. Also, science students have been found to score higher on numerical and reasoning abilities than agriculture and arts students (Chatterjee, 1983). Gaur and Mathur (1974) found high correlation between intelligence and occupational aspirations. Studies on reading show no difference between IQs of good and poor readers (Dash, 1991). Mishra (1989) found that bilinguals were superior in abstract and verbal logical reasoning. R. Singh (2001) reported long attention span in case of highly intelligent boys.

Creativity

Studies have shown positive and significant relationship between intelligence and creativity (for a review, Passi, 1997). The findings of the studies have rather been equivocal. Raj (1978) found that creativity discriminates between high and low intelligent groups. Sengupta (1979) reported that high and low creative students differed in intelligence level. A few studies (Deshmukh, 1979; Kishore, 1981; Mehdi, 1977) have noted positive but low correlation. Gupta and Chandradash (1994) found that intelligent people are more creative. Kamra and Gakhar (1999) reported scientific creativity to be positively related with intelligence. On the other hand, Bhattacharya (1978) found that level of creativity does not affect intelligence. Gupta (1980) found both verbal and non-verbal creativity to be independent of intelligence. Sansanwal and Sharma (1993) observed that scientific creativity was not influenced by intelligence. Muddu (1980) has reported a negative correlation between the two.

Personality

It has been reported that intelligent persons are emotionally stable (Arora, 1992; Murthy, 1966), socially mature (Mulia, 1991; Rao, 1978), altruistic (Tyagi, 1999), committed (Kumari, 1986), adjusted (Kakkar, 1965) and show high self-concept (Sharma & Jaswal, 1999). In comparison to dull children, intelligent children exhibit less anxiety (Patel & Kapadia, 1985) and behaviour problems (Ali, 1967), do not show frustration

(Jethwani, 1986), and are introverted (Vidhu, 1968). They also show high degree of need for order (Patil, 1982) and perform better under ego stress conditions (Gupta & Sharma, 1991). Using Rorschach inkblot test, Adhikari, Adhikari, and Tripathi (1986) found that persons with high IQ (between 111-120) showed integrated personality and greater organization in composition as compared to the subjects with lower IQ (between 80 and 110). Studies related to the personality profiles of delinquents and criminals place them in low intelligence category (Nathawat, 1974; Sivanandan, 1974). Gautam (1971) reported that leaders have high IQ. Also, intelligent people are field independent (Panda, 1991) and extroverted (Sharma & Bansal, 1991-92). D'Souza, Singh and Basavarajappa (1999) reported no relationship between shyness and intelligence.

Information Processing Approach to Intelligence

The PASS (Planning, Attention, Simultaneous, and Successive) model of intelligence (J.P. Das, Naglieri, & Kirby, 1994) has drawn considerable attention of some researchers. Studies (Das & Das, 1984; Dash, Puhan, & Mahapatra, 1985) found that simultaneous processing variables are rationally related to Piaget's concrete operations. Dash and Mahapatra (1989) noted that there was no appreciable developmental change in successive processing in the children between grades 3 and 7. On the other hand, simultaneous processing and planning evinced a clear developmental change. Sahu and Devi (1984) have shown that children (9-11 years old) with greater reading ability performed at a higher level on successive and simultaneous processing tasks. Muralidharan and Srivastava (1995) found facilitatory effect of temple ecology on simultaneous processes. Kar (1989) has shown close relationship between individual differences in strategy deployment in selective attention, search, and planning processes. Kar and Dash (1992) have integrated the studies done within the framework of information integration model as an alternative to the existing models of intelligence. Reviewing the available evidence they argue that coding and planning are relatively invariant modes of information processing. As a sequential model of cognitive development this approach emphasizes on qualitative changes in the efficiency of cognitive processing with development.

CONCLUSION

Research on intelligence in India does not present a very encouraging picture. Though a large number of intelligence tests have been constructed or adapted in India, the nature of these tests leaves much to be desired. The ideas and technology of testing have been borrowed from the West. Researchers have seldom paid attention to the problems of human assessment that arise in the Indian socio-cultural context. As Misra, Sahoo, and Puhan (1997) noted, "borrowing and adapting tests has become a major academic problem threatening the quality of work" (p. 309). Researchers (*e.g.*, Kulkarni & Puhan, 1988; Sinha, 1983; Tripathi, 1982) have identified a number of sources of error arising out of differences between tester and testee, caste, power hierarchy, and a host of other response set effects such as acquiescence and test-taking attitude. They have noted that Indian psychologists need to give up the habit of blind borrowing from the Western culture, avoid duplication of efforts, develop culturally appropriate frameworks and concepts, and relate the concepts to Indian culture.

Mohanty and Puhan (1980) have raised the problems arising out of "imposed etic" approach, particularly in the processes of selection and recruitment. These are due to the fantastic selection ratios in the developing countries including India where there have always been more people than jobs. The emphasis has, therefore, been on keeping the best interest of the employer in view while the interest of the individual seeking the job has largely been ignored. They also point out the difficulty in obtaining an appropriate and, at the same time, reliable and valid criterion against which the validity of the instrument can be assessed.

The situation of testing in India demands a change in our perspective on test construction. Tests sensitive to cognitive as well as affective domains suitable for Indian conditions need to be developed. They should be in tune with the emerging perspectives on intelligence. Also, there is need to emphasize the application of intellectual skills in adaptation to everyday contexts. The assessment procedure should emphasize on obtaining information about the skills and potentials of individuals in the natural course of working. In place of linguistic and logical-mathematical varieties of instruments, there is a need to devise instruments that peep directly at the intelligence-in-operation rather than proceed via the detour of language and logical faculties. Attention to a range of measures designed specifically to tap different facets of the capacity in question would even be more desirable.

Most of the empirical studies on intelligence have been conducted employing those instruments making the results of the studies undependable and suspicious. One also notices lack of an appropriate theoretical framework and methodological rigour in these studies. Time has come when psychologists in India need to be pragmatic, derive their research problems from the Indian socio-cultural context, and develop culturally appropriate conceptualization and tools for the assessment of intelligence.

In sum, the tradition of intelligence testing in India has altogether been an imported one. It has followed the Western tradition and borrowed psychometric concepts since its very inception. In dealing with psychological concepts, as Mukherjee (1980) has noted, the Indian researchers have endorsed an "implicit assumption that the definition of those concepts and their measurement as proposed by Western research workers will also hold good in our cultural context" (p. 6). The difficulty in transferring concepts and tools wholesale from one cultural setting to another has not deterred the test constructors in doing so. The research in the area of test construction in India does "not show much rigour in terms of precision of measurement, in drawing appropriate inferences regarding the constructs which the researcher intends to measure and also in terms of their accuracy of generalization, besides the negligence of a proper conceptualization" (Mukherjee, 1997, p. 678).

5

The Traditional Notion of Intelligence: Analysis of Sanskrit *Suktis* and Hindi Proverbs

Chapter 3 dealt with the limitations of the psychometric notion of intelligence and also the various alternative perspectives that have emerged in recent years in the Western world. It was observed that intelligence is increasingly viewed as a cultural construct (or genre) and its assessment necessarily demands understanding the local definitions of intelligence. This chapter extends the argument further by taking into account the indigenous ideas regarding intelligence as evident in the Indian scholarly texts and folk literature. In particular, it examines the notions of intelligence as reflected in Sanskrit *suktis* and Hindi proverbs.

The Sanskrit language has a living tradition of at least three thousand years stretching into present times. As the common language of the India's cultural growth and as the principal vehicle of its thought for much of this period, it occupies a unique position in the national identity of India. It is replete with inspirational, creative, narrative, descriptive and gnomic compositions of high literary value (Haksar, 2000). Much of the ancient Indian wisdom, written in Sanskrit, is in the form of *suktis* or *subhasitas* (good words). The *suktis* may be small (many consist of only one or two sentences), but are believed to be more serious, miraculous, close to ultimate reality, loaded with hidden meanings. They reflect the essence of the experiences of the foresighted saints as well as the common people. As a small lamp lightens the entire house, the *suktis* reveal the secrets of the living and non-living worlds.

Proverbs (or Maxims) are used extensively by people throughout the globe in social interchanges to sharpen the impact of communication. They help to effectively express one's thoughts and feelings. The use of these short, familiar, fixed and sequential expressions in day-to-day writing and conversation makes language more precise and lively. It is generally held that proverbs represent well-known truths, social norms or moral actions (Gibbs & Beitel, 1995). Rooted in the traditions and practices of a community they often summarize the essence of folk wisdom that has filtered through ages in the form of shared experiences of a community. The beliefs expressed in these abridgements of wisdom are, however, relativistic and explicitly known. Though with the passage of time a few proverbs may lose their relevance, a large majority of them continue to serve as valuable guides for behaviour.

Since the early years of the twentieth century, clinical and educational psychologists, psychiatrists, and neuro-psychologists have used proverbs as a diagnostic tool for evaluating intelligence, psychopathology and brain dysfunctions (*e.g.*, Andreasen, 1977; Van Lancker, 1990). Experimental psychologists have looked at people's understanding of proverbs as indicators of categorization and reasoning processes (*e.g.*, Honeck, Kibler, & Firment, 1987). Developmental psychologists have viewed proverb understanding as one of the key achievements of intellectual functioning in children (*e.g.*, Nippold, Martin, & Erskinne, 1988; Piaget, 1969). Personality psychologists have used proverbs to assess personality traits (*e.g.*, Baumgarten, 1952; Marzolf, 1974). Social psychologists have explored the extent to which proverbial sayings reflect normative aspects of how people think and behave in social situations (*e.g.*, Furnham, 1987; Rogers, 1990). Psycholinguists have studied proverb comprehension to uncover the unconscious mental processes used in making sense of non-literal language (*e.g.*, Gibbs, 1994; Honeck & Temple, 1994; Kemper, 1981).

There are several detailed studies on proverb use and understanding in different cultural contexts (*cf.* Mieder, 1993). The frequent use of proverbs in different contexts and cultures reflects a variety of facets about nature and human behaviour which makes proverbs useful in oral communication, political rhetoric, lyrics, newspaper headlines, book titles, advertising slogans and cartoon captions. The proverbs are related to various themes of human life including body, love, work, friendship, death, as well as general principles about intelligent or reasonable behaviour (Goodwin & Wenzel, 1981). Proverbs related to intelligent behaviour deal with (a) cause-effect reasoning, such as *spare the rod and spoil the child* or *he who lies down with dogs will rise with flees*; (b) Reasoning from effects to causes, such as *where there is smoke, there's fire* and *where bees are there is honey*; (c) reasoning by analogy, such as *grace is to the body what judgement is to mind;* and (d) reasoning from a specific instance to a more general conclusion, such as *once bitten, twice shy* and *swallow does not make a summer*. Proverbs about practical reasoning caution against inappropriate generalizations, such as *don't judge a book by its cover* and *all that glitters is not gold.* Proverbs also caution against faulty reasoning, such as *actions speak louder than words.*

The present study attempted to examine the nature of intelligence as represented in Sanskrit *Suktis* and also as shared in the influential tradition of proverbs available in Hindi language, which is the official language of India and is spoken by largest number of persons (about 39% of the population).

THE CONCEPT OF *BUDDHI*

Buddhi (intelligence) is a varied, all inclusive and integral concept in the Sanskrit literature. A perusal of English-Sanskrit dictionary (Monier-Williams, 1964) reveals that there are as many as 29 words in Sanskrit that are used for 'intelligent person', 27 words for 'intellect', and 18 words for 'intelligence' (Table 5.1). An analysis of these terms indicates that *buddhi,* in general, refers to the following:

(a) the mental vigour or power of forming and retaining concepts;
(b) reason, intellect, mind, discernment, and judgement;
(c) perception, comprehension, apprehension, and understanding;
(d) knowledge of one's self, conscience, will, desire;

(e) presence of mind, ready wit, and skill;
(f) an opinion, view, notion, idea, and conjecture; and
(g) thought about or meditation on.

Table 5.1: Sanskrit Terms used for Intelligent, Intellect and Intelligence

	Sanskrit Terms
Intelligent person	*Buddhimaan, Dheemaan, Matimaan, Medhavi, Manasvi, Subuddhih, Kushalbuddhin, Shuddhdhih, Kritdhih, Subudhh, Sajnanh, Jnani, Jnanwaan, Prajnavan, Manishi, Prekshavan,Kovidah, Jnata, Vidurh, Marmajnah, Vijnah, Vilakshanah, Kushalmatih, Nipunamatih, Chaturah, Chaturbuddhi, Vidagdhah,Vidagadhbuddhi, Kalyanbuddhih.*
Intellect	*Buddhi, Medha, Matih, Manasa, Prajna, Citta, Chetana, Chetam, Chijnam, Bodhah, Samvit, Samvinteeh, Manisha, Upalabddhih,Pratibha, Jnamih, Pratipada, Shemushi, Dhishana, Preksha, Jnandristi, Dhyanam, Bodhshaktih, Chikshantih, Jnanashaktih,Sanjna.*
Intelligence	*Buddhih, Jnanam, Dhee, Medha, Chetana, Chaitanyam, Citta, Chichkshaktih, Vijnata, Kushalata, Kaushalayam, Chaturya, Vaichkshanyam, Vidagdhata, Vaidgdhyam, Suwarta, Shubhawarta, Gurhbhashitam.*

Thus the conception of *buddhi* not only includes cognition but also affective and motivational functions. Also, there has been stress on good intelligence (*Subuddhi*), secret intelligence (*Gurhbhashitam*), and good idea and their communication (*Shubhawarta*) in the Sanskrit literature. In an interesting analysis Rajshekher in a book on poetics entitled *Kavya Mimamsa* has described three types of Buddhi i.e., *Smriti* (memory), *Mati* (view) and *Prajna* (wisdom). They are related to remembering past, understanding present and visualizing future.

Intelligence in the Scholarly Traditions of India

The notion of intelligence in the Indian tradition has been approached in diverse ways in the different schools of thought. It has been characterized in terms of *pratibha* in *Nyaya Vaisesika*, *prajna* in Patanjali's *yoga* system, *vak* in *Tantrika* literature, and *bhavas* in *Samkhya* philosophy. A brief overview of these notions seems in order (also refer Srivastava, Tripathi & Misra, 1995).

Pratibha literally means a flash of light, a revelation. It is often used in the sense of wisdom characterized by immediacy and freshness. It subsumes any kind of knowledge, which is neither sense-born, nor of the nature of an inference. It might be called supra sensory and supra rational appreciation, grasping truth directly, and, therefore, seems to have the same value in Indian philosophy as intuition has in the Western systems (Kaviraj, 1966). In *Agamic* literature the term *pratibha* refers to Highest Divinity, understood as the principle of intelligence and conceived as female. The prime characteristics of this supra-sensory knowledge are immediacy, intense clarity, and transcendentalness (*i.e.*, free from time and space limitations). An intelligent person having realized this higher order knowledge becomes a *mahakarta* (great worker) and *mahabhokta* (great experiencer).

In the Indian philosophical treatises intelligence has usually been treated as a transpersonal state, a process and an entity, the realization of which depends upon one's own effort, persistence and motivation. As Das (1994) noted, the concept of intelligence in the Indian philosophy refers to "waking up, noticing, recognizing, understanding, and comprehending. In contrast to the usual meaning of intelligence, as understood in the Western literature, *Buddhi* (intelligence) includes such things as determination, mental effort, and even feelings and opinions in addition to such intellectual processes as knowledge, discrimination, and decision making" (p. 387). Thus an intelligent person is capable of knowing the intentions of others, is polite and remains away from self-praise, exhibits initiative and interest in work, and lacks rigidity. His keen observation is sharp enough to decipher even the intentions of animals and birds. An intelligent person is always alert and responds appropriately to emergent conditions. He is not disturbed by difficult or harsh situations. He is always ready to fight for the right cause. This situation characterizes practical understanding in real life conditions.

The *Samkhya-Yoga* system asserts that any act of awareness involves three levels of consciousness: *manas*, *ahankar*, and *buddhi*, usually translated as "lower mind", "ego" and "*intellect*", respectively. *Manas* picks up the sensory input, *ahankara* sorts the input according to a continually revised scheme of classification, and *buddhi* assesses the value of the categories that *ahankara* is using. The *Samkhya* school also describes intelligence in terms of eight *bhavas* (*i.e.*, state of being). The *bhavas* are of two types – *sattvika* and *tamsika*. The *sattvika* (pure) *bhavas* constitute *dharma* (virtue), *jnana* (knowledge), *viraga* (non-attachment), and *aisvarya* (power) while *adharma* (non-virtue), *ajnana* (ignorance), *raga* (attachment), and *anaisvarya* (weakness) constitute *tamasika* (impure) *bhavas*.

The *Samkhya* philosophy characterizes *Prakriti* as consisting of three *gunas* (constituents): *Sattva* (lightness), *Rajas* (passion), and *Tamas* (heaviness). Of the three, *sattva* is considered an essence of luminous intelligence, with the tendency for manifestation or reflection, but without mass or gravity, and, therefore, unable to manifest. It promotes movement to a higher level; the psychological makeup of a sattvic doer constitutes a necessary grounding to build wisdom. Under the sattvic mode, each action is felt intrinsically joyous, is performed without any expectation or desire for extrinsic reward. Actions involve austerity of words (speaking words which are good, beautiful, true, and give peace), austerity of mind (silence, self-harmony, loving-kindness and pure heart), and austerity of body (purity, righteousness, chastity, and non-violence). *Sattvic* intelligence perceives the eternal being as unperishable and infinity in finite things. It knows the principle of action and principle of withdrawal from action, knows what ought to be done and what ought not to be done, and can discriminate between freedom and bondage. The *sattvic* does show discrimination and perseverance, and experiences an inner peace that transcends the momentary victories and failures.

The *rajas*, characterized as moving principle, has the energy that counteracts and dispenses the inertia of *tamasa* (Jayakar, 1988). *Rajasic* action is referred to as the level path – it serves to maintain the *status quo*. Passion, thirst, lust, desire, greed are the specific traits associated with the rajasic influence. *Rajasic* people worship power and wealth; being enslaved by their sense cravings, they work invariably for personal gains. There is no clear understanding of what is right or wrong; what should be done and what should not be done. The *rajasic* pleasure is initiated by the sensory desires, it is sweet to begin with, but eventually leads to pain and sorrow.

Tamas has the ingredients of manifestation, such as matter, mass, gravity, volume, and density, but with inertia which makes any independent movement impossible. Activity guided by *tamasic* influence not only impedes a progressive movement (towards wisdom), but also leads the self onto a lower path. It promotes in the doer ignorance, sleepy dullness, delusion, inertia, and negligence. Appropriately depicted as darkness, work in the tamasic mode is performed with a confused mind, without consideration of the consequences, or of one's powers or of the harm that may come upon others, or of loss to oneself. The tamasic self is portrayed as vulgar, arrogant, deceitful, malicious, indolent, despondent, and procrastinating.

It is held that these *gunas* are essentially present in every creation. Their proportion may, however, vary from one creation to the other. Corresponding to each *guna* is a *dosha* (non-quality), which governs all vital events and processes of the human body. *Sattva* is represented by *pitta, rajas* by *vata*, and *tamas* by *kapha*. *Pitta* is responsible for such psychological phenomenon as the holding together of the various elements of the body in their proper form (intelligence, clear conception, courage, fear, anger, delight, confusion, and lucidity), and maintaining the cohesive unity of the body as a whole. *Pitta* is of different types, among which *saadhaka pitta* is reponsible for *buddhi*. Vaagbhata in his *Ashtanga Samgraha* notes that *saadhaka pitta* is responsible for *buddhi, medha* (wisdom), *abhimaan* (self-esteem), *utsaaha* (enthusiasm), and the achievements of one's aspiration (Shanbhag, 1988).

Prakriti remains in an unmanifested state until it is enlivened by *purusa* (consciousness). The first manifestation of *prakriti* to arise from her association with *purusa* is *buddhi* (intellect). In the Indian tradition, intelligence has been treated in terms of wisdom. The *Bhagavad Gita* makes reference to a number of terms to refer to a wise person. They include learner, knower of absolute truth, intelligent person, great soul, sage, self-realized, sober, liberated being, mystic transcendentalist, undeluded, knower of Supreme *Brahman*, knowledgeable, one in divine consciousness, devoted soul, self-controlled, introspective sage, man of steady intelligence, one who sees with equal vision, and one who has conquered mind. A wise person remains situated in equanimity and sameness, equipoise in misery and happiness. Such a person enjoys unlimited happiness, is located in the self (aiming within), and derives pleasure from within. He/she is unbewildered; without false prestige; free from illusion, lust, fear, and anger; is gentle, humble, prideless, non-violent, truthful, modest, determined, tolerant, friendly and forgiving, engaged in good services for all, treats everyone equally, is a natural mediator, has companion, and is adverse to fault finding. The *Bhagavad Gita* assumes that wisdom is not an abstract intellectual engagement; it is a response to real life concerns. Also, it is within the reach of possibilities for which a practical manual has also been prescribed.

A distinction has been made between *pratibha* or intelligence as lower and higher, or bad *(papbuddhi)* and good (*dharmabuddhi*). Good intelligence leads to happiness, pleasure and prosperity, and is constructive. Bad intelligence is destructive and causes unhappiness. This has elsewhere been referred to as *sarala* (or simple and straightforward) and *kutila* (or devious and cunning) intelligence (Badrinath, 1999). Individuals with low level of intelligence are not able to see beyond present whereas an intelligent person goes beyond the immediate, realizing the permanence and truth of the *Brahman*, the highest divine. Such a person distinguishes between what is temporary (*nitya*) and what is permanent (*anitya*). Intelligent persons are equated with adults, whereas people with low intelligence (*ajnanis*) are considered children.

Vidyapati in his book *Purush Pariksha* has distinguished a man from those who merely look like a man (refer Jha, 1999). A man is one who is *purusharthavan*, that is who has attained *purushartha*, the four objects of human life (e.g., *dharma*, *artha*, *kama*, and *moksha*). Such a person is brave, learned and intelligent. Even a brave person, in addition to courage and perseverance shows a sense of discrimination. Thus intelligence is a characteristic of the man. Such a person attains mastery over theory and practice. According to Vidyapati, "He whose wits are beyond measurement, who is far from being either an ill wit (*kubuddhi*) or no-wit (*abuddhi*), he is....Good wit (*subuddhi*)". Thus three types of intelligence have been discerned: *subuddhi* (good wit), *kubuddhi* (ill wit), and *abuddhi* (no wit). A *subuddhi* is acute in wit (*pratibha*), has a sharp memory (*medhavi*), and he whose wits, when affairs present themselves, are nimble and keen in inference. Such a person shows topmost concern for society. A scholar who alienates himself from society and remains absorbed in issues hardly of any concern to life and existence of his society, does not belong to the realm of society. *Kubuddhi* or *Durbuddhi* is of two types: *Bachak* or *thaga* (swindler), characterized by sweet tongued, ruthless, crooked and usurper of others' property; and *Pishun* or *chugalkhor* (calumniator), characterized by ungratefulness, always finding faults in others, and shameless. *Kubuddhi*, being acute in wit, easily manages to reach high office and becomes powerful. He, however, uses his power for the satisfaction of his own greed. A person characterized as *abuddhi* or *nirbuddhi* is devoid of any wit. He cannot afford commonsense; as a result he is not only harmless but worthless. *Abuddhi* is of two types: *Janma barbar* (*abudhhi by birth*) and *sansarga barbar* (*abuddhi* by association).

It is assumed that knowledge constitutes the nature or quality of self (*atman*) acting through mind, reaching out to the objects and making them known to the self. An early reference to the functions of mind in *Aitareya Upanisad* includes the following: *Samjnana* (awareness), *jnana* (perception), *vijnana* (discrimination), *prajnana* (intelligence), *medha* (wisdom), *dṛsti* (insight), *dhṛti* (steadfastness), *mati* (thought), *manisa* (thoughtfulness), *smṛti* (memory), *samkalpa* (conception), *kratu* (purpose), and so on. *Chandoghya Upanishad* also gives a list of mind's functions which incorporates some additional functions such as *citta* (intelligence and thought), *dhyana* (concentrated reflection), and *smer* (rememberness) (Misra, 1999).

The indigenous view considers *vivek* (sense of discrimination) as the biggest asset, which causes happiness and prosperity. It is derived from perceptual analysis, inference, analogical reasoning and materials learned from books and authorities. Enumerating on the relationship between consciousness and the physical structure, Das (1994) observes that pure consciousness is at the top with no material basis. From consciousness evolves the discriminative intelligence or *Buddhi*. The consciousness of one's own identity as an individual evolves out of discriminative and evaluative intelligence. The mental functions evolve secondarily out of intelligence and ego defense. Next to evolve are the five perceptual abilities (*e.g.*, seeing, hearing, smelling, tasting, and kinesthesis) and five motor abilities (*e.g.*, speech, grasping, locomotion, reproduction and excretion). These abilities are then attached to five basic elements, or natural substances: earth, light, water, wind, and space. In contrast to Western psychology the Indian perspective views motor organs as contributing to our experience and knowledge.

ANALYSIS OF SANSKRIT *SUKTIS*

Srivastava and Misra (1999a, 2000) examined the nature of intelligence and the ways it influences behaviour as reflected in the *Sanskrit Suktis*. Three laypersons, having competence for Sanskrit language and with no formal training in psychology, scanned about 20,000 *suktis* contained in Sagar's (1990) *Vishwa Sanskrit Sukti Kosh*, and Verma and Verma's (1985) *Vishwa Sukti Kosh*. They were told to indicate whether a *sukti* was in any way related to 'intelligence' as found in the everyday usage. The present authors examined the *suktis* thus identified and, in case of ambiguity, clarifications were sought. In this way 339 *suktis* having reference to intelligence were identified. It may be noted that the above two volumes contained *suktis* were prepared after analyzing 110 Sanskrit texts.

Each *sukti* was read independently by at least two investigators having knowledge of the historical and spiritual traditions of India, and proficiency in Sanskrit. Based on the meaning contained in a *sukti*, a conceptual or thematic category was assigned. These categories were further grouped into few broad categories on the basis of their conceptual configuration. There was high agreement between the investigators regarding the meaning and grouping of *suktis*.

Analysis revealed four dimensions of intelligence: ***Cognitive Competence, Social Competence, Entrepreneurial Competence, and Emotional Competence***. More than one-third (39%) of the *suktis* stressed on the emotional competence of the intelligent person followed by entrepreneurial competence (26%) and cognitive competence (23%). The social competence was less emphasized (15%).

About one-third of the *suktis* stressed on three important attributes of intelligent persons: ***Control of emotions, Sensitivity to context,*** and ***Hard work*** (Table 5.2). Under control of emotions, a large majority of the *suktis* prescribed that an intelligent person should be able to control his/her anger. It is assumed that anger is the result of *ajnana* (ignorance) that destroys all qualities of man including intelligence. It is considered a type of wine under the influence of which people lose control over their senses and are thus not able to discriminate between right and wrong. Another characteristic of intelligent person is control of impulses (*Jitendriya*). People don't treat properly a person who does not have control over his/her impulses. Arousal, arrogance, jealousy, violence, and finding faults with others are also not observed in an intelligent person.

Sensitivity to a context refers to behaving according to the *desh* (ecology), *kala* (time), and *patra* (person). An intelligent person adapts himself/herself to the changing ecology like a frog. He/she also behaves like a tortoise that withdraws itself into its shell at the time of risk and comes out of the shell in favourable circumstances. An intelligent person recognizes the importance of time and begins work at the right time without losing it and utilises time for his/her personal benefits/advancement. Even small work at the right time proves to be more beneficial and those who properly utilize time don't repent afterwards. Also, recognition of the fact that there are different timings for work and enjoyment is important. Behaving according to the *patra* is also significant. Showing scholarship before ignorant people is considered foolishness. Also, bad people are calmed only by appropriate response, and being simple and generous to such persons is not desirable.

Intelligent persons are hard working. Conversely, hard work makes one intelligent. The Indian scholarly tradition emphasizes the importance of effort in the right direction without which nothing can be achieved. One should not leave effort for fate. As the continuous fall of water softens even a stone, right effort makes things happen. It is only due

Table 5.2: Characteristics of Intelligent Persons as Reported in Sanskrit *Suktis*

Characteristics	*f* (N=339)	*Per cent*
A. Cognitive Competence		
1. Sensitivity to context	36	11
2. Comprehension	5	2
3. Discrimination	5	2
4. Planning	4	1
5. Reflection	13	4
6. Communication	14	4
B. Social Competence		
7. Following norms	8	2
8. Respecting elders/guests	13	4
9. Helping others	9	3
10. Friendship with caution	22	6
C. Entrepreneurial Competence		
11. Unaffected by criticism	3	1
12. Practical consideration	9	3
13. Patience	11	3
14. Vigilance	3	1
15. Commitment	8	2
16. Maintaining secrecy	5	2
17. Hard work	38	11
18. Moderation	9	3
D. Emotional Competence		
19. Optimism	2	-
20. Enthusiasm	2	-
21. Control of emotions	47	14
22. Being alert to contemporary happenings	6	2
23. Kindness	10	3
24. Stability	8	2
25. Self-respect	9	3
26. Politeness	6	2
27. Independence (economic)	4	1
28. Speaking the truth (in context)	12	4
29. Control of ego	16	5
30. Realistic self-appraisal	2	–

to practice that a novice becomes an expert in a particular field of knowledge. The importance of the doctrine of *karma* cannot be ignored in the Indian context, which advocates for doing work without bothering for its consequences. 'As you sow so shall you reap' is the basic philosophy behind the doctrine of *karma*.

Within the category of cognitive competence, in addition to sensitivity to context, included are attributes such as reflection, communication, comprehension, discrimination and planning. ***Reflection,*** according to the *suktis*, refers to prior thinking about pros and cons of an action. It includes evaluation of one's strengths and weaknesses as well as advantages and disadvantages of an action. Also, modality of executing the task should be properly examined. It is recommended that people should not start a work suddenly since this may not lead to the desired consequences and thus can become a source of unhappiness. The **communication ability** is also important. An intelligent person speaks only when necessary, makes his mind clear using minimum words, his/her speech is loaded with hidden meanings, and remains focused on the problem under consideration. Such a person does not speak unpleasant things and communicates only after obtaining permission of the person concerned. An intelligent person is able to draw inferences and comprehend the intentions of others immediately. He is capable of deciphering meanings out of symbols. Such a person discriminates between good and bad, right and wrong, and, thus, is able to plan for the future.

Included among social competence are the characteristics such as following social norms, respecting parents, elders and guests; helping the needy; and remaining in the company of good people. An intelligent person observes social rules; it is his/her *dharma* (duty). Such a person, however, is neither led by the masses, nor leads them as the advantages of such movements are shared by all while disadvantages are thrust upon the leader. An intelligent person helps the needy but refrains from getting acknowledged. Being in the company of good people is another quality of an intelligent person who makes friends cautiously.

In addition to hard work, a few other characteristics related to entrepreneurial competence include patience, vigilance, practical approach, commitment to work, maintaining secrecy till the task is completed, and being unaffected by the criticism were noticed. An intelligent person shows patience in both types of situations: He tolerates bad people's deeds and continuously approaches a task which remains inaccessible. He/she remains alert and adopts a cautious approach. Practicality refers to listening to all voices but doing what one thinks appropriate. Also, it suggests accepting good advices even if children or even bad people have proposed the same and dealing with the problems skilfully. An intelligent person remains focused on the task and successfully accomplishes the same despite several odds. He/she remains unaffected by the adverse circumstances and maintains secrecy about the plan of action till the task is completed.

According to Sanskrit *suktis*, an intelligent person speaks restrained truth, is not an egoist, shows moderation in behaviour, is kind and polite, lives in the present, is self-respecting, has realistic self-appraisal, and is economically independent. He/she speaks the truth but restrains from doing so if it is harmful to the person/society. Being modest is another quality: Excess of anything, be it modesty, politeness, simplicity, arrogance, wealth, etc., is rather not included in the attributes of an intelligent person. Such a person shows respect for the self. He/she does not bow before others for any favour; and at the same time does not indulge in self-praise. Repenting for the past and indulging in daydreaming are not the qualities of an intelligent person. Rather, he/she lives in the present and is also able to assess his strengths and weaknesses. An intelligent person earns his livelihood and spends according to his/her income.

ANALYSIS OF HINDI PROVERBS

Three lay persons having competence in Hindi language and with no formal training in psychology identified 393 proverbs related to intelligent behaviour and intelligent persons after scanning four dictionaries of Hindi proverbs, *i.e.*, Madhav and Misra's, (1965) *Kahawat Kosh*, Sharma's (1983) *Vargikrit Hindi*

Lokokti Kosh, Shukla and Sharma's (1986) *Hindi Lokokti Kosh*, and Kaushik, Shastri, Shastri, and Gupta's (1990) *Muhawara-Lokokti Kosh*. These volumes document about 25,500 proverbs in Hindi. These volumes are not mutually exclusive. As a result, many proverbs are common among them. It may be mentioned that while the volumes by Kaushik *et al.* (1990), and Sharma (1983) covered proverbs spoken in standard Hindi language, Madhav and Misra's (1965) included proverbs spoken in different regional languages of the State of Bihar. Shukla and Sharma (1986) included the proverbs spoken in the State of Madhya Pradesh. On the whole, these volumes contained majority of the proverbs of Hindi language.

Each proverb was read independently by at least two investigators proficient in Hindi language, and having knowledge of the social and cultural traditions. Based on the message and meaning of each proverb, a conceptual category was assigned. These categories were further organized into few broad categories on the basis of their conceptual configuration. There was high agreement between the investigators with regard to the meaning and grouping of proverbs in different categories. In case of disagreement the help of an expert was obtained.

The analysis revealed that the proverbs are largely concerned with three aspects of intelligence, namely structure and determinants of intelligence, characteristics of an intelligent person/behaviour, and characteristics of an unintelligent person/behaviour. Of a total of 393 proverbs, 41 (10%) were related to the structure and determinants of intelligence, 214 (55%) described the characteristics of an intelligent person/behaviour, and 138 (35%) were related to the unintelligent person/behaviour. The following is a summary that emerged after content analyzing the themes present in the proverbs (for details, see Srivastava & Misra, 1996b).

Structure of Intelligence

Table 5.3 contains the details of factors related to the structure and determinants of intelligence. A large number of proverbs (22%) referred to individual and group differences in intellectual competence of people. Few such proverbs are: "All individuals cannot be treated alike", "All the five fingers are not equal", "Individuals differ in their intelligence", and "A crow among the birds, and barbers among the human beings are most intelligent".

Table 5.3: Factors related to the Structure and Determinants of Intelligence as described in Proverbs

Characteristics	*f (n = 41)*
Structural Features	
1. Essential for acquiring knowledge	2
2. Real basis of discrimination	3
3. Thought as supreme wealth	2
4. Considered as the greatest power	2
5. Individual and group differences	9
6. Distribution of intelligent and unintelligent people	4
7. Continuity and discontinuity in intellectual development	6
8. Judgement of intelligent behaviour depends on the outcome received	1
9. Theoretical and practical aspects of intelligence	2
10. Incomplete knowledge is dangerous	3
Determinants	
11. Genetic factors	3
12. Environmental factors	4

Analysis revealed that the Indian tradition believes in two things. First, intelligence gets manifested right from the beginning of life ("A child's sharpness gets manifested in the crib itself"). Second, intellective capacity degenerates after the age of sixty. The analysis shows that the distribution of intelligent and unintelligent people is not guided by a particular physical ecology or region, rather both types of persons are found everywhere (*e.g.*, "Asses are not found in Kabul alone").

Intelligence is considered essential for acquiring knowledge. In fact, it has also been treated synonymously with 'knowledge'. It is thought to be the supreme wealth and the greatest power. Intelligence provides the real basis of discrimination among individuals ("Do not evaluate a person on the basis of his attire or physique, rather on the basis of his heart and mind"). Further, one is judged intelligent on the basis of the outcome of one's actions ("If successful then intelligent, if not successful then unintelligent"). There are two aspects of intelligence – *knowetic* and *pragmatic/procedural*. The practical intelligence is situated in the social context and only few persons are fortunate enough to be endowed with both types of intelligence.

Among the determinants of intelligence, the importance of both genetic and environmental factors has been recognized. The proverbs like "Like father like son" and "Intelligence gets manifested at the time of birth" endorse the belief in genetic bases. However, it is the environment that has received prominence in the Indian folk wisdom. Intelligence is earned through one's own efforts and practice. Exposure to varied environmental contexts is considered important for its development. It is held that "in comparison to bookish knowledge acquiring practical knowledge through pilgrimage and travel (*deshatan*) is in no way inferior", and "travel makes one intelligent". Obviously, it is the social intelligence that has been given primacy in these couplets. Also, the type of people with whom one lives, and the type of food one eats, determines one's mental state. "Spare the rod and spoil the child' is another famous proverb reflecting the importance of environmental factors. However, the significance of external factors such as luck has not altogether been missing in the Indian psyche.

The importance of *Karma* (deeds) hardly needs to be overemphasized while describing the role of genetic and environmental factors. It is believed that a child receives his *Karma* from his parents ("The child grows due to father's efforts, the agricultural output is due to one's own efforts"). This proverb also communicates that the activity or passivity of *Karma* from the previous generations is dependent upon one's own efforts.

Characteristics of the Intelligent People

Analysis of proverbs revealed four broad dimensions of intelligent behaviour: **Cognitive Competence, Social Competence, Entrepreneurial Competence, and Emotional**

Competence (Table 5.4). Out of 214 proverbs, 54 per cent stressed the cognitive competence of the person, 3 per cent the social competence, 30 per cent the entrepreneurial competence, and the remaining 13 per cent the emotional competence.

Table 5.4: Characteristics of an Intelligent Person as described in Hindi Proverbs

Characteristics	*f*	*Percentage (N = 214)*
A. Cognitive Competence		
1. Readiness to learn	8	4
2. Sensitivity to context	38	18
3. Comprehension	12	6
4. Learning (from past experience)	12	6
5. Problem solving	11	5
6. Planning	15	7
7. Reflection	4	2
8. Communication	12	6
B. Social Competence		
9. Observing norms	4	2
10. Serving elders	3	1
C. Entrepreneurial Competence		
11. Practical Orientation	28	13
12. Commitment	1	–
13. Patience	5	2
14. Hard work	11	5
15. Vigilance	7	3
16. Resourcefulness	8	4
17. Goal-directedness	2	1
18. Moderation	3	1
19. Secrecy	2	1
D. Emotional Competence		
20. Self-respect	13	6
21. Confidence	2	1
22. Trustworthiness	2	1
23. Open-mindedness	4	2
24. Self to other orientation	7	3

Within the category of **cognitive competence**, the highest number of proverbs described an intelligent person as one, who **behaves according to the context** (*i.e.*, ecology, time and person). Proverbs such as "Finding fault with the gift is not desirable", "Gift is to be accepted whatever it may be", "Tit for tat", "There is no point in crying over the spilt milk", "By the time you begin medication the child will die", "A farmer who does not work in the month of *Asvin* (plantation season) can't do anything in the month of *Agahan* (harvesting season)", and "Call uncle even to an ass if required" reflect this aspect of intelligent behaviour.

Another important cognitive feature of an intelligent person is **planning**, which is reflected in the following proverbs: "Thinking of tomorrow makes one problem free", "When an intelligent person gets a place to sit, he carves a place to stretch himself", "This winter is not going to be the last one" and "To save the eyes an intelligent person uses proper ointment". Other cognitive abilities are: the **ability to draw inferences** ("For an intelligent person, gestures are sufficient", "The moment the boy called me uncle, I guessed that he has lost his knife", "Humans can make out after hearing half of a story, bulls after hearing the complete story", and "Rod to asses and signals to wise persons"), **learning from past experiences** ("Ram will not visit Janakpur again", "The jackal will not go to the palm tree", "Humans learn from their past experiences"), **finding strategic solutions** of the problems ("What can be achieved by adopting an appropriate strategy cannot be achieved by dictating orders"), by appreciating **cause-effect relationship** ("The quantity of agricultural products depends upon the quality of soil", "By sitting idle one cannot fill the pond with water"), and through **reflection** ("Thinking more than just reading"). After having analyzed different aspects of the problem, an intelligent person places the problem in its proper context. Three **verbal abilities** of intelligent people emerged from this analysis. These are: Good **communication skills** ("Foolish fail to impress anyone no matter how long they speak, intelligent people are able to impress others even by their short speech"), **moderation in speech** ("It is neither good to remain silent for a long period, nor is the habit of excessive talking"), and **giving statements loaded with hidden meaning** ("As are the leaves hidden one within the other in a banana tree, so are the layers of wisdom hidden in a single word of the wise man"). Metaphors and other tools of linguistic expression are used quite frequently.

Though an intelligent person shows **respect for social**

norms ("No matter how important an act may be if it is against social norms, it is not desirable"), he is not led by masses and remains unaffected by criticism ("Despite barking dogs, the procession continues to move"). A few proverbs also emphasized paying respect for and service to the parents and elders.

Under the category of entrepreneurial competence, it emerged from the analysis that intelligent people adopt **practical approach** and remain conscious of the feasibility of various aspects of the problem ("In a situation of losing everything an intelligent person lets the half go for the benefit of the remaining half"). Also, such behaviour is **goal-directed** ("An intelligent person keeps his house in order"), and thus makes focused effort ("Attempting for one goal also makes other goals accessible, running for many goals simultaneously makes everything inaccessible"), **deals with the problem resourcefully** ("Killing two birds with one stone"), and **maintains secrecy** about his future plans ("Wise people keep their plans with themselves"). Analysis revealed that an intelligent person shows emotional characteristics such as **positive self-appreciation** and self-to-other orientation ("First self then God"), **open mindedness** ("Listen to all, do as you like"), **confidence** ("Since the barber's wife is smart, her nail cutter is made of bamboo"), and **trustworthiness**.

MULTIFACETED NATURE OF INTELLIGENCE

The present study focused on understanding the indigenous notion of intelligence as reflected in Sanskrit *Suktis* and Hindi proverbs. Intelligence in the Indian scholarly tradition (also see Das, 1994; Srivastava *et al.*, 1995; Srivastava, 1999b) has been characterized in the sense of wisdom whose prime characteristics are immediacy, freshness, intense clarity and transcendence (that is, free from time and space limitations). It has been treated as an entity, a state, and a process, the realization of which depends upon one's own efforts, persistence and motivation. In contrast to the usual meaning of intelligence as understood in the Western tradition, the Indian view is more intense and inclusive of such things as determination, mental effort, along with feelings and opinions in addition to such intellectual processes as knowledge, discrimination, and decision making.

The structure of intelligence was central to a large number of proverbs. These proverbs may be grouped into three categories. The first category of proverbs emphasizes the operation/functions/or processes of intelligence. Proverbs describing intelligence as essential for acquiring knowledge, as a real basis of discrimination among the masses, continuity/discontinuity in intellectual development, and practical aspects of intelligence fall under this category. The second category covers the proverbs that describe intelligence as a value. In these proverbs intelligence has been described as supreme wealth, greatest power, superior to physical strength, and an accomplishment. Since values are viewed as socially approved goals (Kluckhohn, 1951), there ought to be cultural differences in intelligence as a value. The analysis shows that Indian society accords high priority to intelligence, intelligent behaviour, and intelligent people. Third, there is an attempt to validate the concept of intelligence by describing individual and group differences, as they are perceived in Indian thinking.

The Western theories of intelligence are rooted in a positivist notion of knowledge and empiricist approach toward its understanding. Except Piaget and Vygotsky who approached intelligence in action, the majority of researchers consider intelligence in terms of disposition, ability or attribute of the person that is manifested in physiological, verbal and behavioural forms. In contrast, the Indian conception of intelligence is more process-oriented and tied to the context. For example, most of the proverbs describe the situations in which behaving in a particular mode characterizes intelligence. Also, one is judged intelligent on the basis of the balance of actions and outcomes.

Among the determinants or factors shaping intelligence, the Indian folk wisdom emphasizes on the role of both genetic and environmental factors. The transmission of intellectual characteristics from parents to offspring is a widely held belief. Intelligent children are considered to behave differently from very early in their lives. The role of external factors such as luck or chance has been endorsed. However, there is a strong support to the notion that intelligence is the product of one's own efforts which gets consolidated by practice and exposure to the right kind of environment. In this context, the doctrine of *Karma* (deeds) holds a unique place. Anthropological studies endorse that Hindus believe that they reap the harvest of their own *Karma* and the *Karma* passes through generations from father to son and from mother to daughter. Intelligence is seen as the result of one's own *Karma* and the child inherits it from his/her parents. However, the activity or passivity of this genetic endowment depends upon the child's *Karma*, persistence and motivation. This seems to be more or less similar to Piaget's (1960) *structuralism* where a person actively constructs his cognitive structures by operations and reflections. The realization of higher level of intelligent functioning is somewhat similar to performing operations on operations'.

Components of Intelligence

The analysis of *suktis* and proverbs shows that the Indian view stands at a distance from the psychometric notion of intelligence, which, till recently, was confined, to the cognitive domain. While recognizing the importance of cognitive abilities, it also stresses the emotional characteristics and the behaviours in relation to others as well as competence in performing a task. Thus the Indian view of intelligence is multifaceted, which has four major aspects: **Cognitive Competence, Social Competence, Entrepreneurial Competence,** and **Emotional Competence.**

The *suktis* and proverbs do not place premium on mere possession of cognitive abilities *per se*, rather the use of these abilities in real life situations is stressed. The abilities such as comprehension and discrimination are applied while thinking reflectively. A reflective person, after having heard all sides of the problem, places the problem in its proper context. An intelligent person shows sensitivity to context (*i.e.*behaves according to the ecology or *desh,* time *or kala,* and person or *patra*). Such behaviours demand making generalizations and discriminations on the part of the actor. Also, this kind of thinking leads to the development of associative thinking, rather than abstract thinking. Further, the intelligent person makes long-term planning and takes preventive measures, shows willingness to learn and learns from past experiences; and finds strategic solution of the problem. A couplet from *Panchatantra* (Haksar, 1992, p. 40) avers this view:

> "The great must be managed with meekness,
> And with stratagem the fierce,
> The base should be won with a small gift,
> But equals one must face with valour".

The Indian view does not attach importance to communication alone. Rather, an intelligent person is one who communicates effectively. This is pertinent to India which has a rich oral tradition. In this tradition, *jnana* (knowledge) was never written down but was handed down through mouth from one generation to the other in the form of stories, poems, and verses. The oral tradition emphasized the excellence of *priyamvada* (felicitous speech). A person showing the excellence of *priyamvada* has no eye for obstinate argumentation, though in reasoned discourse he/she is as readily eloquent as the God of speech. He/she has a meticulous sense of place and time. He/she descries through the people at a glance and yet behaves properly towards them. Never does he/she utter a foul word. And to cap it all, he/she is as acutely conscious of his/her failings as he/she is of others (Raina & Srivastava, 2000).

While relating with others not very prominent in the proverbs, *suktis* placed premium on characteristics such as following social norms and showing respect for and service to the parents, elders, and guests. It may be noted that the Indian child rearing practices make a special effort to inculcate in the child a regard for family/social norms as well as for elders (Krishnan, 1998). The Indian tradition views children as a source of old-age security (Mamdani, 1972), a way of enhancing the parent's sense of status, power, and personal pleasure (Singh, Bhargava, & Kumar, 1981), or potential earning members (Weiner, 1990). Thus, the economic value of children in terms of their contribution towards running the family tree and material help offered by them are given primacy over their psychological value such as children are the sources of pleasure and love and make life meaningful (Srivastava, 1997). Helping the needy is another social behaviour of an intelligent person. Further, an intelligent person remains in the company of good people. Or, alternatively, it may also be said that being in the company of good people nurtures intelligence. A larger number of *suktis* gave primacy to the latter view.

In the Indian tradition a person is judged intelligent in relation to his/her performance on the task. An intelligent person adopts a practical approach towards finding solution of a problem. Not behaving like an 'ideologue', an intelligent person remains tied to the reality and responds according to the demands of the task. Thus, there is plasticity in the behaviour of an intelligent person. Hard work is another characteristic, which has been greatly emphasized by the *suktis* and proverbs. It relates to the principle of *yoga* as competence in work forms an important aspect of Indian thinking. In addition, an intelligent person shows patience, remains vigilant, adopts various strategies to solve a problem, and remains focussed on the goal. The proverbs have made a special mention of two attributes of intelligent persons: moderation in behaviour and maintaining secrecy till the task is complete.

An intelligent person is able to control his/her emotions. Control of emotions is related to desires. The concept of *jitendriya* in the Indian context refers to a person who is able to manage and regulate the emotions. Such a person has full control over his/her impulses and actions. There are other concepts in the Indian thought too, such as *nishkama karma* (non-attachment) and the practices of yoga, which refer to emotional self-regulation. Yogic and religious practices including observance of fasts (*vratas*) help one to develop control over one's impulses. The *Bhagavad Gita* combines the virtues of detachment and impulse control in personality type called *Sthitaprajna*, implying one whose intellect is stable. Truthfulness has been another highly valued characteristic in the Indian people. The Greek traveller Megasthenes, who visited India in the fourth century BC, was amazed at not encountering a single individual—in this land where the Ganga flows—who knew what it was to tell a lie. *Satyam vada, dharmam chara* (be truthful in speech, be good and right in whatever you do) has been the motto of Indian tradition. It is, however, believed that one should not tell the truth that is harmful to the society. It is assumed that truth is not truth in itself; rather, it is the welfare of all human beings which constitutes truth. The attributes, such as, kindness and politeness make an intelligent person sensitive to others. Stability in behaviour, self respect and realistic self-appraisal make a person dependable and trust worthy. Such a person neither repents for the past, nor indulges in unrealistic planning for the future; rather, lives in the present. Avoiding excess of anything and adopting a middle path is also observed in the intelligent people.

In conclusion, intelligence, according to the Indian view, is not limited to the success of individual or personal achievements alone. Rather, it aims at achieving a common good. Also, intelligence stands for an adaptive potentiality of a person across different domains of life. Not restricted to the cognitive domain alone, this adaptive potentiality consists of a range of skills that equip one to overcome life problems and to grow and become what one wants to achieve in personal as well as social domains. Thus, the Indian view presents a model of an intelligent person who with his/her cognitive and emotional/personality characteristics attempts to achieve the collective and personal goals in life. The understanding of one's environment constitutes a major part of intelligence (Baral & Das, 2004).

6

Bhagavad Gita: An Indian Discourse on Wisdom*

C. SUVASINI, GIRISHWAR MISRA, AND ASHOK K. SRIVASTAVA

This chapter presents an analysis of ancient Indian text of the *Srimad Bhagavad Gita* (BG) with a view to delineate the concept of intelligence and wisdom. This presentation of BG is based upon the following interpretations: Yogi (1967), Prabhupada (1989), Maheshwar (1978) and Mascaro (1962). The discourse of *Bhagavad Gita* was set in the great battlefield of Kurukshetra. It was a dialogue between Arjuna and Lord Kṛsna. Lord Kṛsna proposed and elaborated a theory of intelligence or wisdom in response to the problem posed by Arjuna. The great War of Kurukshetra had commenced. Pandavas and Kauravas, the two warring factions had assembled on the battlefield. The Kaurava warriors had blown their conches, thereby signalling the start of the war. At this crucial moment, Arjuna, the great Pandava warrior, began to doubt his resolve to fight. Seeing that his opposition comprised of his own relatives and friends put him in a very conflicting situation. To fight meant to injure, and possibly destroy his own kith and kin. Affluence, pleasure, even sovereignty of the world seemed worthless to Arjuna if they were to be gained at the cost of his near and dear ones.

---

* *Based on this analysis, a paper titled "Psychology of wisdom: Western and eastern perspectives" was published in Journal of Indian Psychology, 2000, 18 (1& 2), 1-32,* by the authors.

Simultaneously, the call of duty beckoned him. Arjuna was a *Kshatriya* and it was his moral duty to fight. Arjuna was torn between reason and emotion. Moreover, there were other considerations. The very act of killing was sinful and would have negative repercussions on the killer. The destruction would ruin a harmonious social order (caste and family) that had been upheld for long. Faced with a problem of such staggering proportions, Arjuna was in a quandary. He was severely distressed. He is described as stupefied, paralyzed, distraught and despondent. He was in a state of suspension and overwhelmed with sorrow. His skin was burning all over, his mouth was quivering and he was unable to stand. His mind was in a whirl. He had thought as much as he could, but of no avail. He did not know what to do – to fight, or to leave the battlefield, or to fight poorly so as to ensure his own defeat and destruction. He had reached the zenith of his own thinking. At this momentous hour, all his activities had come to a standstill. With hope, Arjuna then surrendered to his charioteer, Lord Kṛsna for guidance. In response, Lord Kṛsna threw open to Arjuna a whole new perspective on reality. This brought an altogether new realm of existence which helped him to have a better understanding of the reality that Arjuna was currently embedded in. Kṛsna's discourse is analyzed here so as to trace the process of wisdom and put it in proper perspective.

ACTIVITY IN THE DOMAIN OF PHENOMENAL REALITY

Ordinary mortals live in the realm of *Prakriti* – the reality. This phenomenal reality is ephemeral; it came into being in the course of contact of material nature with *Purush*. Material nature is characterized by non-conscious activity; spiritual nature is passive, pure sentience. Reflections of both, material and spiritual nature, appear in the phenomenal world. Importantly, consciousness did not emerge at a certain point in the evolution of phenomenal reality; it was present at its very birth/inception. The phenomenal reality is referred to as the Field of Activity. It consists of following 24 basic elements:

(a) 5 great elements (earth, water, fire, air and ether)
(b) 5 sense organs (eyes, ears, nose, tongue and skin)

(c) 5 motor organs (voice, hands, legs, arms and genitals)
(d) Mind, which is classified along with the sense and motor organs
(e) False ego or the sense of self ('I') as experienced by ordinary human beings.
(f) Intelligence
(g) Unmanifested stage of the three modes *(gunas)* of nature (*Sattva, Rajas, Tamas*)
(h) Five objects of the senses (smell, sound, touch, taste and form)

Interactions among these elements give rise to distress, happiness, desire and hatred. The field of activity is typified in the metaphor of the body. In such a world is embedded a self whose identity is derived from the sum total of the physio-psychological apparatus available to man. The average man, then thinks of himself largely (or even entirely) by referring to his physical, mental and behavioural features or attributes. All activities that take place in the phenomenal world unavoidably bring in a tripartite differentiation between the doer, the doing and the task done (and between the knower, the process of knowing and the known). Within the self/doer/knower, there are five causes, which jointly operate in bringing about an action. These include the body, the false ego (lower 'I am'), the receptive and motor organs, the various impulses to action (desires, motivations) and Fate (influence of divine forces, *samskaras* – inherited unconscious sense impressions). It is recognized that human behaviour is highly variegated; individuals behave differently from each other, and also differently across different situations and at different times. An explanation for this variation is offered. The phenomenal world is forever in restless activity and is hence always hanging. The self embedded within this reality is, therefore, also in a state of permanent flux. The composition of the causes is also not fixed – it changes over time. The different selves (and correspondingly the different knowers/doers/composition of causes within the self) are segregated into three ideal categories – *sattvic guna* (mode of goodness), *rajasic guna* (mode of passion) and *tamasic guna* (mode of ignorance). The categories are held to be ideal types, it is understood that doers and knowers are in existence adulterated. Just as there are three types of doers/knowers, similarly there are also three types of doings/knowings and three types of things done/knowledge. There is correspondence between the three levels. For example, a *rajasic* doer engages in a *rajasic* kind of activity which results in a *rajasic* outcome. Thus each activity that takes place in the phenomenal reality can as a whole be characterized as predominantly *sattvic, rajasic* or *tamasic.*

Sattvic Mode

The *sattvic* influence is regarded most favourable of being intelligent and gaining wisdom. It promotes movement to a higher level; the psychological make-up of a *sattvic* doer constitutes a necessary grounding upon which to build up wisdom. Under the spell of *sattvic guna,* sacrifices are performed in accordance with the scriptures. Each action is felt to be intrinsically joyous, is performed without any expectation or desire for extrinsic reward. Actions involve austerity of words (speaking words which are good, beautiful, true and give peace), austerity of mind (silence, self-harmony, loving-kindness, and pure heart) and austerity of body (purity, righteousness, chastity and non-violence). Sacrifices and other kinds of holy work are understood as duty that one is bound to perform. Work is neither looked at lustily, nor shirked from. A self embedded in the *sattvic* reality attains intelligence and earthly happiness (each a material reflection of possessions of the truly wise). *Sattvic* intelligence perceives the eternal being in perishables and infinity in finite things. It knows the principle of action and the principle of withdrawal from action, knows what ought to be done and what ought not to be done, what is to be feared and what is not to be feared, and can discriminate between freedom and bondage. There is freedom from the chain of selfish attachments, and from egotism (*i.e.* from egoistic inclinations). The *sattvic* doer shows determination and perseverance and experiences an inner peace that transcends the momentary victories and failures. Pleasure in the *sattvic* realm begins as sorrow but eventually leads to pure joy.

Rajasic Mode

Rajasic mode is considered less helpful in the process of attaining wisdom. *Rajasic* action is referred to as the level path – it serves to maintain the *status quo* of the *Rajasic* self. Passion, thirst, lust, desire and greed are the specific traits associated with *rajasic* influence. *Rajasic* people worship power and wealth; being enslaved by their sense cravings, they work invariably for personal gains. In the *rajasic* realm, sacrifices are performed and the threefold harmony (of body, mind and words) is practiced to seek worldly honour, reward and reputation. Work is seen negatively, experienced as too much of an effort; often work is abandoned because of the fear of pain it may cause. Being closely bound to actions (for anticipation of reward), the *rajasic* self frequently encounters fleeting pain and fleeting pleasure. The *rajasic* vision holds the world as constituted by many diversities and divisions. In the *rajasic* world, there are many things, each having its own limitations (well-defined, narrow boundaries). There is no clear understanding of what is right or wrong; what should be done and what should not be done. The *rajasic* pleasure is initiated by sensory desires; it is sweet to begin with, but eventually leads to pain and sorrow.

Tamasic Mode

Activity guided by *tamasic* influence does not just impede a progressive movement (towards wisdom), but also leads the self downward onto a lower path. It promotes in the doer ignorance, sleepy dullness, delusion, inertia and negligence. Appropriately depicted as darkness, work in the *tamasic* mode is performed with a confused mind, without consideration of the consequences, or of one's powers or of the harm that may come upon others, or of loss to oneself. Such work rebounds to increase the ignorance embedding the *tamasic* self. In practice of the threefold harmony, the *tamasic* doer substitutes self-torture for self-control; sometimes self-control is aimed at hurting another. In the *tamasic* realm, the self experiences no harmony. The *tamasic* self is portrayed as vulgar, arrogant, deceitful, malicious, indolent, despondent and procrastinating.

In the *tamasic* understanding, wrong is thought of as correct and things are perceived in a distorted perspective. In the *tamasic* vision, any thing may be seen as if it were everything – this narrow perception is oblivious to the diversity and multiplicity available to *rajasic* understanding and is ignorant of the oneness that is experienced in *sattvic* insight. It is a delusion from beginning to the end.

RELATIONSHIP BETWEEN SELF AND ITS ACTIVITY

In the phenomenal reality, there exists a bi-directional influence between self and the activity it engages in. The karmic laws dictate the nature of this connection. In general, the relationship is such that there is sustainment of both the self and its action. For example, actions performed under the *sattvic* influence promote *sattvic* qualities in the self which then further encourages *sattvic* actions by the self. However, on some very important details, the relationship differs among the modes of material nature.

A *sattvic* doer engages in action without any expectation or hope for reward. *Sattvic* action performed as duty is not purposeful or instrumental. Its intrinsic worth or quality liberates the doer from attachments. Such liberation draws the self towards wisdom; this movement then urges the self to further engage in a similar action (*i.e.* action not aimed at fugitive results). If *sattvic* actions are conscientiously practiced, then the self can arrive at the highest point of psycho-spiritual development. This would involve shedding of its *rajasic* and *tamasic* propensities. Such a self, characterized by purely (or predominantly) *sattvic* qualities, possesses divine nature. Some of the traits characterizing such a *sattvic* self include freedom from fear, pride and anger; truth, righteousness, consistency in sacred learning and contemplation, study of scriptures, non-violence and steadiness. Having arrived at the frontiers of development in the phenomenal world, if the self persists in *sattvic* activities, transcendence of the phenomenal world can be attained. This is the course for acquiring wisdom.

Under the spell of *rajasic* influence, the self acts to attain certain fruitful ends. Since motivated actions are intrinsically binding, they have repercussions on the self such that the self is further compelled to act similarly (*i.e.* to gain something). If the self falls prey to such entrapments, then there is an ascendancy of *rajasic* influence. When the *rajasic guna* dominates (or completely permeates) the self, it is said to possess a demoniac nature. Such a self is deceitful, insolent, conceited and ignorant. A person having demonical nature does not know what should or should not be done. He/she possesses very little discriminative capacity. He/she perceives the world to have no moral foundation. He/she considers lust to be the sole cause of birth; he/she does not accept that there are laws of creation. He/she is full of insatiable material longings that impel him/her to engage in impure work. He/she considers slaying his enemies. He/she is enclosed within a network of delusions. He/she seeks refuge in anger and lust. A very serious danger is that indulgence in *rajasic* activities threatens to collapse the self into the *tamasic* mode. Greed, desire and wrath are described as the three gates to *tamasic* hell. Then, any possibility of elevation would also severely diminish (or altogether disappear).

Ordinary humans (with their limited selves) desiring pleasure, put to use their physical and mental endowments. They engage in action – physical, verbal or mental – aimed at obtaining pleasure. This enterprise can occur at either gross or subtler planes. For example, one can either enjoy eating good food; alternatively one can recollect an earlier eating experience and derive pleasure. In either case, because they fulfil man's primary desire, such pleasure giving experiences are sought after, and are repeatedly engaged in. Eventually pleasure-seeking people become deeply attached to those experiences and objects from which they get so much joy. Everything would be fine except for one hitch: human experiences are part of a phenomenal world, which has rather bothersome features – events are temporary and reality is ever-changing. No pleasurable experience lasts forever and the joy obtained from it is not permanent. An attachment to the object/experience remains, just as its memory lingers. Inability to engage in the experience and acquire the object then causes intense grief. Worse still, the entire process is entrapping. Because of karmic laws operating in the phenomenal world, consequences of actions rebound on the individual. They push the individual to further engage in pleasure seeking, which causes greater unhappiness. This process gets more and more entrenched, and the individual becomes trapped in the hellish swamp of phenomenal reality. Thus, pleasure seeking in the phenomenal world is inherently tied to suffering and sorrow.

Overcoming Suffering through Wisdom

That human beings occupy an inherently pain-causing phenomenal world did not, in Kṛsna's discourse, lead to despair and hopelessness. Kṛsna's delivery was optimistic and constructive – it specified several means through which human beings could put an end to their suffering. In this context three essential pathways to wisdom – the path of knowledge, the path of action, and the path of devotion are proposed. It is also hinted that each of these corresponds to a distinct life style. For example, a hermit adopts the path of knowledge and the path of action is suited to a householder. In addition, it is asserted that knowledge, action and devotion are sequential, successive stages in the course of attaining wisdom which is a differentiated process.

It seems that wisdom is a holistically transforming process. Several changes in the nature of self come about a becoming wise. *Bhagavad Gita* highlights many particular changes in the nature of self which collectively portray the process of wisdom.

SANKHYA YOGA : THE ABSOLUTE REALM OF ETERNAL BLISS

A primary factor in attaining wisdom is becoming cognizant of the absolute reality different from the temporary phenomenal reality. A detailed portrayal of this reality is given in chapter 2 of the *Bhagavad Gita*. While phenomenal reality is manifest, absolute reality in its constitutional nature is unmanifest. In this 'other-reality', the duality between self and world, inner and outer, subjective and objective is absent. With such blurred distinctions, this reality is constituted by the oneness of entire cosmology. It is interchangeably referred to as The True Self or *Brahman*. The experience (of self) located in this realm is of an oceanic oneness with the whole of existence. In this state, the boundaries of the individual soul are collapsed resulting in an expansive experience of self. The self becomes *Atman*, the transcendental being. With his/her limitations existing no more, such a person feels transcendentally free, and immensely blissful. The joy that springs from this experience can fully consummate a man's desire for pleasure. The most appealing feature of this reality is that it is lasting. At various points, this reality has been described as eternal, indestructible, immutable, never changing and permanent. It follows that the happiness, which features in this realm, is also ever-lasting, it is not susceptible to the frenzied changes that characterize the phenomenal world.

The self in the permanent realm is also eternal. Unlike the human body-mind aggregate, this self neither takes birth, nor dies. Kṛsna describes it as being unborn, immutable, indestructible and ancient. It cannot be slain. To become wise, the nature of this self needs to be clearly grasped and realized. Becoming aware of, and understanding the nature of the absolute world, necessarily involves understanding the phenomenal world as well. Each must be recognized as independent unit, complete in itself. Then the phenomenal world must be seen for what it truly is – a permanently shifting equilibrium operated by the ceaseless interplay of the three modes – *sattva, rajas,* and *tamas.* Such an understanding shall compel one to appreciate the sheer enormity of the activities that take place in the phenomenal setting. Only an appreciation is possible, the complexity of the activity-loaded phenomenal world is itself deep. However, even a simplistic knowledge of the operations of the phenomenal world is desirable. This is because from such an understanding, one can deduce and understand which actions are right (*i.e.* they help evolution in phenomenal reality) and which actions are wrong (*i.e.* they hinder evolution, promote retrogression).

An important development in the awakening is that over and above the field of phenomenal activity, there lies a knower of the field. The knower constitutes the absolute consciousness. A differentiation between the field of activity and its knower can be drawn at the cosmic level, and at the level of an individual human being (the two levels, in fact, run parallel). In Chapter 7 of the *Bhagavad Gita,* a differentiation between phenomenal and absolute realm is brought about with a specific focus. The non-conscious quality of phenomenal, material nature and in contrast, pure consciousness that constitutes absolute reality is highlighted. The multiplicity and variegatedness of phenomenal reality are sketched. As opposed to this, absolute reality is an undifferentiated oneness. Attaining wisdom requires discernment along these dimensions between the absolute and relative realms.

The process of differentiating between the field of activity and the knower of the field with respect to oneself primarily involves becoming deeply cognizant of the consciousness within oneself. Then one must know that this individual consciousness is a spark (a fragment) of a more expansive cosmic consciousness. This fragment has entered into the phenomenal world and has drawn around its centre, several sense organs, motor organs and mind to create, the psycho-physiological aggregate known as the human being. In doing so, this spark of consciousness has become entangled and embroiled in this phenomenal reality. It is this consciousness within oneself that experiences pleasure and suffering. It becomes available through the instruments of mind and sense organs. However, when extracted from the body within which it is embedded (*i.e.* when withdrawn from the phenomenal realm), this individual consciousness becomes inactive. Being passive; in its pure state it is a silent witness to the happenings at the phenomenal realm. It is an uninvolved knower. Thus, in gaining wisdom, one has to become aware of the knower within one's material body, and after doing so, differentiate between the field of activity and the knower of the field. This has been described in chapter 13 of the *Bhagavad Gita*.

The knower within the material body is held to be a fragment of the self in the Absolute. This self is the knower without the boundaries of an individual consciousness. This in effect means that in the Absolute Reality, the self is essentially renounced of actions. This is the teaching of chapter 4 of the *Bhagavad Gita*. The self is basically inactive. It does not engage in activities but is a mere witness to activities. Correlative to the understanding that the knower/the self is in essence an inactive entity, is the realization that all the activities that occur in the phenomenal reality entirely arise from the interplay of the three modes of material nature. This means that even the functioning of human individual in the phenomenal realm is in actuality directed by the material modes. This is asserted in chapter 14 of the *Bhagavad Gita*.

A metaphorical portrayal of phenomenal reality is offered in chapter 15 of the *Bhagavad Gita*. The whole of phenomenal reality is likened to a tree seemingly indestructible. The roots of this tree are situated upwards, they originated from *Brahman*. The branches of this tree extend downwards, and are spread all round. The tips of the branches constitute the sensory organs. The twigs are the objects of the senses. The tree also has roots stretching downwards. The subsidiary roots are the various attachments and aversions. The secondary roots are the tendencies towards piety and impiety. This tree is nourished by the three material modes. The phenomenal man is located (entangled) within the ubiquitous expansions of this tree. From within, he cannot see the tree clearly or completely. He wanders from branch to branch, mindlessly and in confusion. His journey is not discontinued when a particular body-psyche configuration is lost (*i.e.* one death). After a brief pause, another body is assumed and the movement renewed. The location of man within this tree determines, and is determined by the activities he engages in. The travelling within this tree can be both horizontal and vertical (*i.e.* ascent/descent). A horizontal movement will serve to sustain his psychic status. A decent will lead to developments that are antithetical to the wisdom process (*e.g.* greater entanglement). Ascending along the tree will promote psycho-spiritual elevation within limits. Wisdom involves a true comprehension of the nature of this tree. For this, it is required that one should step out of this tree. This stepping out amounts to a cutting down of this tree. The indestructibility of this tree is only apparent. Detachment is the psychological weaponry that can bring this about. To sum up the process of becoming wise requires:

1. an awareness (of the existence) of Absolute reality,
2. an understanding of the nature of Absolute reality,
3. a whole new insight into the phenomenal world within which one is embedded, and
4. a sharp differentiation between the two realms.

The above comprehension, identified as the first stage in becoming wise (Yogi, 1967), has been labelled as the Sankhya Yoga. It is achieved through an experiential process, wherein the self undergoes a holistic transformation. It becomes available when one attains transcendental consciousness through an active practice of *dhyana* or meditation. The practice of meditation has been described as the self (consciousness, not the phenomenal identity) unfolding itself by itself to itself; as the self seeing the self. Chapter 6 of the *Bhagavad Gita* is a practical manual, which lists the steps of meditation, and several precautions that need to be taken for meditation to be effective. Such meditation culminates in one becoming the Absolute consciousness (which is commensurable to its understanding). From this vantage point, a truer picture of phenomenal reality comes into view.

Karma Yoga

Its basic objective is to leave the world of phenomenal reality and enter into the Absolute realm. In transcendental consciousness, the Absolute reality is reached only for brief spells – the idea now is to remain there permanently – even as one is engaged in the daily business of life. This calls for a permeation of the experience of Absolute consciousness into the activities one is engaged in within the world of phenomenal reality. Such a practice is called *karma yoga*.

At this point a distinction between the recluse and the householder style of living needs to be made. The differentiation between the two overlaps with the differentiation between *sankhya yoga* and *karma yoga*. It has been interpreted that a recluse refrains from activities while a householder is actively engaged. A recluse engages in mental speculation (which is activity in the phenomenal realm) while the householder is involved in several physical activities (Yogi, 1967). *Karma yoga* is hence applicable/valid to both orders of life. Being situated in Absolute consciousness, bliss, peace and everlasting joy become naturally or spontaneously available. That this experience is absolutely flawless is the most important fact. Once this state is reached, there is no incentive left to act for the sake of obtaining pleasure (*i.e.* pleasure of the phenomenal world). An alternative is to withdraw from the field of activity in the phenomenal world altogether. This, however, is considered not possible as long as one is still associated with the phenomenal world (as in possessing a body). The logical move is to follow *karma yoga* as elaborated in chapter 3 of the *Bhagavad Gita*. In addition to suiting to the needs of one becoming wise, *karma yoga* makes important positive contributions to the process. The causal relation between actor and activity is (just as ever) bi-directional.

In *karma yoga*, one performs actions called *yajna* or acts of sacrifice. Under this is included a wide range of activities, only a small part of which consists of rituals to please gods. According to *Yogi* (1967), the acts of *yajna:*

- are performed when situated in absolute consciousness
- contribute to process of becoming wise
- help to maintain the flow of phenomenal reality in a desired direction, and
- help in fulfilment of desires in a manner that is harmonious with the laws of phenomenal nature. Although mostly free of desires, there is not yet a complete transcendence of material desires. This is in keeping with the treatment of wisdom as a process.

Primarily, *yajnas* are not motivated by a desire to seek or enhance pleasure. In performance of actions, there is detachment from such interests. The individual (having attained a degree of wisdom) can distinguish between right action and wrong action. Above all, the entire material apparatus (body, mind, sense organs) is subjected to the processes of phenomenal nature. The individual is brought in harmony with the stream of evolution. The mind is inclined to act so as to further the wheels of natural forces. There is a natural decline of desires which may obstruct cosmic evolution. There is correspondingly a strengthening of desires which promotes this evolution. Performing sacred rituals can fulfil such desires. Under such circumstances, man spontaneously engages in actions which respond to needs of the time. Such actions refer to one's allotted duty, his *dharmic* prescriptions. In performing his *dharma*, an individual also helps preserve a social order needed for harmony in the society. Moreover, ordinary people emulate the wise—this is also positive. Finally, since such actions enjoy the favour of the forces of nature, their performance requires no effort on the part of the doer. Thus actions in *karma yoga* help maintain the phenomenal reality and support its development. Simultaneously, they also contribute to an individual's development towards wisdom. This is brought about through renunciation of action, a process opposed yet complementary to action in *karma yoga*. This is discussed in chapter 5 of the *Bhagavad Gita*. Renunciation means loss. The process of attaining the Absolute self (experiencing of knower) is accompanied by a loss of one's identity in the phenomenal reality. The latter is called renunciation. Once the Absolute self is reached, one realizes that one (knower) is truly detached from the world of action. The inactive nature of the self/knower becomes an experiential reality.

Transcendental consciousness being infused into everyday life, one is no longer touched by external contact. One does not rejoice in the pleasure of phenomenal realm, nor does one experience material suffering. One resists anger and desire springing in the phenomenal psyche. One submits authorship of all actions to the three material modes. Such a self does not act or cause action to be undertaken. There is recognition that several activities such as seeing, hearing, touching, smelling are performed by the complex of the body-mind-intellect-sense organs; that one is merely a witness. With this awakening one renounces all the fruits of one's activities. After all, if one is not causing these actions, why must one reap the benefits (or suffer the consequences) resulting from them? One, therefore, offers to the material powers all the results of one's activities. This translates into not reacting with positive (or negative) emotions to the consequences (desirable or undesirable) of one's actions. Such a mode of renunciation has been discussed in chapter 18 of the *Bhagavad Gita*.

Work of the kind described above is *sattvic* in nature. It promotes *sattvic* qualities in the doer which is conducive to becoming wise. Most important, in the *sattvic* realm, laws of *karma* operate to disentangle one from the entrapments of the phenomenal world. This withdrawal from phenomenal associations is the other side of moving closer to the realm of the Absolute. In fact, the two processes are complementary, each facilitates the other. Such work (in the *sattvic* mode) has been prescribed in chapter 17 of the *Bhagavad Gita*. Engagement in *sattvic* activities leads to the acquisition of divine qualities. These have been listed in chapter 16 of the *Bhagavad Gita*, and have already been referred to.

Work in the *sattvic* mode, and cultivation of divine traits are not ends in themselves. They are necessary steps to reaching the summit of development (in wisdom) within phenomenal reality. The final objective, after arriving at the frontiers of the phenomenal realm, is to transcend it altogether. Such transcendence is brought about as follows. *Sattvic* action results in loosening of the bonds with the phenomenal world. Absence of purposeful activities leads to gradual decline in accumulated karmic repercussions. Eventually, there is a complete dissolution of karmic effects. Once this is achieved, there is within oneself no cause that requires phenomenal reality for its fulfilment. With this emptying out (of *karmas*) there is no purpose to be served in returning to the phenomenal reality. There is, in fact, no return to the phenomenal reality. Such a self truly transcends phenomenal reality and becomes free from the cycle of life and death. Simultaneously, there is a profound immersion in the realm of the Absolute. Through practice of *karma yoga*, the knowledge acquired in *sankhya yoga* becomes an experiential reality. The Absolute realm reached earlier only in transcendental consciousness becomes a way to be. With the permeation of Absolute consciousness into one's daily activities, an integration of the two realms—Absolute and phenomenal is achieved. Such an experiential integration is called cosmic consciousness (Yogi, 1967), a state subsequent (and higher) to transcendental consciousness in the movement towards wisdom. Parallel to the attainment of cosmic consciousness is modification in the meditation practice where each facilitates the other.

Bhakti Yoga

Bhakti Yoga, the path of devotion, is described in chapter 12 of the *Bhagavad Gita*. Some researchers (*e.g.*, Goel, 1986; Prabhupada, 1989) regard it an independent route to wisdom, an alternative to *sankhya* and *karma yoga*. Another interpretation (Yogi, 1967) is that *bhakti yoga* is subsequent to and built upon the achievements of *sankhya* and *karma yoga*. Through *bhakti* or devotion, cosmic consciousness gives way to godly consciousness. Recently, Orme-Johnson, Zimmerman and Hawkings (1997) have differentiated between God consciousness and Unity consciousness. God consciousness is characterized by a feeling of love and devotion for God. In Unity consciousness, one becomes integrated with the cosmic psyche. In *bhakti yoga*, the devotee aims for a personal one-to-one relationship with the personal God. He/she actively worships a human form of God – remembering him through each living moment with focused mind that does not wander. Chanting of certain phrases is recommended to bring this state of mind (Prabhupada, 1989). In this worship, there is devotion, dedication, dependence and surrender to the God. There must also be faith in the potency of this practice. Eventually, the devotee attains God-consciousness, which is a profound awareness of an all-pervading oneness. The realm of being (absolute consciousness) and activity (phenomenal reality) which were distinct (but held together in *karma yoga*) now merge into a singularity. Their separate identities get dissolved. God-consciousness is supra-intelligence; it therefore cannot be grasped through instruments of the intellect. It is marked by an experience of unbounded love for God. Since everything is seen as God, the love is also naturally all-pervasive. Initially, the devotee is separate from God, although in an intimate and personal bounding with him. Eventually, however, there is an extinction of this separate identity, the worshipper and the worshipped fuse into a single unity.

God-consciousness comes as awareness that all manifestations in the phenomenal world are in essence God. Thus, in the devotee's vision the taste of water, the fragrance of earth, the light of the sun and moon, the digesting fire in the body of living entities are all God. The holy sacrifices, the offerings made in their sacrifices, the butter and the fire in the offerings, and the penance involved are in actuality God. God's opulence in the phenomenal world are innumerable, a small sample is given in chapter 10 of the *Bhagavad Gita*. In God-consciousness, thus, an understanding emerges that God is all-pervasive and through in the entire range of phenomenal reality and omniscient. Corresponding to this is the awakening to the essential oneness that underlies the apparent variegation of the phenomenal reality. It is recognized that God is not subsumed or exhausted by his phenomenal manifestations. In fact, all of the phenomenal opulence is supported only by a fraction of God's being.

In God-consciousness comes the awareness that God brings forth all creation. It is realized that the manifest universe has its origin in God and that the creation begins with the partitioning of single God-conscious from the material nature. The former is infused into the latter and the wheels of nature are set into motion. It is realized that God supports the entire creation; that the material universe rests upon God. This is picturized as pearls resting upon a string and as the wind resting upon the vastness of ethereal space. However, once created, God is relatively detached from the happenings in the phenomenal realm. He merely watches in silence, uninvolved and unaffected (this is analogous to the knower in the individual). Finally, God also brings about the dissolution of the phenomenal world when he winds it all up into himself. The nature of God that one becomes aware of in God-consciousness is given in chapters 8, 9 and 10 of *Bhagavad Gita*. Remembering God at the moment of death (*i.e.* being in God-consciousness) is said to liberate one from the phenomenal world. Thus, through the practice of *Bhakti Yoga*, one becomes aware of the oneness of God that permeates, underlies and supports all the diversities of phenomenal reality. One experiences sublime love for this God, meaning for all existence. Accompanying this is an alteration in the experience of meditation.

CHARACTERIZING THE WISE

Individuals can be distinguished by several traits peculiar to the category of wise people. A more or less exhaustive listing of the characteristics of wise people from *Bhagavad Gita* is presented here. *Bhagavad Gita* makes reference to a number of terms to refer to a wise person. They include learned, knower of absolute truth/seer of truth, intelligent person, great soul, sage, self realized, sober, liberated/liberated in Supreme, mystic transcendentalist, undiluted, knower of Supreme *Brahman*, one in complete knowledge, one in divine consciousness, devoted soul, self controlled, introspective sage, man of steady intelligence, one who sees with equal vision, and one who has conquered the mind. Also, there are many terms for the state of experiencing wisdom. They include attainment of *Brahman* conception, ultimate destination, transcendental perfection, promotion of God's spiritual nature, situated in transcendence, in a transcendental position, arrival to spiritual kingdom/spiritual sky, self situated, self realized, eternal situation, transcendental consciousness, attainment of Supreme, and spiritually situated. The experiential, social and psychological characteristics of wise people as given in *Bhagavad Gita* are described in the following section.

Experiential Characteristics

Situated in Equanimity and Sameness—This state is reflected in the following behavioural/experiential characterization: Same in misery and happiness, equipoise in fear and anxiety, steady in success and failure, no affection for good or evil, does not hate illumination, attachment or illusion when they are present or long for them when they disappear, mind established in sameness and equanimity, even- mindedness amid pleasant and unpleasant events, and same in honour and dishonour, in desirable and undesirable situations.

Experiences Bliss and Contentment—This refers to the following experiences: Enjoys unlimited happiness and rejoices; enjoys transcendental peace, supreme happiness becomes accessible and attains tranquillity. A wise person is satisfied with gain that comes of its own accord, is fully satiated, not interested in material happiness and has no expectation of honour.

Located in the Self—This category involves perception of self as an object and reflected in terms like self-connected, self intelligent, established in self, aiming within, self-realized, self-illuminated, a man in himself and able to see the self.

Joy from Within—This category emphasizes on the intrinsic sources of pleasure: Enjoyment in the self, happy from within, actively enjoying within, takes pleasure in self and satisfied in self alone.

Removed from the Field of Senses—This category deals with the behaviours and experiences involved in withdrawing from the physical world. A wise person gives up the sense of proprietorship over possessions, freedom from attachment, and detachment, transcendental to three modes of material nature/unattached to three modes. While seeing, hearing, touching, smelling, eating, walking, dreaming, breathing, talking, giving up, accepting, opening, closing knows that sense organs are engaged with them—he is aloof from them, gives up material desire for sense gratification, free from material contamination, freedom from entanglement with children, wife, home and the rest and general mass of people, renunciation and intelligence is not entangled.

Freedom from Suffering—This category refers to the emotional state: A wise person is one who is free from care and from all sources of distress, does not grieve or lament, does not get agitated on encountering the unpleasant and not agitated in mind in the midst of threefold miseries.

Social Characteristics

These characteristics include the following: Unbewildered, free from faults, without false prestige, false ego, and false association; free from illusion, lust, fear and anger; purified, perfect, righteous, fully cleansed of misgivings, educated, gentle, humble, prideless, nonviolent, simple, clean, steadfast, sinless, performs sacrifices, austere, truthful, modest, determined, fortitude, vigour, free from greed, tolerant, non-envious/free from envy, friendly, forgiving, no one is agitated due to him, he is not disturbed by people, without an enemy, kind, does not become enemy's enemy, engaged in good services for all, does not need to depend upon/take shelter among living beings, treats everyone (*e.g.* friends, benefactors, pious and envious, sinners) with equal intelligence, mediates between belligerents, is a neutral mediator, has compassion, is averse to fault-finding and charitable.

Psychological Characteristics

A wise person subscribes to the following and behaves accordingly:

(a) *Activity performed by Material Nature:* Activities are being performed by material nature in all respects; none other than the *Gunas* perform activities.
(b) *Self is Non-doer*: The self, though dwelling in the body, never does anything.
(c) *Self is Transcendental*: The self is transcendental, the self is inexhaustible, the self is beyond material nature.
(d) *Discrimination between Knower and Field*: Knows the difference between body and knower of the body, understands living entity, material, material nature and modes of material nature.
(e) *Vision of Oneness*: Sees the super soul equally situated everywhere, in all living entities, sees all living entities in self, sees as same everywhere, sees the expansion not separated identities, regards as same a lump of earth, a stone, and gold, sees with equal vision a learned, a cow, an elephant, a dog and a dog-eater.
(f) *Controlled Senses*: Not attached to external sense pleasure, conquered senses, winds up senses from sense objects, has subjugated his sense, able to tolerate lust and anger/not disturbed when lust appears.
(g) *Disciplined Mind and Intelligence*: Has regulated/controlled mind and intelligence, mind is steady, has disciplined mind and its activities.
(h) *Acts without Attachment*: Performs no fruitive activities although fully engaged in it, works only for keeping body and soul together, performs prescribed duties without attachment, performs duties equiposed, acts with intelligence, senses and mind only for the purpose of purification, work is something obligatory, not bound by actions.
(i) *Renounces Fruits of Actions:* Renounces fruits of all endeavours, views work for the sake of sacrifice, neither hates nor desires fruits of activities, free from auspicious and inauspicious results of work, abandons all attachment to success and failure, does not take shelter in fruitive results.
(j) *Works in Eternity*: Merges work entirely into

transcendence, in full consciousness, gives up results to Lord.

(k) *Essentially Inactive:* Living in material body, does not do anything or cause anything to be done, restrained from material and mental activities, does not engage in the senses, in sense-gratification, does not take part in sources of misery, does not take delight in sensory enjoyments.

(l) *Free from Karmas*: Does not acquire sinful reactions, free from all sins, free from all reactions to the past deeds.

(m) *Freedom from Life/Death Cycle*: No rebirth in the temporary world, not born at the time of creation, or disturbed at the time of dissolution, liberated from the bondage of birth and death, cessation of material existence.

(n) *Devotional Activities*: Always engaged in devotion with determination, in full faith always thinking of God within himself, renders transcendental loving service, fully situated in God/fully in God, in constant touch with Supreme.

Lord Kṛsna's exposition on wisdom aimed at alleviating Arjuna's suffering. Its purpose was to put an end to the state of suspension that Arjuna found in himself. Being aware of the absolute realm of existence, Arjuna had access to a fresh perspective on phenomenal reality in which he was situated. Since suffering is intrinsic to phenomenal reality, he would continue to experience grief, so long as he was entrapped in this reality. Kṛsna's discourse offered wisdom to Arjuna. Then he would experience love, peace and joy. He would recognize that his loved ones would not perish their true-selves, and would remain even after their temporary bodies disintegrated. He would know his earlier anxiety over their death was unnecessary. Kṛsna's teachings suggested that Arjuna should perform his moral duty without attachment or aversion to the consequences that would result. He would incur no sin whatsoever. Moreover such action would be in harmony with evolutionary processes and would not, as he had earlier imagined, damage the social order. Also, in witnessing the

Universal form, Arjuna had already seen the results of the war. He had come to know that the Pandavas would emerge victorious, and the Kauravas would lose in the Kurukshetra war. In this witnessing of the future also, Arjuna's present took shape. He saw himself participating in the war. In fact, by the end of Kṛsna's discourse, Arjuna had attained wisdom. He had become an integrated being, a devotee of God and an enlightened person. His grief had vanished. He was filled with bliss. His conflicts and doubts had disappeared. He lifted his bow and arrow with a firm mind and proceeded to fight on the battlefield.

CONCLUSION

The themes of holism and dynamism present in *Bhagwad Gita* offer an interesting theoretical framework for the construct of wisdom. The holistic understanding has generated a concept of wisdom, in which all of its multiple aspects are incorporated. Moreover, these different features are not treated as separate strands; they are brought together as an integrated theme. The *Bhagavad Gita*'s treatise on wisdom is truly all-inclusive and exhaustive. It leaves no facet of wisdom untouched. The factor of dynamism has resulted in a processual treatment of wisdom. In *Bhagavad Gita,* wisdom is stage-like and develops over time. This concern with the temporal dimension of wisdom has rendered it richer, and more alive. The salient aspects of this approach to wisdom may be summarised as follows:

(i) The *Bhagavad Gita* condemns the human aspiration to gain human control over nature. It considers such an endeavour 'faulty' as it inevitably results in man becoming entangled in the processes of nature. Still, it has expounded an elaborate theory on the functioning of the cosmos. Bringing into picture the permanent realm, it differentiates between the permanent and temporary realm on several dimensions. Man and society are presented as integral constituents of this cosmos. Further, wise people use this knowledge in a manner that is harmonious with, and not opposed to, the flow of nature.

(ii) Wisdom in the *Bhagavad Gita* is not an abstract intellectual engagement; it is a response to real life concerns. Real problems constitute the starting point for wisdom. It is aimed at putting an end to suffering in life. Furthermore, such concerns and conflicts are equally pertinent even today. In fact, Arjuna's case can be regarded as a concrete, historical image employed to initiate a dialogue on issues which are part and parcel of the human nature. The view of wisdom ennunciated in *Bhagavad Gita* is pragmatically oriented as it serves as a compelling guide to action. The *karma yoga* is a manual for practicing wisdom in action and promotes cosmic evolution.

(iii) In the *Bhagavad Gita*, there is both an appreciation of and elaboration on the trappings, which are regarded as intrinsic to the world. Wisdom's foremost objective is to make people free from these entrapments. Emancipation is central to such wisdom. In becoming wise, one transcends the temporary world. This freedom is experienced as unbounded love in *bhakti yoga*. But the experience of bliss is much earlier even in the path of wisdom.

(iv) The technical, pragmatic and emancipatory interests are not in conflict with each other. In fact, they are not even independent dimensions of wisdom. They operate jointly and simultaneously, serving and complementing one another. It is the knowledge in *sankhya yoga* which provides rationale for the practice of *karma yoga* that leads to emancipation. Then, again, it is because of the brief spells of transcendence (in absolute consciousness) that the knowledge of *sankhya yoga* becomes experientially available. Also, it is the bliss encountered in moments of transcendence, which provides impetus to undertake the formidable path of *karma yoga*. The difficult process of withdrawing oneself from the unmindful attraction of sense objects is made easier by the experience of transcendental joy. Because of the latter, *karma yoga* becomes intrinsically rewarding and immensely enjoyable from the start.

(v) The *Bhagavad Gita* recognizes that human beings are usually motivated by a desire to seek pleasure. Wisdom offers a viable solution for this kind of blind hedonism. In becoming wise, one experiences bliss which comes without any negative repercussions. In having wisdom, man's desire to seek pleasure is fully consummated. Also, wise people possess certain distinct affective characteristics. For example, they are happy and without fear or pride. Wisdom involves a new cognitive orientation to reality having scope for absolute reality and permanent self. The cognitive apparatus undergoes modification and physical reality is cognized differently. The wise is able to see as one of the multiple aspects of reality. Their self-perceptions change, as they tend to perceive themselves as immortal and expansive. Wise people demonstrate characteristic ways of behaving. They engage in morally appropriate actions. Wisdom in *Bhagavad Gita* is concerned with issues of morality. Arjuna's conflicts were essentially moral dilemmas. The solution to moral problems lies in acquiring wisdom. Wise people recognize simultaneously at the level of the absolute reality and at the level of temporary reality. They engage in action which facilitates their individual evolution (*i.e.* draws them closer to absolute reality), and concurrently benefits cosmic processes (*i.e.* at the level of temporary reality). The *Bhagavad Gita* suggests that virtuous behaviour is both required for, and that results from becoming wise. Such wisdom is automatically of service to society. Wisdom facilitates 'matching', a concept proposed by Marriott (Collins, 1991). Matching ".... Refers to the cohesive articulation or proper ordering of things, especially human society ...." (Collins, 1991). It is similar to the Sanskrit term, *dharma*. Wise people have sense of being attuned to their social world. Their behaviour is appropriate and properly suited to the demands of the situation.

(vi) In the *Bhagavad Gita*, there is an appreciation of individual differences. It is recognized that people aspiring for wisdom may possess different temperaments. Wisdom in the *Bhagavad Gita* caters to these differences. Each person can adopt a route to wisdom which is best suited to his or her life style and psychological make-up.

(vii) In becoming wise, the identity of a person is transformed. The wise person experiences himself as eternal, indestructible, and also inactive. Through the practice of *karma yoga*, absolute consciousness evolves into cosmic consciousness. The expansive experience of self is deeply established. Cosmic consciousness then develops into God consciousness. In this process the wise person becomes profoundly aware of the oneness underlying separate identities. Eventually his identity merges with that of God. Moreover, this self-transformation is holistic. The limited human being, on gaining wisdom begins to identify with the entire cosmos and the self becomes all-inclusive.

(viii) The most optimistic message of the *Bhagavad Gita* is that wisdom is possible—ordinary mortals can attain it. Wisdom in the *Bhagavad Gita* is not a hypothetical abstraction; it is within the reach of possibilities. What is more, this is not an empty statement. It is substantiated by specification of techniques which would lead to wisdom. In *karma yoga*, a practical manual for becoming wise is offered. Such wisdom can be validated only by experiencing it; one may subject it to empirical investigations.

(ix) Thus *Bhagavad Gita* presents a very comprehensive theory of wisdom. Wisdom in the *Bhagavad Gita* jointly satisfies the triple Habermasian requirements of serving technical, pragmatic and emancipatory interests. It is agreeable to ordinary mortals, in that it promises fulfilment to their pleasure-seeking impulses. This wisdom ushers in, new and more accurate forms of cognizing and perceiving. Further, it results in ethical action.

Wisdom in the *Bhagavad Gita* is inclusive and holistic—all aspects of the self are considered and they remain integrated.

It is also stage-like. It is more of a process, and less of a state. The process of wisdom is a process of self-transformation and self-evolution. Most of all, it is an attitude towards life processes. This attitude, central to wisdom is acquired early in the process. As a state, wisdom is a point where all conceivable virtues converge. While promoting the development of an individual, wisdom is also beneficial to the society, of which the individual is a part.

7

Lay People's Understanding and Use of Intelligence: A Multicentric Study*

Attempts were made in chapter 5 to discern the notion of intelligence from the indigenous thought in the Indian tradition, particularly Sanskrit *suktis* and proverbs in Hindi. The analysis indicated four broad aspects of intelligence: ***Cognitive Competence, Social Competence, Entrepreneurial Competence,*** and ***Emotional Competence.*** It was noted that the Indian notion of intelligence stands at a distance from the prevailing western view which till recently placed heavy premium on reasoning and problem solving abilities. The last chapter provided an account of wisdom in *Bhagvad Gita* and expanded the discourse to include different levels of reality. In the Indian view a person is judged intelligent if he or she is competent in social problem solving and is generally pro-social in orientation. Intelligence is not confined to the success of the individual alone; rather it aims at achieving the common good. This chapter reports our effort to situate the understanding of intelligence in the lives of people and their experiences. It was empirically attempted by interviewing the lay people about different aspects of intelligence. Before presenting the details of the study we may briefly examine certain aspects of the world view that shapes Indian mind.

The Indian world view maintains the position that human life is a source or medium (*sadhana*) of fulfilment, both spiritual as well as material. The four *purusharthas* (life goals) –

---

* The study was conducted in collaboration with Professors Adesh Agarwal, P. Prakash, B.G. Singh and Dr. Shah Alam.

dharma (virtue), *artha* (wealth), *kama* (desire), and *moksha* (salvation)–clearly reflected these concerns. The fact that Indian economy has primarily been agricultural led to the development of common characteristics including deep loyalty to the family or clan. Interdependence, sharing and harmony constituted the basic values. In recent years, however, it is increasingly realized that the traditional Indian culture has undergone transformation under the impact of western education, urbanization, and industrialization (see Srivastava, 1995 for details). To Srinivas (1966), some of these changes are: *Sanskritisation* or a lower caste person behaving like a higher *(brahman)* caste; secularization (or less importance to religious beliefs); modernization, industrialization, and urbanization (movement of large numbers of people from rural to urban centres; and westernization (change in behaviour patterns resulting due to western cultural ethos). In this context, it becomes imperative to understand the notion of intelligence as prevalent in the contemporary Indian society.

To this end, a multi-centric study involving participants from diverse socio-cultural contexts, schooling, age, and sex was conducted. The data were collected from five centres, namely Delhi, Ajmer, Gorakhpur, Raipur, and Mysore. These localities represented north, south, western, and central regions of India. Variations are also observed in terms of language spoken, and physical ecology such as desert, tribal, agricultural, and metropolitan localities.

In the context of Indian society, urbanization and schooling constitute important contextual variables having a far-reaching significance. The degree of urbanization shows diverse trends with about 26 per cent people living in urban areas and the remaining 74 per cent in the rural areas. According to Census of India – 2001, the literacy rate is 65.37 per cent (Male=75.85%, Females=54.16%), with further large variations in rural and urban areas. The country is struggling to achieve the goal of the universalization of elementary education. Schooling, in terms of process and inputs, provides a formal set-up that is expected to promote knowledge, attitude and skills necessary for survival and growth in modern days. The cognitive, social, and affective consequences of schooling are, however, not very clear (Dash & Mishra, 1989; Dash & Mohanty, 1996).

The consequences of urbanization and schooling are related to the developmental stage of a person. In a predominantly collectivist society like India the roles, relationships, obligations, etc., are largely guided by one's position in relation to the significant others. Autonomy and dependence both operate in different ways across various life stages. That too varies in rural and urban settings and with exposure to schooling. For instance, an educated person retires at 60 years of age from formal occupational duties while no such notion operates in the life of unschooled people who continue to work till their health allows. Also, the notion of time, nature and degree of commitment, involvement, interest, etc., are organized in qualitatively different ways. In the West, Erikson (1963) suggested stages of development and drew attention to the changing values and conflicts as people progress through life stages. The nature of adaptative demands and related strategies tend to vary across adolescence, adulthood, midlife, and old age. In this way age-related differences are expected in the construal of intelligence.

Socialization in India is prominently gendered and discrimination due to gender is quite visible in the Indian society (Anandalakshmy, 1994). For a vast majority, home and work happen to be two separate domains associated with masculine and feminine roles, respectively. Women are expected to excel in interpersonal relations, in home-based activities and in affective regulations. They are also supposed to follow a different code of conduct from that of men. As a result, there are diverse societal expectations from the two sexes. This scene, however, is gradually changing with an increase in the number of women entering to the organized sector and joining positions of greater responsibility which require initiative, decision making, and planning.

The Indian socio-cultural scenario, therefore, presents a complex pattern. Keeping this in view, this study explored the similarities and differences in the construal of intelligence in diverse groups of lay people. Since intelligence refers to the adaptational demands of a particular context, variations were expected in the notions of intelligence due to factors such as urbanization, schooling, age, and gender.

METHOD

Participants

A sample of 1885 participants was drawn from five localities in India, *i.e.*, Gorakhpur (n=400), Mysore (n=400), Ajmer (n=285), Raipur (n=400), and Delhi (n=400), representing the northern, southern, western, and central parts of India as well as a metropolitan city (which is also the capital city), respectively. The participants varied along the dimensions of ecological setting (rural/urban), schooling (schooled/ unschooled), age (12-14 years or grade 8 students, 16-18 years or grade 12 students, 20-25 years, 45-50 years, and 60+ years), and sex (male and female) (for details see Tables 7.1 and 7.2). Persons having completed primary education (at least 5 years of schooling, 4 years in case of Mysore) were considered schooled. Since different eco-cultural settings vary in their adaptive demands, it was reasoned that these would be reflected in diversity in conceptualizing intelligence and intellectual skills. As such, care was taken to ensure the representation of participants from diverse occupational backgrounds.

The choice of locations was partly determined by the availability of collaborating investigators and partly on the consideration that the locations should be as divergent as feasible. Delhi, the capital city of India and one of the metropolis, is inhabited by people migrated from different parts of the country with diverse religious, social, and cultural practices. Though Gorakhpur, Raipur, and Ajmer are located in Hindi-speaking belt, the dialects spoken are distinctly different. Also, located in the northern part of India, Gorakhpur represents an agricultural mode of economy. Raipur is in the tribal belt in central India. Ajmer is a desert area in the western part of the country. Mysore is one of the prominent places in the southern part of India. The southern peninsula of India occupies a distinct place since ancient time in many respects such as history, language, culture, and so forth.

Table 7.1: Details of Sample from Delhi, Raipur, Mysore and Gorakhpur (N = 1600; 400 from each centre)*

Age in Year	*Urban*				*Rural*			
	Schooled		*Unschooled*		*Schooled*		*Unschooled*	
	M	*F*	*M*	*F*	*M*	*F*	*M*	*F*
12-14	10	10	5	5	10	10	5	5
16-18	10	10	5	5	10	10	5	5
20-25	10	10	5	5	10	10	5	5
45-50	10	10	5	5	10	10	5	5
60+	10	10	5	5	10	10	5	5

* The table shows distribution of participants at one centre and likewise participants from other centres were also selected.

Table 7.2: Details of Sample from Ajmer Centre (N=285)

Age in Year	*Urban*				*Rural*			
	Schooled		*Unschooled*		*Schooled*		*Unschooled*	
	M	*F*	*M*	*F*	*M*	*F*	*M*	*F*
12-14	10	10	5	5	10	10	5	5
16-18	10	10	5	5	10	10	5	5
20-25	10	10	5	5	10	10	5	5
45-50	10	10	5	5	10	10	5	5
60+	10	10	5	5	10	10	5	5

Measure

To appreciate laypersons' understanding and use of 'intelligence', an interview guide was prepared, which contained 8 questions of open-ended type. It was tried out on a small sample (N=20). The schedule focused on the salient features of an intelligent person/behaviour, the criteria they used for deciding about these characteristics, rating of their own intelligence, factors which facilitate the development of intelligence, situational variations in the expression of intelligence, and the relationship between intelligence and emotional competence. The specific items of the interview guide were as follows:

1. *Attributes of Intelligent People:* In our day-to-day experience we find some people to be very intelligent

while others behave in an unintelligent ways. In your view, what are the attributes/characteristics/behaviours of an intelligent person?

2. *Basis of Identifying the Characteristic Features of Intelligent People:* On what basis you have decided about these characteristics of an intelligent person? Did you use certain criteria or norm? Please describe them.
3. *Intelligence in Different Domains:* It is often seen that some people are intelligent in work situations (*e.g.*, office, school, agricultural activities) but are not so intelligent in social situations (*e.g.*, family matters, peer groups, neighbourhood relations). How do you think about this situation?
4. Does a behaviour which is considered intelligent in one situation, also considered intelligent in all other contexts?
5. *Self-Rating of Intelligence:* How intelligent are you? (Rating on a 5 point scale where 5=highly intelligent and 1= highly unintelligent, in work, social contexts, and in learning situations).
6. *Factors Facilitating Development of Intelligence:* In your view what are the factors that facilitate the development of intelligence?
7. (a) Is intelligence a gift of God?
   (b) Can intelligence be enhanced by training?
8. *Familiarity with Intelligence Tests:* Have you ever seen or used a test of intelligence? If yes, please tell your view about how appropriate are they in measuring intelligence?

Procedure

The investigators approached the participants individually either at their places of work or at their homes and, after establishing rapport, interviewed them. The investigators in the form of written notes recorded the responses verbatim. The responses were later content analyzed. Each response was scrutinized independently by two investigators and its meaning was determined. Based on the meaning contained in each response, a conceptual category was assigned to it. These categories were further grouped into a few broad themes on the basis of their conceptual configuration and emphasis. There was high agreement between the investigators regarding the meaning and category of the responses.

RESULTS

Characteristics of an Intelligent Person

Number of Attributes

In response to the question 'what are the attributes/characteristics/behaviours of an intelligent person, participants yielded a total of 7,931 attributes (M=4.21; range= 2-12) of the intelligent people. Table 7.3 shows that highest numbers of attributes were proposed by the participants from Delhi (31%), which was followed by Gorakhpur (25%), Ajmer (16%), Raipur (15%), and Mysore (13%), respectively. The urban participants yielded larger number of attributes (60%) than their rural counterparts (40%). The urban-rural differences across five localities were significant (*Chi-square* (4)=300.19, $P < 0.01$). The only exception was Gorakhpur where rural participants reported relatively greater number of attributes. The urban participants from Delhi and Raipur reported twice more characteristics than their rural counterparts (see Fig. 6.1). The schooled and unschooled participants without regard to their residential background supplied equal number of responses. Though there was no difference in the number of attributes supplied by males and females in the urban area (each supplied about 30% attributes), rural males provided 20.5 per cent attributes as compared to 19.7 per cent attributes supplied by rural females. Also, females from Gorakhpur reported higher number of attributes than their male counterparts (Fig. 7.2). Table 7.4 reveals that higher number of attributes was elicited by the urban participants in the age group of 20-25 years (15%) and 60+ years (13%). The remaining three groups each yielded about 11 per cent attributes. In contrast, it were the rural participants in the age group of 20-25 years who supplied least number of attributes (7%), followed by 16-18 years (8%), 60+years (8%), 12-14 years (9%), and 45-50 years (9%) (Fig. 7.3). The difference in the number of attributes with age was significant [*Chi-square* (4)=35.06, $P<.01$].

Table 7.3: Number of Attributes of an Intelligent Person (Per cent Frequencies)

Locality	Urban				Rural			
	SM	SF	UM	UF	SM	SF	UM	UF
Delhi (N=2436)	12	10	20	23	9	7	9	10
Gorakhpur (N=1958)	14	13	9	11	12	13	12	16
Raipur (N=1158)	22	20	16	15	8	7	6	6
Ajmer (N=1301)	14	17	14	10	17	10	9	9
Mysore (N=1078)	18	19	15	10	12	8	8	10

SM = Schooled Male UM = Unschooled Male
SF = Schooled Female UF = Unschooled Female

* The number in parenthesis indicates the total number of attributes reported by participants of the particular locality.

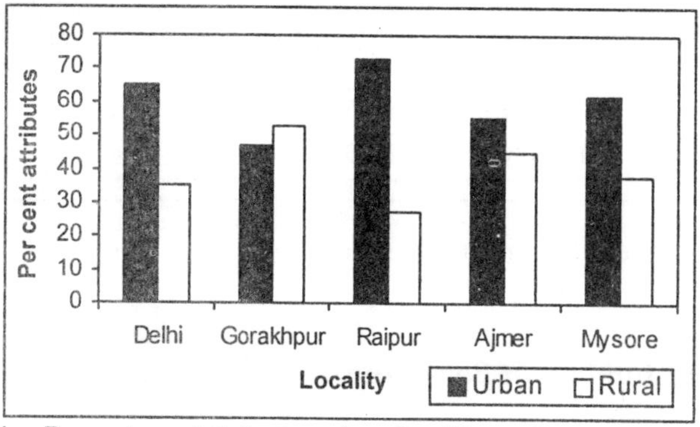

Fig. 7.1: Percentage Attributes of an Intelligent Person reported by Urban and Rural Participants.

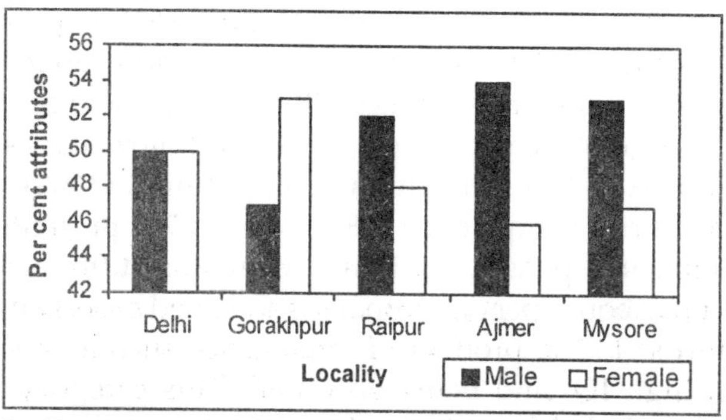

Fig. 7.2: Percentage Attributes of an Intelligent Person Reported by Males and Females

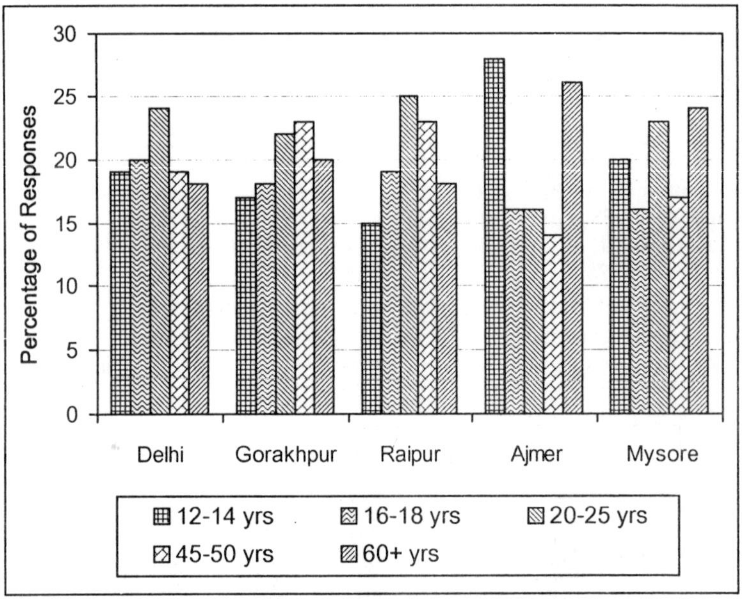

Fig. 7.3 : Percentage of Attributes Reported by Lay Persons of Various Age Groups

Facets of Intelligent Behaviour

A thematic analysis of laypeople's responses, pooled from the five centers, yielded four broad conceptual dimensions of intelligent behaviour. These were: **Cognitive Competence, Social Competence, Entrepreneurial competence,** and **Emotional Competence**. Of these, 30 per cent responses were related to cognitive competence, which was followed by social competence (27%), emotional competence (19%), and entrepreneurial competence (18%). Figure 7.4 presents the distribution of responses. In addition, there was a fifth category, constituting about 6 per cent responses and titled miscellaneous, that referred to the product of intelligence such as good in studies, high IQ, and being educated. This category was, however, excluded from the final analysis.

Table 7.4: Total Number of Attributes Reported by Lay Persons of Various Age groups (*Per cent Frequencies*)

Locality	*Age Groups*				
	12-14	*16-18*	*20-25*	*45-50*	*60+*
Delhi (N=2436)					
Urban	11%	13	17	11	13
Rural	8	7	7	8	5
Gorakhpur (N=1958)					
Urban	8	9	11	10	9
Rural	9	9	11	13	11
Raipur (N=1158)					
Urban	10	13	19	16	14
Rural	5	6	6	7	4
Ajmer (N=1301)					
Urban	15	8	8	8	14
Rural	13	8	8	6	12
Mysore (N=1078)					
Urban	12	8	14	10	15
Rural	8	8	9	7	9

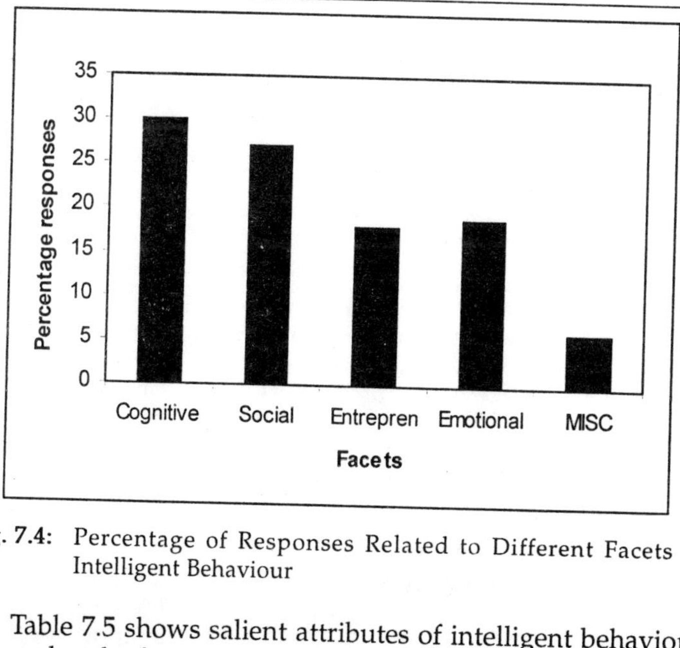

Fig. 7.4: Percentage of Responses Related to Different Facets of Intelligent Behaviour

Table 7.5 shows salient attributes of intelligent behaviour covered under four major conceptual dimensions. The cognitive competence involved sensitivity to context, reflection, communication, decision-making, and learning; social competence included helping the needy, obedience, service to elders, following norms, and carrying family responsibilities; emotional competence included control of emotions, honesty, empathy, religious, health consciousness, sensitive, polite, good conduct, and economic independence; and entrepreneurial competence reffered to hardworking, systematic, commitment, efficient, responsible, patience, and disciplined. These were prominently reported by lay people belonging to different groups from all the centres.

Sensitivity to context refers to the belief about the significance of relationship amongst person (*patra*), time (*kala*), and place or ecology (*desh*). Communication is another characteristic of an intelligent person. An intelligent person speaks when necessary, makes his/her mind clear using minimum words, his/her speech is loaded with hidden meanings, and remains focused on the problem under consideration. Also, such a person weighs and evaluates various alternatives (reflective thinking) before arriving at a decision. He examines what is good and what is bad in a given context. Such a person plans for the future and learns from past experiences.

Table 7.5: Salient Attributes of Intelligent Behaviour covered under the Four Conceptual Dimensions

Cognitive Competence	*Social Competence*	*Entrepreneurial Competence*	*Emotional Competence*
Context sensitivity Reflection Communication Decision Making Learning Planning	Helping the needy Service to elders Obedience Following norms Carrying family responsibilities Friendliness Involvement in group behaviour Non-extravagant	Hardwork Systematic work Commitment Efficiency Responsiblity Patience Discipline	Control of emotions Honesty Empathy Religiosity Confidence Health consciousness Sensitivity Politeness Good conduct Economic independence Adjustment

The Indian conception of intelligence is, as the study reveals, situated more in the practices and performances distributed across several domains. For example, respect for and service to elders, parents, and guests; being obedient, following social norms, being non-extravagant, and carrying family responsibilities were prominently reported under social competence. The entrepreneurial competence refers to the manner in which a person approaches and accomplishes a task. Three major concerns pertaining to task accomplishment are noted: systematic and efficient pursuance of a task; responsibility, hard work, discipline and patience. Under emotional competence, the laypeople reported that an intelligent person is one who is able to control his/her emotions, particularly emotions such as anger, jealousy, hatred, etc. Attributes such as speaking truth, empathy, honesty, politeness and humility make a person sensitive to other persons. Also, an intelligent person is health conscious and self-sufficient.

Table 7.6 shows that urban participants provided a significantly greater number of features related to all the four facets of intelligence than their rural counterparts. The schooled group reported a relatively greater number of characteristics pertaining to all the aspects except social competence which was emphasized more by the unschooled participants. The difference in the frequency of responses due to schooling was significant. Figure 7.5 indicates that while urban schooled participants stressed more on cognition, the urban and rural unschooled people laid premium on social competence. As regards gender differences, females yielded greater number of responses related to social and emotional competence than males. It may be noted (see Fig. 7.6) that cognition was highly emphasized by both males and females irrespective of their habitat. Social competence was equally emphasized by rural females and was second in order among urban females. Urban males laid similar emphasis on social and emotional competence. The age differences were also significant. Participants in the age group of 20-25 years supplied more features related to cognitive and entrepreneurial competencies. In contrast, social and emotional competencies were reported more by the older participants aged 60+ years. Figures 7.7 and 7.8 present interesting results. Rural participants of all ages (except 20-25 years) stressed social competence more or equally than cognitive competence. In contrast, cognitive competence was emphasized only by urban participants aged 20-25 and 60+ years.

Table 7.6: Frequencies for Various Facets of Intelligent Behaviour

	COMPETENCE AREAS				
Groups	*Cognitive*	*Social*	*Entrepreneurial*	*Emotional*	*Chi-Square (df= 3)*
Locality					
Urban	1,516	1,130	840	964	136.82**
Rural	902	998	602	531	
Schooling					
Schooled	1,369	986	773	757	59.11**
Unschooled	1,049	1,160	669	738	
Sex					
Male	1,157	906	812	802	14.37**
Female	1,125	982	681	817	
Age (*in years*)					
12-14	388	391	311	335	40.96**
16-18	416	364	319	303	(df=12)
20-25	562	459	321	367	
45-50	438	437	299	342	
60+	422	511	308	404	

** $P < .01$.

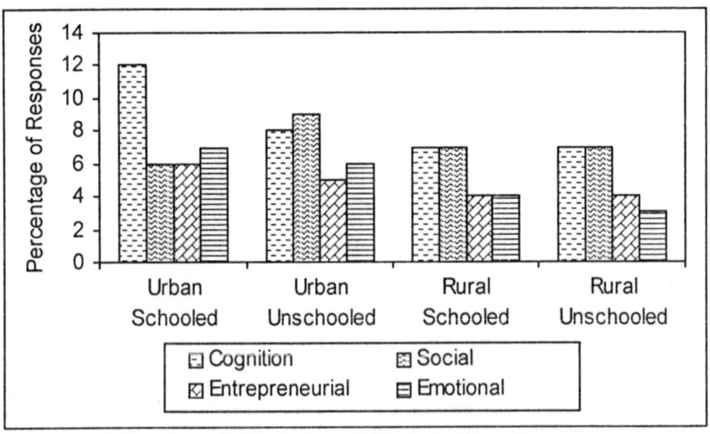

Fig. 7.5 : Schooling and Facets of Intelligence

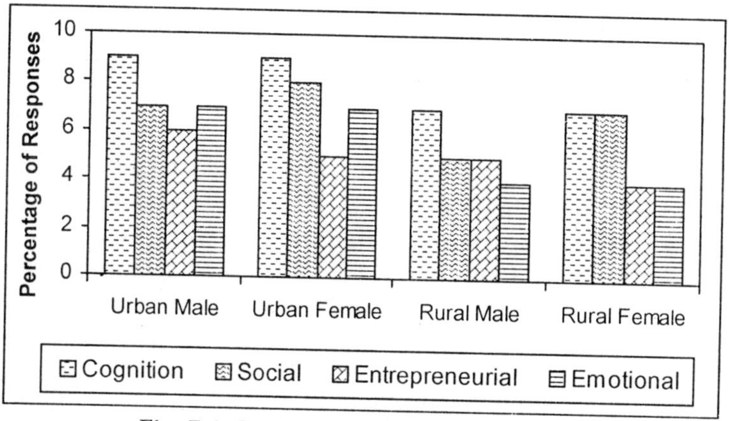

Fig. 7.6: Gender and Facets of Intelligence

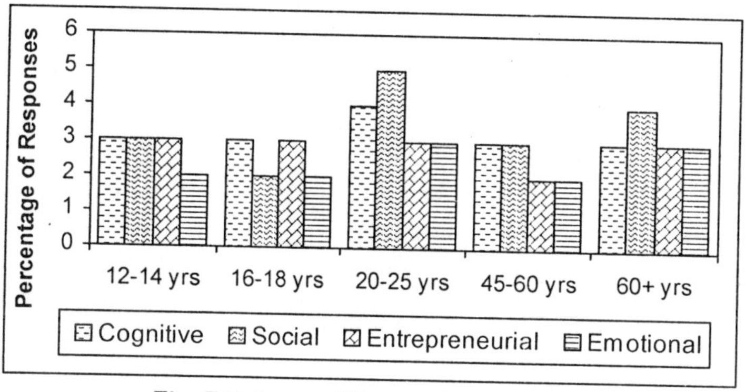

Fig. 7.7: Age and Facets of Intelligence

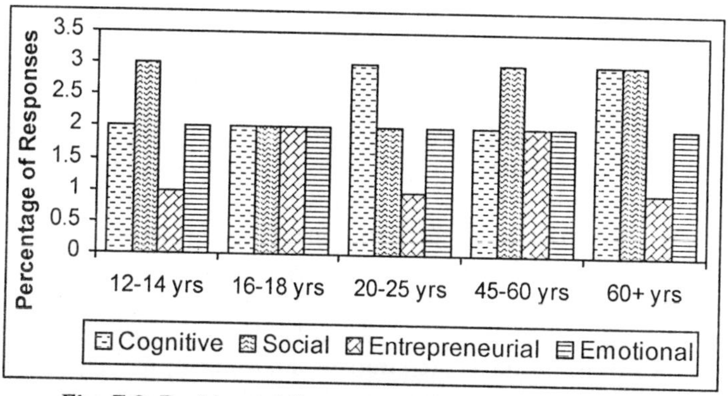

Fig. 7.8: Residential Context and Facets of Intelligence

Characteristics of Intelligent Persons: Effect of Locality and Schooling

Table 7.7 contains the features of intelligent persons as reported by the lay people across locality (residential background) and schooling. An analysis of these responses indicates four major dimensions of intelligent behaviour. These are: **Cognitive Competence, Social Competence, Entrepreneurial Competence, and Emotional Competence.**

Among the aspects of cognitive competence, majority of the participants agreed that an intelligent person shows sensitivity to the context, is reflective, communicates effectively, gives statements loaded with hidden meaning, and is able to take decisions. The urban-schooled participants more frequently reported these qualities than urban unschooled and rural participants. Some additional cognitive qualities such as attentiveness, remaining informed, foresightedness, planning for the future, and knowing one's strengths and limitations were also stated by the participants from Ajmer. A few sporadic responses like an intelligent person shows presence of mind, willingness to learn, draws lessons from past experiences as well as learns faster, and has strong memory were also obtained. The pattern of responses from the participants of Delhi and Gorakhpur was similar. The participants from the Raipur yielded limited number of cognitive qualities while the responses of participants from the Ajmer were considerably varied. Abilities such as planning and comprehension were given greater weightage by the participants from Ajmer and Mysore.

The unschooled participants more frequently ceded the aspects of social competence than the urban schooled ones. The results indicate that an intelligent person displays respect for and service to the parents, elders, and guests; is obedient, helps the needy by providing adequate counselling or otherwise, and follows social norms. Such a person is friendly with others, remains in the company of good people, actively takes part in the welfare activities, and is non-extravagant. The unschooled participants from Delhi and Gorakhpur also viewed intelligence as situated in such activities as carrying out family responsibilities and maintaining unity in the family. The lay people from Ajmer additionally reported intelligent persons to be facilitators. The respondents from Mysore reported two social characteristics of an intelligent person—helping the needy and participating in group welfare activities.

Under the category of entrepreneurial competence, while a large number of schooled participants considered an intelligent person as one who systematically pursues his task and is efficient, majority of the unschooled participants viewed him/her as committed and hard working. Handling the task with seriousness, patience, responsibility, and discipline are some other features of an intelligent person. In addition, the participants from Delhi reported an intelligent person as successful, coordinates various activities, holds scientific orientation, and is able to take preventive measures.

The unschooled respondents more frequently reported the characteristics related to emotional competence. To them, an intelligent person is honest, polite, clever, religious, health conscious, and has control over emotions, tries to achieve economic independence, and does not interfere in others' work. Some less frequent responses endorsed that an intelligent person shows empathy, curiosity, and self-confidence, is of sensitive nature, adjusting, has good conduct and leadership qualities. While the participants from Mysore reported fewer emotional characteristics, the responses of lay people from Gorakhpur and Riapur were diverse.

Table 7.8 shows the differences in conceptualization of intelligence in relation to the residential background of lay people. The cognitive competence, in general, was more stressed by the urban respondents (except Raipur). In contrast, the rural participants gave relatively greater weightage to social competence. This difference, however, was not observed in the responses of participants from Raipur and Ajmer. Except Delhi participants, entrepreneurial competence was greatly emphasized by the rural participants. The urban participants were high on the reporting of characteristics related to emotional competence. The urban-rural differences were significant only in case of Delhi participants.

Table 7.7: Characteristics of an Intelligent Person as Reported by Lay People (Schooled and Unschooled)

(*Per-cent Frequencies*)

Characteristics	*Delhi*				*Gorakhpur*				*Raipur*				*Ajmer*				*Mysore*	
	Urban		*Rural*		*Urban*		*Rural*		*Urban*		*Rural*		*Urban*		*Rural*			
	S	*U*	*S*	*U*	*S*	*U*	*S*	*U*	*S*	*U*	*S*	*U*	*S*	*U*	*S*	*U*	*S*	*U*
A. Cognitive																		
1. Presence of Mind	–	–	–	–	2	–	–	–	–	–	–	–	–	–				
2. Attention	–	–	–	–	–	–	–	–	–	–	–	–	3	3	2	6	–	–
3. Readiness to learn	1	2	–	–	–	–	–	–	–	–	–	–	1	1	1	1	–	–
4. Being Informed	1	–	–	–	–	–	–	–	–	–	–	–	3.3		5	4	–	–
5. Sensitivity to Context	15	7	4	3	9	5	11	9	6	5	8	10	2	2	2	–		
6. Comprehension	1	1	1	1	–	–	–	–	–	–	–	–	2	2	–	–	14	14
7. Learning (Past Experience)	2	–	1	–	3	–	1	1	–	–	–	–	1	1	–	–	–	–
8. Memory	1	1	–	–	–	–	2	–	–	–	–	–	–	–	–	–	2	2
9. Problem Solving	1	–	–	–	–	–	–	–	–	–	–	–	–	–	–	–	–	–
10. Decision Making	6	3			2	2	6	2	5	4	–	–	5	3	8	2	–	–
11. Planning	–	–	1	1	–	–	–	–	–	–	–	–	3	2	3	–	5	–
12. Farsightedness	1	–	–	–	2	–	–	–	–	–	–	–	2	3	2	5	13	8
13. Reflection	8	4	8	12	14	5	8	7	11	10	8	11	7	6	8	3	–	–
14. Resourcefulness	2	–	–	–	–	–	–	–	–	–	–	–	–	–	–	–	–	–
15. Communication	7	6	10	9	11	6	6	7	–	–	6	7	2	3	14	2	–	–
16. Meta–Cognition	–	–	–	–	–	–	–	–	–	–	–	–	2	–	2	2	–	–
	46	24	25	26	43	18	34	26	22	19	22	28	33	29	47	25	34	24

(*Cond.*)

Table 7.7 (*Contd.*)

Characteristics	*Delhi*				*Gorakhpur*				*Raipur*				*Ajmer*				*Mysore*	
	Urban		*Rural*		*Urban*		*Rural*		*Urban*		*Rural*		*Urban*		*Rural*			
	S	*U*	*S*	*U*	*S*	*U*	*S*	*U*	*S*	*U*	*S*	*U*	*S*	*U*	*S*	*U*	*S*	*U*
B. Social Competence																		
17. Follows norms	2	3	–	–	4	17	3	1	4	3	–	–	2	2	1	6	–	–
18. Service to elders/guests	3	11	19	19	3	2	10	10	–	5	8	8	12	6	6	4	–	–
19. Obedience	10	8	4	4	9	11	9	13	–	–	3	3	–	11	9	9	–	–
20. Helpful	7	7	11	11	–	–	5	6	7	15	2	3	13	9	8	10	5	12
21. Family Unity/Responsibilities	1	4	3	3	1	4	–	–	–	–	–	–	–	–	–	–	–	–
22. Friendliness	2	2	4	4	–	3	–	–	1	1	3	1	–	–	–	–	–	–
23. Has Good Company	–	–	2	2	–	–	–	2	–	–	–	–	–	–	–	–	–	–
24. Participation in Group Work	–	–	–	–	2	–	2	2	–	–	–	–	–	3	5	7	3	5
25. Encouragement	–	–	–	–	–	–	–	–	–	–	–	–	–	2	–	–	–	–
26. Good Etiquettes	–	–	1	–	–	–	2	3	3	–	–	–	–	–	–	–	–	–
27. Non–Extravagent	–	1			1	1			3	3	2	2	–	–	–	–	–	–
	25	36	44	43	20	38	31	37	18	27	18	17	27	33	29	36	8	17
C. Entrepreneurial																		
28. Systematic	–	–	3	3	4	3	2	1	4	1	5	3	–	–	–	–	–	–
29. Commitment	–	–	–	–	–	–	1	–	3	–	2	1	–	–	–	–	9	15
30. Hard work	1	3	1	1	–	4	–	–	3	5	4	5	–	–	–	3	5	6

(*Contd.*)

Table 7.7 (*Contd.*)

Characteristics	*Delhi*				*Gorakhpur*				*Raipur*				*Ajmer*				*Mysore*	
	Urban		*Rural*		*Urban*		*Rural*		*Urban*		*Rural*		*Urban*		*Rural*			
	S	*U*	*S*	*U*	*S*	*U*	*S*	*U*	*S*	*U*	*S*	*U*	*S*	*U*	*S*	*U*	*S*	*U*
31. Serious	–	–	–	–	1	–	–	–	–	–	–	–	12	11	10	12	–	–
32. Practical	–	–	1	–	–	–	–	–	–	–	–	–	1	1	1	1	–	–
33. Efficient	7	3	–	–	4	1	2	2	–	–	7	9	–	–	–	–	15	7
34. Responsible	1	2	–	–	–	–	3	3	2	1	–	–	–	–	–	–	4	4
35. Disciplined	–	–	2	1	2	1	2	–	1	3	1	2	–	–	–	–	–	–
36. Patience	1	1	1	–	3	2	8	9	3	–	3	3	1	1	1	1	–	–
37. Successful	1	2	1	1	–	–	–	–	–	–	–	–	–	–	–	–	–	–
38. Good Coordinator	–	–	3	1	–	–	–	–	–	–	–	–	–	–	–	–	–	–
39. Goal–Directedness	–	–	–	–	2	–	–	–	–	–	–	–	–	–	–	–	–	–
40. Scientific Orientation	5	4	–	–	–	–	–	–	–	–	–	–	–	–	–	–	–	–
41. Preventive Measures	–	–	1	–	–	–	–	–	–	–	–	–	–	–	–	–	–	–
	16	15	13	7	16	11	18	15	16	10	22	23	14	13	12	17	33	32
D. Emotional																		
42. Empathy	1	2	–	1	–	–	2	1	–	–	–	–	–	–	1	–	–	–
43. Honesty	2	3	–	1	2	1	1	2	2	3	2	2	1	1	–	–	2	1
44. Emotional Control	6	9	–	1	5	6	2	2	5	5	6	1	–	–	–	7	–	–
45. Positive Attitude	1	–	–	–	–	–	–	–	–	–	–	–	–	–	–	–	–	–
46. Self Respect	–	1	–	–	–	–	–	–	–	–	–	–	–	–	–	–	–	–
47. Cleverness	1	2	–	–	–	4	–	–	–	–	–	–	–	1	1	3	–	–
48. Humility	–	1	–	–	–	–	–	–	–	–	–	–	–	–	–	–	–	–

(*Contd.*)

Table 6.7 (*Contd.*)

Characteristics	*Delhi*				*Gorakhpur*				*Raipur*				*Ajmer*				*Mysore*	
	Urban		*Rural*		*Urban*		*Rural*		*Urban*		*Rural*		*Urban*		*Rural*			
	S	*U*	*S*	*U*	*S*	*U*	*S*	*U*	*S*	*U*	*S*	*U*	*S*	*U*	*S*	*U*	*S*	*U*
49. Religiosity	1	2	–	–	–	1	–	3	1	1	1	4	1	1	–	–	–	–
50. Confidence	–	1	1	1	–	1	2	1	3	1	–	–	–	–	–	–	2	–
51. Health Consciousness	–	2	2	2	1	2	–	4	3	4	7	7	–	–	–	–	3	–
52. Sensitivity	1	2	–	–	–	–	–	–	2	1	1	1	–	–	–	–	–	–
53. Non–Obtrusive nature	–	–	1	1	–	–	–	3	–	–	–	–	–	–	–	–	–	–
54. Independence (Economic)	–	–	2	4	–	4	–	–	4	4	–	–	–	–	–	–	–	–
55. Politeness	–	–	–	2			1	–	7	9	3	2	9	10	10	10	–	–
56. Quietness	–	–	2	–	–	–	–	–	–	–	–	–	–	–	–	–	1	1
57. Adjustment	–	–	–	–	2	–	1	1	3	–	–	–	–	–	–	–	–	–
58. Straightforwardness	–	–	–	–	–	–	–	–	–	–	–	–	10	5	–	–	–	–
59. Curiosity	–	–	–	–	1	2	2	–	–	–	–	–			–	1	–	–
60. Leadership	–	–	–	–	2	1	–	–	–	–	–	–	2	2	–	–	–	–
61. Egoism	–	–	–	–	–	–	–	–	3	6	1	1	–	–	–	–	–	–
62. Humanitarian approach	–	–	–	–	–	–	–	–	–	–	–	–	3	5	–	1	–	–
63. Good Conduct	–	–	1	2	2	1	3	3	4	4	6	2	–	–	–	–	–	–
64. Fearlessness	–	–	–	–	–	–	3	2	–	–	–	–	–	–	–	–	–	–
	13	25	9	15	15	23	17	22	37	38	27	20	26	25	12	22	8	2

(*Contd.*)

Table 7.7 (*Contd.*)

Characteristics	*Delhi*				*Gorakhpur*				*Raipur*				*Ajmer*				*Mysore*	
	Urban		*Rural*		*Urban*		*Rural*		*Urban*		*Rural*		*Urban*		*Rural*			
	S	*U*	*S*	*U*	*S*	*U*	*S*	*U*	*S*	*U*	*S*	*U*	*S*	*U*	*S*	*U*	*S*	*U*
E. Misc.																		
65. Education	–		9	9	6	10	–	–	3	1	6	7	–	–	–	–	12	15
66. Good in Studies	–	–	–	–	–	–	–	–	4	5	5	5	–	–	–	–	–	–
67. High IQ	–	–	–	–	–	–	–	–	–	–	–	–	–	–	–	–	5	10
	–	–	9	11	6	10	–	–	7	6	11	12	–	–	–	–	–	–

S = Schooled U = Unschooled

* Data at Mysore Centre were not analyzed for schooled and Unschooled participants at the interface of their urban-rural habitat.

Table 7.8: Dimensions of Intelligent Behaviour Reported by Urban and Rural Participants

(Per cent Frequencies)

Locality	*Cognitive*	*Social*	*Entrepre-neurial*	*Emotional*	*MISC.*	*Chi Square (df=4)*
Delhi						
Urban	35	30	15	20	–	11.32*
Rural	25	45	11	14	5	
Gorakhpur						
Urban	32	27	15	19	7	1.96
Rural	30	30	17	20	3	
Raipur						
Urban	21	20	13	37	9	6.34
Rural	25	17	23	24	11	
Ajmer						
Urban	33	30	13	24	–	0.56
Rural	35	30	15	20	–	
Mysore						
Urban	31	6	31	8	24	6.45
Rural	21	12	42	6	19	
Overall						
Urban	34	25	14	23	4	4.43
Rural	27	28	17	18	10	

* *P*<.05

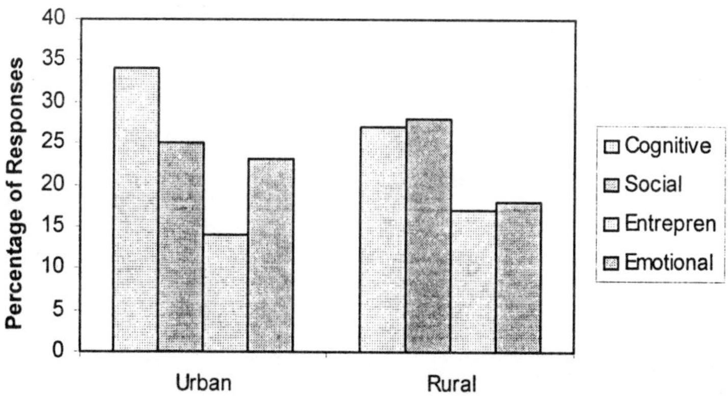

Fig. 7.9: Facets of Intelligence reported by Urban and Rural Participants

The schooled participants more frequently reported the cognitive and entrepreneurial competencies (Table 7.9). In contrast, their unschooled counterparts gave greater emphasis on social and emotional competencies (Fig. 7.10). It may be noted that the differences in the per centage of responses as related to schooling were significant for the Mysore participants only.

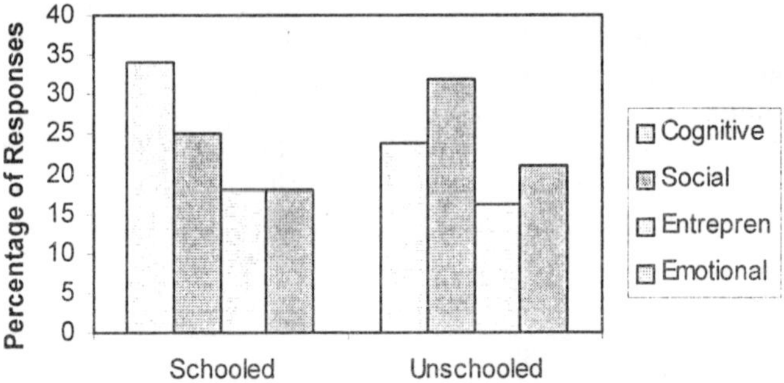

Fig. 7.10: Percentage of Responses related to Facets of Intelligence reported by Schooled and Unschooled Participants

Table 7.9: Dimensions of Intelligent Behaviour reported by Schooled and Unschooled Participants

(Per cent Frequencies)

Locality	*Cognitive*	*Social*	*Entrepre-neurial*	*Emotional*	*Misc.*	*Chi-Square (df=4)*
Delhi						
Schooled	36	34	15	11	4	5.33
Unschooled	25	40	11	19	5	
Gorakhpur						
Schooled	39	28	17	16	–	5.90
Unschooled	26	38	13	23	–	
Raipur						
Schooled	22	18	19	32	9	0.80
Unschooled	24	22	17	29	8	
Ajmer						
Schooled	40	28	13	19	–	3.83
Unschooled	27	35	15	23	–	
Mysore						
Schooled	34	8	33	8	17	9.49*
Unschooled	24	17	32	2	25	
Overall						
Schooled	34	25	18	18	5	3.27
Unschooled	24	32	16	21	7	

* $P < .05$

An attempt was made to find out the major trends in lay people's responses as a function of their schooling. Towards this end, frequencies were pooled together without regard to locality and were rank ordered. Of these, five highly and five least ceded characteristics of intelligent persons are reported in Table 6.10. Participants agreed that an intelligent person shows sensitivity to the context and helps the needy. While the maximum number of urban-schooled participants reported reflection, they also ceded that an intelligent person communicates effectively, and is able to take decisions. All these characteristics refer to one or the other form of self-determination or intentionality in thought and action. The urban unschooled and rural (schooled and unschooled) groups gave priority to social competence including obedience, service to elders and guests, and helping the needy. The cognitive competence was accorded second priority by these groups. Among the least ceded attributes, emotional and entrepreneurial competencies emerged in a major way. Participants endorsed that an intelligent person remains conscious about his health, is polite, is honest, is committed, and pursues a task systematically. The rural participants also reported 'following social norms' as an important aspect of intelligence.

Table 7.10: Characteristics of Intelligent Persons given by Lay People Varying in Schooling

Urban		*Rural*	
Schooled	*Unschooled*	*Schooled*	*Unschooled*
Highly Ceded Characteristics			
Reflection	Obedience	Service to elders	Service to elders
Context sensitivity	Helping	Communicability	Reflection
Helping	Context sensitivity	Reflection	Obedience
Communicability	Communicability	Helping	Helping
Decision Making	Decision Making	Context sensitivity	Context sensitivity
Least Ceded Characteristics			
Health consciousness	Patience	Following Norms	Decision Making
Patience			
Patience	Systematic	Honesty	Honesty
Honesty	Health	Seriousness	Following Norms
Commitment	Commitment	Health	Systematic
Systematic	Honesty	Systematic	Hardworking

Gender Differences

Table 7.11 shows gender differences in the characteristics of intelligent persons. The participants of both sexes equally mentioned aspects of cognitive competence such as sensitivity to context, decision-making and communication. Decision-making was more emphasized by the urban respondents. Males tended to consider an intelligent person as 'reflective'—the one who after having considered all sides of the problem, places the same in its proper context and then takes decisions. The characteristics such as willingness to learn, learning from past experiences and learning faster, and foresightedness were reported by greater number of males.

The female participants gave primacy to social competence. In particular, a large number of females than males agreed that an intelligent person follows social norms, respects and serves the parents, elders, and guests, is obedient, helps the needy by providing adequate counselling or otherwise, is friendly and non-extravagant. More females than males from Delhi and Gorakhpur viewed intelligence situated in such activities as maintaining unity in the family and carrying out the family responsibilities. The rural participants from Delhi and Gorakhpur considered that an intelligent person remains in the company of good people. Participation in group work was endorsed by larger number of males than females from the localities other than Delhi. The urban males from Ajmer also saw intelligent people as encouraging.

Among the features related to entrepreneurial competence, the study indicated that males described an intelligent person more frequently as one who systematically pursues a task, is committed, is hard working, adopts a practical approach and thus remains tied to the reality, and shows patience. The participants from Ajmer, irrespective of gender, indicated seriousness, efficiency, responsibility, and discipline as the features of intelligent people. More number of males from Delhi also considered an intelligent person as successful, good manager, and having scientific orientation. The goal-directed behaviour of intelligent persons was reported by the urban participants from Gorakhpur.

Table 7.11: Characteristics of an Intelligent Person by Lay People's Sex

(*Per cent Frequencies*)

Characteristics	*Delhi*				*Gorakhpur*				*Raipur*				*Ajmer*				*Mysore*	
	Urban		*Rural*		*Urban*		*Rural*		*Urban*		*Rural*		*Urban*		*Rural*			
	M	*F*	*M*	*F*	*M*	*F*	*M*	*F*	*M*	*F*	*M*	*F*	*M*	*F*	*M*	*F*	*M*	*F*
A. Cognitive																		
1. Presence of Mind	–	–	–	–	2	1	–	–	–	–	–	–	–	–	–	–	–	–
2. Attention	–	–	–	–	–	–	–	–	–	–	–	–	4	5	3	4	–	–
3. Readiness to learn	2	1	–	–	–	–	–	–	–	–	–	–	2	–	1	1	–	–
4. Being Informed	1	–	–	–	–	–	–	–	–	–	–	–	2	5	4	5	–	–
5. Sensitivity to Context	10	9	3	3	6	9	9	9	5	6	9	8	2	3	2	1	–	–
6. Comprehension	1	1	–	1	–	–	–	–	–	–	–	–	1	2	–	–	15	14
7. Learning (Speed & Past Exp)	4	3	1	1	4	–	1	1	–	–	–	–	2	–	–	–	–	–
8. Memory	–	–	–	–	–	–	1	1	–	–	–	–	–	–	–	–	2	3
9. Problem Solving	1	–	–	–	–	–	–	–	–	–	–	–	–	–	–	–	–	–
10. Decision Making	4	4			2	1	4	5	6	4			5	5	6	5	–	–
11. Planning	–	–	1	1	–	–	–	–	–	–	–	–	3	3	4	6	2	2
12. Farsightedness	1	–	–	–	1	2	–	–	–	–	–	–	4	1	3	3	12	10
13. Reflection	7	4	11	8	12	9	9	7	11	10	13	6	7	8	6	6	–	–
14. Resourcefulness	1	1	–	–	–	–	–	–	–	–	–	–	–	–	–	–	–	–
15. Communication	7	7	8	12	11	8	7	6	–	–	7	6	2	2	3	3	–	–
16. Meta-Cognition	–	–	–	–	–	–	–	–	–	–	–	–	1	2	2	1	–	–
	16	30	24	26	38	30	31	29	22	20	•29	20	35	36	34	35	31	29

(*Contd.*)

Table 7.11 : (Contd.)

Characteristics	Delhi				Gorakhpur				Raipur				Ajmer				Mysore	
	Urban		Rural		Urban		Rural		Urban		Rural		Urban		Rural			
	M	F	M	F	M	F	M	F	M	F	M	F	M	F	M	F	M	F
B. Social Competence																		
17. Following Norms	4	2	2	1	8	11	2	2	4	6	–	–	2	2	3	3	–	–
18. Service to elders/guests	6	9	18	21	1	3	8	12	4	1	7	9	10	8	8	7	–	–
19. Obedience	8	9	5	6	4	6	4	7	–	–	–	–	2	2	2	2	–	–
20. Helpful	3	7	11	10	2	–	6	5	8	12	3	2	10	13	9	9	6	5
21. Family Unity/Responsibilities	1	5	4	3	2	3	–	–	–	–	–	–	–	–	–	–	–	–
22. Friendliness	1		2	4	1	2	–	–	1	1	–	2	–	–	–	–	–	–
23. Has Good Company	–	–	3	1	–	–	1	1	–	–	–	–	–	–	–	–	–	–
24. Participation in Group Work	–	–	1	1	2	2			–	2			6	1	5	6	5	4
25. Encouragement	–	–	–	–	–	–	–	–	–	–	–	–	1	–	–	–	–	–
26. Good Etiquettes	–	–	1	1	–	–	–	–	2	1	–	–	–	–	–	–	–	–
27. Non-Extravagant	1	1			–	1	–	–	2	3	2	3	–	–	–	–	–	–
	24	35	46	47	19	27	23	29	21	24	14	18	31	26	27	27	11	9
C. Entrepreneurial																		
28. Systematic approach	–	–	3	3	4	3	1	2	3	2	7	2	–	–	–	–	–	–
29. Commitment	–	–	–	–	–	–	1	–	2	1	2	1	–	–	–	–	14	15
30. Hard work	2	2	2	1	5	2			5	4	5	5	–	–	–	–	5	5
31. Seriousness	–	–	–	–	1	1	–	–	–	–	–	–	11	11	11	11	–	–
32. Practical view	–	–	–	1	–	–	–	–	–	–	–	–	2	–	1	1	–	–
33. Efficiency	5	3	–	–	4	2	2	2	–	–	6	10	–	–	–	–	6	7

(Contd.)

Tabale 7.11 (*Contd.*)

Characteristics	*Delhi*				*Gorakhpur*				*Raipur*				*Ajmer*				*Mysore*	
	Urban		*Rural*		*Urban*		*Rural*		*Urban*		*Rural*		*Urban*		*Rural*			
	M	*F*	*M*	*F*	*M*	*F*	*M*	*F*	*M*	*F*	*M*	*F*	*M*	*F*	*M*	*F*	*M*	*F*
34. Responsibility	1	3	–	–	–	–	3	3	2	1	–	–	–	–	–	–	4	4
35. Discipline	–	–	2	1	1	2	1	1	2	2	2	2	–	–	–	–	–	–
36. Patience	1	1	1	1	2	2	8	9	1	2	4	2	1	1	6	1	–	–
37. Success	2	1	1	1	–	–	–	–	–	–	–	–	–	–	–	–	–	–
38. Good Coordination	–	–	1	3	–	–	–	–	–	–	–	–	–	–	–	–	–	–
39. Goal-Orientation	–	–	–	–	2	1	–	–	–	–	–	–	–	–	–	–	–	–
40. Scientific Orientation	5	3	–	–	–	–	–	–	–	–	–	–	–	–	–	–	–	–
	16	13	11	11	19	13	16	17	15	12	26	22	14	12	18	13	29	31
D. Emotional																		
41. Empathy	1	1	1	1	–	–	3	–	2	3	–	–	–	–	1	–	–	–
42. Honesty	3	2	–	1	2	–	–	2	2	3	2	3	–	1	–	–	2	2
43. Emotional Control	11	8	4	1	5	7	2	2	9	1	5	2	–	–	–	–	–	–
44. Positive Attitude	1	–	–	–	–	–	–	–	–	–	–	–	–	–	–	–	–	–
45. Self Respect	1	1	–	–	–	–	–	–	–	–	–	–	–	–	–	–	–	–
46. Cleverness	2	1	–	–	3	1	–	–	–	–	–	–	–	2	2	2	–	–
47. Humility	1	1	–	–	–	–	–	–	–	–	–	–	–	–	–	–	–	–
48. Religiousness	–	2	–	–	–	1	2	1	1	1	1	4	1	1	–	–	–	–

(*Contd.*)

Table 7.11 (*Contd.*)

Characteristics	*Delhi*				*Gorakhpur*				*Raipur*				*Ajmer*				*Mysore*	
	Urban		*Rural*		*Urban*		*Rural*		*Urban*		*Rural*		*Urban*		*Rural*			
	M	*F*	*M*	*F*	*M*	*F*	*M*	*F*	*M*	*F*	*M*	*F*	*M*	*F*	*M*	*F*	*M*	*F*
49. Confidence	1	1	2	2	1	1	1	2	2	2	–	–	–	–	–	–	1	1
50. Health Consciousness	–	2	2	2	1	1	2	2	2	2	6	8	–	–	–	–	2	1
51. Sensitivity	–	1	–	–	–	–	–	–	–	–	1	–	–	–	–	–	–	–
52. Non-Obtrusive	–	–	1	1	–	–	–	3	–	–	–	–	–	–	–	–	–	–
53. Independence (Economic)	–	–	2	3	2	2	–	–	3	5	–	–	–	–	–	–	–	–
54. Politeness	–	–	2	1	–	–	1	–	7	8	2	1	8	9	8	10	–	–
55. Quietness	–	–	1	1	–	–	–	–	–	–	–	–	–	–	–	–	2	4
56. Adjustment	–	–	–	–	1	2	1	1	1	2	–	–	–	–	–	–	–	–
57. Straightforwardness	–	–	–	–	–	–	–	–	–	–	–	–	6	8	8	11	–	–
58. Curiosity	–	–	–	–	1	1	1	1	–	–	–	–	–	–	–	–	–	–
59. Leadership	–	–	–	–	1	1	–	–	–	–	–	–	2	1	1	1	–	–
60. Egoism	–	–	–	–	–	–	–	–	4	5	1	1					–	–
61. Humanitarian approach	–	–	–	–	–	–	–	–	–	–	–	–	3	4	1	1	–	–
62. Good Conduct	–	–	2	1	1	2	3	3	3	3	5	4	–	–	–	–	–	–
63. Fearlessness	–	–	–	–	–	–	3	2	–	–	–	–	–	–	–	–	–	–
64. Speaking truth (in context)	2	2	2	2	1	1	1	1	1	1	1	1	–	–	–	–	–	–
	23	22	19	16	19	20	20	20	37	36	24	24	20	26	21	25	7	8

(*Contd.*)

Table 7.11 (*Contd.*)

Characteristics	*Delhi*				*Gorakhpur*				*Raipur*				*Ajmer*				*Mysore*	
	Urban		*Rural*		*Urban*		*Rural*		*Urban*		*Rural*		*Urban*		*Rural*			
	M	*F*	*M*	*F*	*M*	*F*	*M*	*F*	*M*	*F*	*M*	*F*	*M*	*F*	*M*	*F*	*M*	*F*
E. Misc																		
65. Education	–	–	–	–	5	10			2	2	4	9	–	–	–	–	–	–
66. Good in Studies	–	–	–	–	–	–	7	5	3	6	3	6	–	–	–	–	14	14
67. High IQ	–	–	–	–	–	–	–	–	–	–	–	1	–	–	–	–	8	9
	–	–	–	–	5	10	7	5	5	8	7	16	–	–	–	–	22	23

M = Male F = Female

* Due to communication gap, data at Mysore centre were not analyzed for male and female participants at the interface of their urban-rural habitat.

In all 24 characteristics related to emotional competence were reported by the lay people. Out of these, honesty, religiousness, health consciousness, non-interference in others' work, politeness, adjustment, and straightforwardness were more frequently reported by the female participants. The males, on the other hand, stressed more on empathy and emotional control. The features such as good conduct and speaking restrained truth were mentioned by the participants from Delhi, Gorakhpur and Raipur. The lay people from Delhi agreed that an intelligent person displays positive attitude, shows self-respect, and is humble. More females than males considered an intelligent person as educated and good in studies.

Table 7.12 shows that cognitive and entrepreneurial competencies were more frequently ceded by the male participants. Females, on the other hand, were high on social competence (see Figure 7.11). The participants of both sexes

Table 7.12: Facets of Intelligent Behaviour reported by Male and Female Respondents (*Per cent Frequencies*)

Locality	*Cognitive*	*Social*	*Entrepreneurial*	*Emotional*	*Misc.*	*Chi Square (df=4)*
Delhi						
Male	32	34	14	20	–	0.58
Female	28	41	12	19	–	
Gorakhpur						
Male	35	21	18	20	6	1.83
Female	30	28	15	20	7	
Raipur						
Male	26	18	21	31	4	2.12
Female	20	21	17	30	2	
Ajmer						
Male	35	29	16	20	–	1.04
Female	36	26	13	25	–	
Mysore						
Male	31	11	29	7	22	0.42
Female	29	9	31	8	23	
Overall						
Male	31	24	18	21	6	1.10
Female	28	27	16	22	7	

equally reported various attributes of emotional competence. A similar pattern is observed for the miscellaneous responses. The sex difference in the pattern of responses was, however, not significant.

Five highly ceded and five least ceded features of intelligent persons as endorsed by males and females are given in Table 7.13. Prominent among the responses of urban males was control of emotions. Also, service to elders emerged as an important quality of intelligent persons among the group of urban female (5 rank), rural male (2 rank), and rural female (1 rank). Good conduct was also sometimes reported as an important indicator of intelligence.

Table 7.13 : Characteristics of Intelligent Persons by Lay People's Sex

Urban		*Rural*	
Male	*Female*	*Male*	*Female*
Highly Ceded Characteristics			
Reflection	Helping	Reflection	Service to elders
Emotional control	Reflection	Service to elders	Communicability
Context sensitivity	Context Sensitivity	Helping	Helping
Helping	Following Norms	Context sensitivity	Reflection
Following Norms	Service to elders	Communicability	Context sensitivity
Least Ceded Characteristics			
Patience	Health Conciousness	Honesty	Emotionally controlled
Good Conduct	Good conduct	Efficiency	Efficiency
Health consciousness	Systematic	Health Consciousness	Good conduct
Honesty	Patience	Following norms	Hardworking
Systematic	Efficiency	Decision making	Honesty

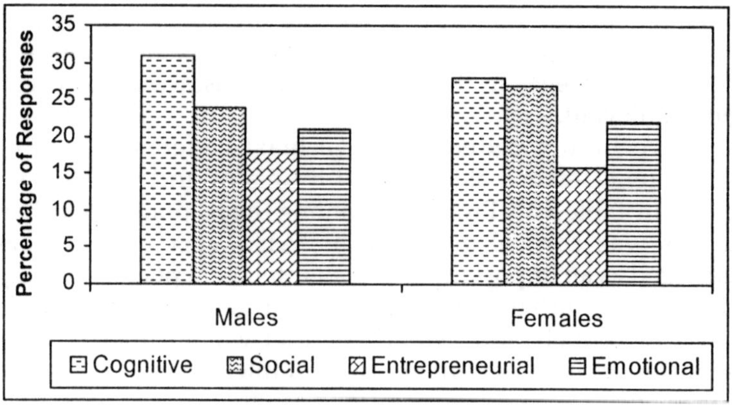

Fig. 7.11: Percentage of Different Facets of Intelligence as reported by Males and Females

Age Related Changes

Tables 7.14 and 7.15 show that sensitivity to context was emphasized more by the lay people from urban areas in the age group of 12-14 years and rural participants aged 20-25 years. Reporting of abilities such as communication and reflection decreased with age. They were more stressed by 16-18 years followed by 20-25 year old participants. The 45-50 year old participants emphasized more on decision-making. Among other cognitive competencies, remaining attentive and informed were frequently endorsed by the participants in the age group of 60+; willingness to learn, planning, foresightedness, and knowing one's strengths and weaknesses by 45-50 year old; and comprehension and learning from past experiences by 16-18 years old participants.

Within the category of social competence, following social norms, obedience, and participation in group work were supplied more frequently by the older people followed by the adults from 45-50 year age group. The elderly participants (aged 60+ year) from Gorakhpur also considered maintaining unity in the family and carrying out family's responsibilities as essential features of the intelligent people. Young rural participants, particularly in the age group of 12-14 years, stressed on paying respect for and service to parents, elders, and guests. Helping others by providing appropriate counselling or otherwise was emphasized by the lay people aged 16-18 years, followed by 20-25, 60+, and 45-50 years, respectively. Participants, irrespective of their age, agreed that an intelligent person should not be extravagant.

The features related to entrepreneurial competence were more frequently endorsed by the younger participants (in the age group of 12-14 and 16-18 years). To them, an intelligent person is committed, hard working, serious, systematic and disciplined. The 20-25 year old people considered an intelligent person as systematic and accepting responsibilities. The elderly participants gave more weightage to efficiency and patience.

Within the category of emotional competence, lay people in the age groups of 12-14 years and 60+ years gave equal weightage to emotional control and speaking the truth. Urban participants reported these qualities more frequently than their rural counterparts. The older participants (60+ years) also gave more weightage to emotional competence such as religiousness, health consciousness and good conduct. While the former two characteristics were more stressed by urban participants, rural participants, in comparison to their urban counterparts, gave more weightage to good conduct. The urban participants aged 14-16 years frequently reported honesty.

Table 7.16 shows that cognitive competencies were given relatively greater weightage by the participants of all age groups which was followed by social, emotional and entrepreneurial competencies (see Fig. 7.12). The lay people in the age group of 20-25 years, which was followed by 16-18 years and 45-50 year old participants, reported cognitive competencies more frequently. The elderly participants more frequently endorsed the social and emotional competencies. The entrepreneurial competence was greatly ceded by the participants in the age group of 16-18 years, which was followed by age groups 12-14 years, 20-25 years, and 45-50 years. The age differences in the reporting of these characteristics were significant only in the group of Mysore participants.

Table 7.14: Characteristics of an Intelligent Person by Lay People's Age in Urban Areas (Per Cent Frequencies)

Characteristics	Delhi					Gorakhpur					Raipur					Ajmer					Mysore				
	12-14	16-18	20-25	45-50	60+	12-14	16-18	20-25	45-50	60+	12-14	16-18	20-25	45-50	60+	12-14	16-18	20-25	45-50	60+	12-14	16-18	20-25	45-50	60+
A. Cognitive																									
1. Presence of Mind	–	–	–	–	–	–	3	2	1	–	–	–	–	–	–	–	–	–	–	–	–	–	–	–	–
2. Attention	–	–	–	–	–	–	–	–	–	–	–	–	–	–	–	3	6	4	1	3	–	–	–	–	–
3. Readiness to learn	–	–	–	–	2	–	–	–	–	–	–	–	–	–	–	–	1	–	2	1	–	–	–	–	–
4. Being Informed	–	–	–	–	–	–	–	–	–	–	–	–	–	–	–	–	–	–	–	–	–	–	–	–	–
5. Sensitivity to Context	–	–	–	–	8	13	4	8	6	7	8	6	4	6	5	2	1	1	1	4					
6. Comprehension	–	–	2	–	–											3	1	–	2	1	5	16	16	5	8
7. Learning (Speed & Past Experience	3	3	3	2	1	1	3	1	2	3	–	–	–	–	–	–	1	1	3	1	–	–	–	–	–
8. Memory	–	1	1	–	–	–	–	–	–	–	–	–	–	–	–	–	–	–	–	–	–	–	6	4	1
9. Problem Solving	–	1	1	1	–	–	–	–	–	–	–	–	–	–	–	–	–	–	–	–	–	–	–	–	–
10. Decision Making	5	4	4	3	2	–	1	2	2	2	3	5	6	5	4	7	1	5	4	4	–	–	–	–	–
11. Planning	–	–	–	–	–	–	–	–	–	–	–	–	–	–	–	2	2	4	5	2			4	5	6
12. Farsightedness	–	–	1	1	–	–	1	2	1	1	–	–	–	–	–	3	1	–	2	6			20	30	15
13. Reflection	4	7	5	7	2	8	12	10	13	8	11	11	9	9	14	6	11	6	9	5	–	–	–	–	–
14. Resourcefulness	1	1	1	–	1	–	–	–	–	–	–	–	–	–	–	–	–	–	–	–	–	–	–	–	–
15. Communication	6	9	5	10	4	10	12	8	7	9	–	–	–	–	–	2	2	2	2	1	–	–	–	–	–
16. Meta-Cognition	–	–	–	–	–	–	–	–	–	–	–	–	–	–	–	1	–	1	2	1	–	–	–	–	–
	28	38	37	36	20	32	36	33	32	30	22	22	19	20	23	32	28	26	34	35	5	16	46	44	30
B. Social Competence																									
17. Following Norms	3	3	3	3	3	13	7	9	6	13	1	4	3	6	2	1	4	–	2	3	–	–	–	–	–
18. Service to elders/guests	6	8	8	10	8	–	5	–	3	3	9	6	2	–	–	12	9	7	3	12	–	–	–	–	–

(*Contd.*)

Table 7.14: (*Contd.*)

Characteristics	*Delhi*					*Gorakhpur*					*Raipur*					*Ajmer*					*Mysore*				
	12-14	*16-18*	*20-25*	*45-50*	*60+*	*12-14*	*16-18*	*20-25*	*45-50*	*60+*	*12-14*	*16-18*	*20-25*	*45-50*	*60+*	*12-14*	*16-18*	*20-25*	*45-50*	*60+*	*12-14*	*16-18*	*20-25*	*45-50*	*60+*
19. Obedience	13	8	5	10	9	–	–	5	6	5	–	–	–	–	–	4	–	2	2	2	–	–	–	–	–
20. Helpful	8	7	5	5	9	–	–	3	5	–	7	13	9	12	10	8	12	15	13	8	3	10	–	–	–
21. Family Unity/ Responsibilities	–	2	3	1	7	3	1	1	2	5	–	–	–	–	–	–	–	–	–	–	–	–	–	–	–
22. Friendliness	–	–	–	–	–	3	1	1	1	1	–	1	2	2	–	–	–	–	–	–	–	–	–	–	–
23. Has Good Company	3	1	2	1	1	–	–	–	–	–	–	–	–	–	–	–	–	–	–	–	–	–	–	–	–
24. Participation in Group Work	–	–	–	–	–	–	1	1	3	–	–	–	–	–	–	3	–	2	3	10	5	4	–	–	–
25. Encouragement	–	–	–	–	2	–	–	–	–	–	–	–	–	–	–	1	–	1	1	–	–	–	–	–	–
26. Good Etiquettes	–	–	–	–	–	–	–	–	–	–	2	1	3	2	–	–	–	–	–	–	–	–	–	–	–
27. Non-Extravagant	–	–	–	–	–	4	4	1	1	–	2	2	4	3	2	–	–	–	–	–	–	–	–	–	–
	33	29	26	30	39	23	19	21	27	27	21	27	23	25	14	29	25	27	24	35	8	14	–	–	–
C. Entrepreneurial																									
28. Systematic approach	–	–	–	–	–	3	3	7	3	1	2	3	4	2	2	–	–	–	–	–	–	–	–	–	–
29. Commitment	–	–	–	–	–	–	–	–	–	–	–	–	1	3	2	–	–	–	–	–	33	24	10	12	–
30. Hard work	4	3	1	1	2	6	4	1	3	3	3	4	4	3	7	–	–	–	–	–	14	10	–	–	–
31. Seriousness	–	–	–	–	–	–	1	1	1	1	–	–	–	–	–	15	18	17	7	10	–	–	–	–	–
32. Practical approach	–	–	–	–	–	–	–	–	–	–	–	–	–	–	–	–	1	1	3	1	–	–	–	–	–
33. Efficiency	2	2	6	8	1	–	1	3	4	4	–	–	–	–	–	–	–	–	–	–	–	–	–	24	17
34. Responsibility	1	4	2	1	1	–	–	–	–	–	–	–	2	3	3	–	–	–	–	–	–	–	18	5	13
35. Discipline	–	–	–	–	–	1	3	2	1	1	6	2	2	2	–	–	–	–	–	–	–	–	–	–	–
36. Patience	–	–	2	–	2	1	2	1	3	4	–	–	2	1	4	1	1	–	1	2	–	–	–	–	–
37. Successful	4	3	2	–	1	–	–	–	–	–	–	–	–	–	–	–	–	–	–	–	–	–	–	–	–

(*Contd.*)

Table 7.14 (*Contd.*)

Characteristics	*Delhi*					*Gorakhpur*					*Raipur*					*Ajmer*					*Mysore*				
	12-14	*16-18*	*20-25*	*45-50*	*60+*	*12-14*	*16-18*	*20-25*	*45-50*	*60+*	*12-14*	*16-18*	*20-25*	*45-50*	*60+*	*12-14*	*16-18*	*20-25*	*45-50*	*60+*	*12-14*	*16-18*	*20-25*	*45-50*	*60+*
38. Good Coordination	–	–	–	–	–	–	–	–	–	–	–	–	–	–	–	–	–	–	–	–	–	–	–	–	–
39. Goal-Directedness	–	–	–	–	–	–	1	3	2	1	–	–	–	–	–	–	–	–	–	–	–	–	–	–	–
40. Scientific Orientation	5	6	5	4	2	–	–	–	–	–	–	–	–	–	–	–	–	–	–	–	–	–	–	–	–
41. Preventive Measure	–	–	–	–	–	–	–	–	–	–		–	–	–	–	–	–	–	–	–	–	–	–	–	–
	16	18	18	14	9	11	15	18	17	15	11	9	15	14	18	16	20	18	11	13	47	34	28	41	30
D. Emotional																									
42. Empathy	1	1	2	–	3	–	–	–	–	–	3	3	5	2	2	–	–	–	–	–	–	–	–	–	–
43. Honesty	6	2	1	2	2	1	1	2	1	2	2	3	2	3	2	1	3	–	3	–	2	7	5	2	3
44. Emotional Control	8	5	7	7	12	10	7	3	5	5	4	2	5	6	8	–	–	–	–	–	–	–	–	–	–
45. Positive Attitude	–	–	1	–	–	–	–	–	–	–	–	–	–	–	–	–	–	–	–	–	–	–	–	–	–
46. Self Respect	–	1	1	–	1	–	–	–	–	–	–	–	–	–	–	–	–	–	–	–	–	–	–	–	–
47. Cleverness	2	–	1	3	1	2	3	1	2	1	–	–	–	–	–	4	–	2	2	2					
48. Humility	–	1	–	1	1	–	–	–	–	–	–	–	–	–	–	–	–	–	–	–	–	–	–	–	–
	–	–	–	–	–	–	–	–	–	–	–	–	–	–	–	–	–	–	–	–	–	–	–	–	–
49. Religiosity	–	–	1	2	4	–	–	2	1	2	2	1	1	–	1	1	2	4	2	1	–	–	–	–	–
50. Confidence	–	–	–	2	1	1	1	1	1	1	2	3	2	1	2	–	–	–	–	–	–	–	–	–	5
51. Health Conscious	1	2	2	1	–	2	1	2	1	2	3	1	2	1	2	–	–	–	–	–	–	–	5	–	15
52. Sensitivity	2	1	2	–	3	–	–	–	–	–	–	–	–	–	–	–	–	–	–	–	–	–	–	–	–
53. Non-Obtrusive nature	–	–	–	–	–	–	–	–	–	–	–	–	–	–	–	–	–	–	–	–	–	–	–	–	–
54. Independence (Economic)	–	–	–	–	–	4	4	1	1	–	3	5	4	4	4	–	–	–	–	–	–	–	–	–	–

(*Contd.*)

Table 7.14 (*Contd.*)

Characteristics	*Delhi*					*Gorakhpur*					*Raipur*					*Ajmer*					*Mysore*				
	12-14	*16-18*	*20-25*	*45-50*	*60+*	*12-14*	*16-18*	*20-25*	*45-50*	*60+*	*12-14*	*16-18*	*20-25*	*45-50*	*60+*	*12-14*	*16-18*	*20-25*	*45-50*	*60+*	*12-14*	*16-18*	*20-25*	*45-50*	*60+*
55. Politeness	–	–	–	–	–	–	–	–	–	–		8	10	9	4	6	8	12	9	–	–	–	–	–	–
56. Quiteness	–	–	–	–	–	–	–	–	–	–	–	–	–	–	–	–	–	–	–	–	–	–	6	2	1
57. Adjusting	–	–	–	–	–	–	1	2	3	1	–	–	2	3	2	–	–	–	–	–	–	–	–	–	–
58. Straightforwardness	–	–	–	–	–	–	–	–	–	–	–	–	–	–	–	3	5	4	4	2	–	–	–	–	–
59. Curiosity	–	–	–	–	–	–	2	2	2	1	–	–	–	–	–	–	–	–	–	–	–	–	–	–	–
60. Leadership	–	–	–	–	–	–	2	3	1	–	–	–	–	–	–	1	1	5	6	2	–	–	–	–	–
61. Egoist attitude	–	–	–	–	–	–	–	–	–	–	4	3	3	6	7	–	–	–	–	–	–	–	–	–	
62. Humanitarian	–	–	–	–	–		–	–	–	–	–	–	–	–	–	5	4	5	3	2	–	–	–	–	–
63. Good Conduct	–	–	–	–	–	1	3	2	1	1	2	3	2	4	3	–	–	–	–	–	–	–	–	–	–
64. Fearlessness	–	–	–	–	–											–	–	–	–	–	–	–	–	–	–
65. Speaking the truth (in context)	3	2	1	2	4	2	1	2	1	2	2	3	1	1	1	–	–	–	–	–	–	–	–	–	–
	23	15	19	20	32	23	26	23	20	18	35	37	38	35	40	23	27	29	31	17	2	7	16	4	24
E. Misc.																									
66. Education	–	–	–	–	–	11	5	5	4	10	4	2	1	2	3	–	–	–	–	–	–	–	–	–	–
67. Good in Studies	–	–	–	–	–	–	–	–	–	–	7	3	4	4	2	–	–	–	–	–	21	14	10	11	16
68. High IQ	–	–	–	–	–	–	–	–	–	–	–	–	–	–	–	–	–	–	–	–	17	15	–	–	–
	–	–	–	–	–	11	5	5	4	10	11	5	5	6	5	–	–	–	–	–	38	29	10	11	16

Table 7.15 : Characteristics of an Intelligent Person by Lay People's Age in Rural Areas

(Per cent Frequencies)

Characteristics	*Delhi*					*Gorakhpur*					*Raipur*					*Ajmer*				
	12-14	*16-18*	*20-25*	*45-50*	*60+*	*12-14*	*16-18*	*20-25*	*45-50*	*60+*	*12-14*	*16-18*	*20-25*	*45-50*	*60+*	*12-14*	*16-18*	*20-25*	*45-50*	*60+*
A. Cognitive																				
1. Presence of Mind	–	–	–	–	–	–	–	–	–	–	–	–	–	–	–	–	–	–	–	–
2. Attention	–	–	–	–	–	–	–	–	–	–	–	–	–	–	–	5	–	2	–	8
3. Readiness to learn	–	–	–	–	–	–	–	–	–	–	–	–	–	–	–	1	–	1	4	1
4. Being Informed	–	–	–	–	–	–	–	–	–	–	–	–	–	–	–	4	5	5	4	5
5. Sensitivity to Context	5	3	4	2	2	9	8	15	6	10	7	9	10	9	8	1	2	5	1	–
6. Comprehension	2	2	–	–	–	–	–	–	–	–	–	–	–	–	–	–	–	–	–	–
7. Learning (Speed & Past Experience	2	1	–	1	–	1	1	1	–	–	–	–	–	–	–	–	–	–	–	–
8. Memory	–	–	–	–	–	–	3	2	1	–	–	–	–	–	–	–	–	–	–	–
9. Problem Solving	–	–	–	–	–						–	–	–	–	–	–	–	–	–	–
10. Decision Making	–	–	–	–	–	3	3	7	4	5	–	–	–	–	–	3	6	7	8	5
11. Planning	2	–	–	1	2	–	–	–	–	–	–	–	–	–	–	8	3	3	5	1
12. Farsightedness						–	–	–	–	–	–	–	–	–	–	4	1	2	4	3
13. Reflection	5	10	13	8	14	7	8	10	8	5	3	13	11	7	16	8	6	10	3	2
14. Resourcefulness	–	–	–	–	–	–	–	–	–	–	–	–	–	–	–	7	1	4	2	2
15. Communication	9	11	14	8	5	5	7	5	7	6	1	10	6	5	10	–	–	–	–	–
16. Meta-Cognition	–	–	–	–	–	–	–	–	–	–	–	–	–	–	–	1	5	1	4	–
	25	27	31	20	23	25	30	40	26	26	11	32	27	21	34	42	29	40	35	27

(Contd.)

Table 7.15 : (*Contd.*)

Characteristics	*Delhi*					*Gorakhpur*					*Raipur*					*Ajmer*				
	12-14	*16-18*	*20-25*	*45-50*	*60+*	*12-14*	*16-18*	*20-25*	*45-50*	*60+*	*12-14*	*16-18*	*20-25*	*45-50*	*60+*	*12-14*	*16-18*	*20-25*	*45-50*	*60+*
B. Social Competence																				
17. Following Norms	1	2	2	3	1	–	1	1	4	3	–	–	–	–	–	1	3	5	3	4
18. Service to elders/ guests	23	21	19	15	18	20	12	6	7	7	12	7	5	9	5	8	5	7	4	10
19. Obedience	7	5	4	6	5	3	2	6	5	13	–	–	–	–	–	3	3	–	7	3
20. Help	10	12	8	11	14	6	6	5	4	6	3	–	3	2	4	5	9	13	8	10
21. Family Unity/ Responsibilities	–	–	5	4	6	–	–	–	–	–	–	–	–	–	–	–	–	–	–	–
22. Friendliness	3	4	3	3	1	–	–	–	–	–	2	2	1	2	3	–	–	–	–	–
23. Has Good Company	2	2	2	3	2	1	–	–	2	–	–	–	–	–	–	–	–	–	–	–
24. Participation in Group Work	–	–	–	–	–	–	–	3	4	2	–	–	3	3		4	7	7	4	7
25. Encouraging	–	–	–	–	–	–	–	–	–	–	–	–	–	–	–	–	–	–	–	–
26. Good Etiquettes	–	1	1	1	1	–	–	–	–	–	–	–	–	–	–	–	–	–	–	–
27. Non-Extravagant	–	–	–	–	–	–	–	–	–	–	1	1	3	3	2	–	–	–	–	–
	46	47	44	46	48	30	21	21	26	31	18	10	15	19	14	21	27	32	26	34
C. Entrepreneurial																				
28. Systematic approach	2	5	3	3	2	–	2	2	2	–	3	6	6	5	3	–	–	–	–	–
29. Commitment						–	1	–	–	1	1	2	3	–	–	–	–	–	–	–
30. Hardwork	1	3	–	2	–	–	–	–	–	–	7	6	3	4	3	–	–	–	–	–
31. Seriousness	–	–	–	–	–	–	–	–	–	–	–	–	–	–	–	13	18	7	9	8

(*Contd.*)

Table 7.15 : (*Contd.*)

Characteristics	*Delhi*					*Gorakhpur*					*Raipur*					*Ajmer*				
	12-14	*16-18*	*20-25*	*45-50*	*60+*	*12-14*	*16-18*	*20-25*	*45-50*	*60+*	*12-14*	*16-18*	*20-25*	*45-50*	*60+*	*12-14*	*16-18*	*20-25*	*45-50*	*60+*
32. Practical approach	2	1	–	–	–	–	–	–	–	–	–	–	–	–	–	–	4	2	1	–
33. Efficiency	–	–	–	–	–	5	1	2	2	1	11	8	8	7	5	–	–	–	–	–
34. Responsibility	–	–	–	–	–	1	–	2	6	5	–	–	–	–	–	–	–	–	–	–
35. Discipline	2	1	1	1	1	3	1	–	–	–	–	1	2	2	3	–	–	–	–	–
36. Patience	–	1	1	1	2	7	11	9	9	9	1	3	4	3	4	–	4	4	4	7
37. Successful	1	2	1	1	1	–	–	–	–	–	–	–	–	–	–	–	–	–	–	–
38. Good Coordination	3	2	2	3	1	–	–	–	–	–	–	–	–	–	–	–	–	–	–	–
39. Goal-Directedness	–	–	–	–	–	–	–	–	–	–	–	–	–	–	–	–	–	–	–	–
40. Scientific Orientation	–	–	–	–	–	–	–	–	–	–	–	–	–	–	–	–	–	–	–	–
41. Preventive Measure	2	–	–	1	2	–	–	–	–	–	–	–	–	–	–	–	–	–	–	–
	13	15	8	12	9	16	16	15	19	16	23	26	26	21	18	13	26	13	14	15
D. Emotional																				
42. Empathy	1	1	1	2	1	4	1	1	1	1	–	–	–	–	–	–	1	1	–	–
43. Honesty	1	–	1	2	–	1	1	–	–	3	1	2	3	3	2	–	–	–	–	–
44. Emotional Control	4	2	3	1	–	1	2	2	2	4	3	6	3	3	1		–	–	–	–
45. Positive Attitude	–	–	–	–	–	–	–	–	–	–	–	–	–	–	–		–	–	–	–
46. Self Respect	–	–	–	–	–	–	–	–	–	–	–	–	–	–	–		–	–	–	–
47. Cleverness	–	–	–	–	–	–	–	–	–	–	–	–	–	–	–	3	4	2	3	1
48. Humility	–	–	–	–	–	–	–	–	–	–	–	–	–	–	–	–	–	–	–	–
49. Religiosity	–	–	–	–	–	1	2	2	2	2	5	1	1	2	3	–	–	–	–	–
50. Confidence	–	1	2	2	2	1	3	2	2	1	–	–	–	–	–	–	–	–	–	–
51. Health Consciousness	4	1	1	1	4	3	3	1	2	1	5	7	7	8	8	–	–	–	–	–

(*Contd.*)

Table 7.15 : (*Contd.*)

Characteristics	*Delhi*					*Gorakhpur*					*Raipur*					*Ajmer*				
	12-14	*16-18*	*20-25*	*45-50*	*60+*	*12-14*	*16-18*	*20-25*	*45-50*	*60+*	*12-14*	*16-18*	*20-25*	*45-50*	*60+*	*12-14*	*16-18*	*20-25*	*45-50*	*60+*
52. Sensitivity	–	–	–	–	–	–	–	–	–	–	1	1	1	2	–	–	–	–	–	–
53. Non-Obtrusive attitude	1	–	1	2	1	1	3	–	4	–	–	–	–	–	–	–	–	–	–	–
54. Independence (Economic)	–	3	2	3	5	–	–	–	–	–	–	–	–	–	–	–	–	–	–	–
55. Politeness	1	1	1	3	1	2	1	–	–	–	5	1	-	1	3	10	5	8	13	12
56. Quietness	1	–	1	2	1	–	–	–	–	–	–	–	–	–	–	–	–	–	–	–
57. Adjustment	–	–	–	–	–	1	1	2	2	–	–	–	–	–	–	–	–	–	–	–
58. Straightforwardness	–	–	–	–	–	–	–	–	–	–	–	–	–	–	–	11	4	4	9	10
59. Curiosity	–	–	–	–	–	1	3	1	1	–	–	–	–	–	–	–	–	–	–	–
60. Leadership	–	–	–	–	–	–	–	–	–	–	–	–	–	–	–	–	3	–	–	–
61. Egoist attitude	–	–	–	–	–	–	–	–	–	–	3	1	–	1	1	–	–	–	–	–
62. Humanitarian approach	–	–	–	–	–	–	–	–	–	–	–	–	–	–	–	–	1	–	–	1
63. Good Conduct	1	2	2	2	2	2	4	3	3	3	4	1	5	5	7	–	–	–	–	–
64. Fearlessness						2	3	3	3	3	–	–	–	–	–	–	–	–	–	–
65. Speaking truth (in context)	2	–	2	2	3	2	1	2	2	2	–	–	1	2	–	–	–	–	–	–
	16	11	18	22	20	22	28	19	24	20	27	20	21	27	25	24	18	15	25	24
E. Misc.																				
66. Education	–	–	–	–	–	–	–	–	–	–	10	7	6	7	3	–	–	–	–	–
67. Good in Studies	–	–	–	–	–	7	5	5	5	7	11	2	3	4	4	–	–	–	–	–
68. High IQ	–	–	–	–	–	–	–	–	–	–	–	3	2	1	2	–	–	–	–	–
	–	–	–	–	–	7	5	5	5	7	21	12	11	12	9	–	–	–	–	–

Table 7.16: Characteristics of an Intelligent Person by Lay People's Age in Rural Areas

(Per Cent Frequencies)

Locality	*Cognitive*	*Social*	*Entrepreneurial*	*Emotional*	*Misc.*	*Chi-Square (df = 4)*
Delhi						
12-14 Yrs	26	39	15	20	–	11.12
16-18 Yrs	33	38	16	13	–	
20-25 Yrs	34	35	13	18	–	
45-50 Yrs	28	38	13	21	–	
60+ Yrs	22	43	9	26	–	
Gorakhpur						
12-14 Yrs	29	27	14	22	8	10.55
16-18 Yrs	28	20	15	27	10	
20-25 Yrs	37	21	16	21	5	
45-50 Yrs	29	27	18	22	4	
60+ Yrs	28	27	15	19	11	
Raipur						
12-14 Yrs	17	20	17	31	–	11.79
16-18 Yrs	27	18	17	28	–	
20-25 Yrs	23	19	20	30	–	
45-50 Yrs	21	22	18	31	–	
60+ Yrs	29	14	18	33	–	
Ajmer						
12-14 Yrs	37	25	15	23	–	9.65
16-18 Yrs	29	26	23	22	–	
20-25 Yrs	32	30	16	22	–	
45-50 Yrs	35	24	13	28	–	
60+ Yrs	31	35	14	20	–	
Mysore						
12-14 Yrs	5	8	47	2	38	135.08**
16-18 Yrs	16	14	34	7	29	
20-25 Yrs	46	–	28	16	10	
45-50 Yrs	44	–	41	4	11	
60+ Yrs	30	–	30	24	16	
Overall						
12-14 Yrs	25	25	18	22	10	5.69
16-18 Yrs	29	24	20	21	6	
20-25 Yrs	33	23	18	22	4	
45-50 Yrs	29	25	18	23	5	
60+ Yrs	27	26	16	24	7	

** $P < .01$

Table 7.17 : Characteristics of Intelligent Persons by Lay People's Age

Urban					*Rural*				
12-14	*16-18*	*20-25*	*45-50*	*60+*	*12-14*	*16-18*	*20-25*	*45-50*	*60+*
Highly Ceded Characteristics									
Context sensitive	Reflective	Helping	Reflective	Reflective	Service to elders	Service to elders	Reflective	Service to elders	Service to elders
Service to elders	Helping	Reflective	Helping	Helping	Reflective	Reflective	Service to elders	Reflective	Helping
Commitment	Service to elders	Context sensitive	Efficiency	Service to elders	Context sensitive	Helping	Context sensitive	Context sensitive	Communi cability
Reflection	Context sensitive	Emotional control	Context sensitive	Context sensitive	Helping	Communi cability	Helping	Obedience	Patience
Emotional control	Communi cability	Following norms	Emotional control	Emotional control	Politeness	Context sensitive	Communi-cability	Communi cability	Obedience
Least Ceded Characteristics									
Religiousness	Patience	Hard working	Speaking truth	Cleverness	Speaking truth	Religiousness	Religiousness	Religiousness	Honesty
Non-extra-vagant	Religiousness	Cleverness	Health conscious	Systematic	Honesty	Empathy	Honesty	Honesty	Religious-ness
Health conscious	Efficiency	Patience	Religious-ness	Non-extra vagant	Emotional control	Honesty	Hard working	Empathy	Emotional control
Systematic	Cleverness	Religious-ness	Patience	Speaking truth	Patience	Hard working	Friendliness	Efficiency	Religious-ness
Honesty	Health conscious	Health conscious	Systematic	Honesty	Decision making	Efficiency	Politeness	Seriousness	Efficiency

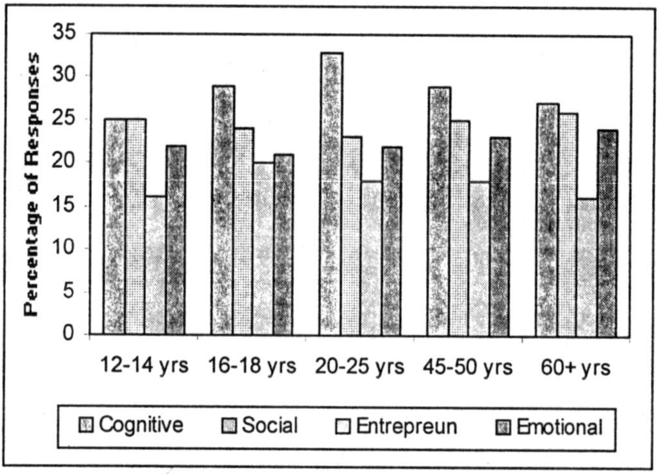

Fig. 7.12: Percentage of Responses Related to Different Aspects of Intelligence by Lay People's Age

Service to elders was prominently reported by the rural participants of all the age groups and also by urban participants in the age groups of 12-14, 45-50, and 60+ years (Table 7.17). Participants agreed that intelligent persons are reflective, help others and show sensitivity to the context. The elderly urban respondents more frequently reported control of emotions. The older participants showed greater concern for the characteristics related to social and emotional competence. Among least ceded characteristics, some additional qualities such as being non-extravagant, religiousness, honesty, speaking truth, hard work, and empathy also surfaced. The rural participants above 60+ years reported control of emotions more frequently.

Criteria for Identifying the Characteristics of Intelligent Persons

Lay people were asked to state the criteria that they employed for reporting the characteristics of intelligent persons. Majority of the participants reported the characteristics of intelligent people on the basis of their personal experiences (Table 7.18). In particular, personal experiences formed the basis for a larger number of rural elderly participants (45-50 and 60+ age groups). Quite a large number of lay people, particularly urban, had also observed intelligent people behaving in these ways. The participants from Ajmer and Mysore also used 'interaction with others' as the criteria for describing the characteristics of intelligent people. A small number of participants from Delhi and Gorakhpur had heard or studied about these characteristics of intelligent persons.

Table 7.18: Criteria for deciding Characteristics of Intelligent Persons

(Per cent Frequencies)

Locality		*Personal Experience*	*Observation*	*Study of Literature*	*Interaction with others*
Delhi	U	56	35	4	6
	R	89	15	–	2
Gorakhpur	U	73	24	–	3
	R	56	33	2	9
Raipur	U	27	73	–	–
	R	52	48	–	–
Ajmer	U	62	16	–	22
	R	55	19	–	26
Mysore	U	50	40	–	10
	R	57	36	–	7

Intelligence and Performance

Table 7.19 shows that being judged as intelligent is related to the successful accomplishment of a task. In the opinion of a large number of participants, particularly rural people, only those persons who are able to achieve their goal are judged intelligent (If successful, intelligent).

Self Appraisal of Intelligence

When asked about how intelligent are you, only about 3 per cent participants rated themselves as having very low intelligence and about 13 per cent as having low intelligence in work situation (Table 7.20). Not a single male, particularly schooled one, considered himself/herself to be of low intelligence. Majority of the participants considered themselves high on intelligence, which was followed by the category of undecided responses. This seems to reflect the fact that intelligence constitutes a strong element of one's self-esteem and self-worth. Though undecided responses were common to participants of all categories, it was maximally endorsed by the participants in the age groups of 20-25 and 60+ years. Few participants (about 11 per cent) also rated themselves very high on intelligence. A similar pattern is observed for ratings in social and academic contexts with the difference that the number of participants rating themselves 'very high' increased as compared to work situation. Also, a large majority (79%) of non-schooled participants were undecided about their academic intelligence.

Table 7.19: Percentage of Respondents agreeing that Judgement of being Intelligent is Task Dependent

Locality		*Yes*	*No*
Delhi	U	74*	26
	R	84	16
Gorakhpur	U	71	29
	R	67	33
Raipur	U	63	37
	R	54	46
Ajmer	U	60	40
	R	72	28
Mysore	U	57	43
	R	61	40

*Highest in case of 60+

Table 7.20: Respondents' Rating of Self Intelligence on a 5-Point Scale (1 = Very Low, 5 = Very High)

Locality		*Work Situation*					*Social Context*					*Academic Context*				
		1	*2*	*3*	*4*	*5*	*1*	*2*	*3*	*4*	*5*	*1*	*2*	*3*	*4*	*5*
Delhi	U	3	4	31	53	9	2	8	31	40	20	5	5	27	39	24
	R	5	9	53	31	7	2	6	36	42	14	2	11	33	38	17
Gorakhpur	U	1	10	20	63	6	2	8	20	60	10	5	24	21	37	13
	R	3	18	29	37	13	2	16	25	44	13	6	19	17	32	26
Raipur	U	-	16	50	25	9	4	19	34	28	15	-	20	33	29	18
	R	2	17	55	20	6	3	21	47	26	3	2	16	48	30	4
Ajmer	U	1	10	30	38	21	22	11	18	46	23	6	17	27	35	15
	R	6	10	26	32	25	11	16	31	27	15	8	20	25	31	16
Mysore	U	2	15	43	33	7	1	16	50	28	5	1	21	48	24	6
	R	2	17	41	34	6	1	23	52	23	1	2	27	46	23	2

U = Urban, R = Rural

Factors Facilitating Development of Intelligence

Table 7.21 lists the factors that, according to the lay people, influence the development of intelligence. Factors such as education, family environment/rituals, child rearing practices, the social group, nutrition, and reading of healthy materials were endorsed by all categories of participants. Also, parental education, economic status of the family, mass-media,

Table 7.21: Factors Facilitating the Development of Intelligence

(Per cent Frequencies)

	Delhi		*Gorakhpur*		*Raipur*		*Ajmer*		*Mysore*	
	U	*R*	*U*	*R*	*U*	*R*	*U*	*R*	*U*	*R*
1. **Schooling**										
Education	13	27	29	20	22	26	13	11	26	27
School Environment	6	–	2	5	–	–	7	9	–	–
2. **Family**										
Family Environment/ rituals	15	19	22	23	15	18	23	21	31	31
Parental Education	6	–	2	7	–	–	7	6	–	–
Child-rearing practices	10	8	8	5	10	–	4	5	–	–
Financial Status	2	–	3	5	–	–	5	6	8	11
3. **Social**										
Good Company	10	20	13	11	14	17	16	18	4	3
Obedience	5	–	3	–	–	–	–	–	–	–
Peer Group	2	–	–	–	–	–	–	–	–	–
4. **Biological**										
Nutrition	10	14	2	4	14	24	7	8	–	–
Physical Health	2	–	–	–	8	–	–	–	–	–
5. **Environmental**										
Mass-media	4	8	–	4	5	–	–	–	–	–
Opportunity to progress (Interaction with others)	4	–	10	2	–	–	–	–	12	15
6. **Personal**										
Reading of healthy materials	7	–	–	6	12	11	–	3	13	8
Hardwork	4	4	2	–	–	–	4	–	–	–
Willingness to learn	–	–	–	–	–	–	–	–	6	5
Emotional control	–	–	–	–	–	–	4	3	–	–
Disciplined life	–	–	–	–	–	–	4	1	–	–
Miscellaneous	–	–	4	8	–	–	–	9	–	–

U = Urban R = Rural

opportunities to interact with learned people, hard work, and disciplined life style were reported to facilitate the development of intelligence. The family environment, study of good materials and nutrition were stressed by the older participants aged 60+ years. The unschooled females least frequently mentioned the child-rearing practices. Education and nutrition were more emphasised by the younger participants in the age groups of 12-14 and 16-18 years.

Some General Observations

When asked whether intelligence is a gift of god, more than half of the participants, except the ones from Delhi, reported in affirmation. At the same time, about three-fourth of the respondents were of the opinion that intelligence can be increased with training. Very few participants had seen a test of intelligence. Also, wide variations were observed with regard to the adequacy of the test items. While very few respondents from Delhi and Gorakhpur considered that these tests appropriately measure intelligence, more number of participants from Raipur, Ajmer and Mysore responded to it in affirmation.

Discussion

The main objective of the study was to discern the notion of intelligence as understood and used by the lay people in India. To tap possible variation in the conceptualization of intelligence, data were collected from five regions of India. The participants varied along the dimensions of ecological context, schooling, sex, and age. The analysis revealed that intelligence is a highly valued construct. Each participant, on an average, reported about four characteristics (range 2 to 12) of an intelligent person. Though urban and metropolitan participants reported larger number of attributes, the rural participants at places even endorsed more features. Also, unschooled and female participants were not far behind so far as reporting the characteristics of an intelligent person was concerned. This establishes the fact that behaving in an intelligent way is highly valued in the Indian context.

The present findings tend to indicate that intelligence is conceptualized differently in the Indian context than the Western view which, until recently, placed a heavy premium on reasoning and cognitive problem solving. The Indian view, in addition to the cognitive attributes, also takes cognizance of the individual's competence in social problem solving, displaying pro-social dispositions, and the manner in which a task is approached, initiated, and accomplished. In this way the Indian view is more close to the notion of intelligence prevalent in African and certain Asian countries. Although one-third of the lay people's responses were related to the cognitive competence, two-third of the responses focused on social competence, emotional competence and entrepreneurial competence. Further, urban, schooled, and male participants emphasized relatively more on cognitive competence and features related to entrepreneurial competence. In contrast, social and emotional competencies were relatively more valued by the rural, unschooled, and female respondents.

The lay people endorsed four cognitive abilities prominently. These were: Sensitivity to context, communication, reflection, and decision-making. Sensitivity to context refers to the beliefs about the significance of person (*patra*), time (*kala*), and ecology (*desh*). A behaviour that is judged intelligent for a given place, time and person may or may not be considered intelligent for other times, places and persons. Whether something is good or bad, positive or negative depends on the context, particularly social context. The idea of *dharma* also leans heavily towards context. It recommends to speak truth, but the truth is not absolute; rather, it is one which helps others. Dependency on context leads to the development of associative, rather than abstract thinking (J.B.P. Sinha & Kanungo, 1997). It is probably due to the associative mode of that Indians include social competence and emotional competence into their conceptualization of intelligence. Indians favour relational mode of self-construal in which connectivity and interdependence are emphasized. The Indian view attaches importance to communication. In order to be considered intelligent, one needs to communicate effectively. This is expected in a country like India, having rich oral tradition. In this tradition knowledge was never written down but was handed down orally from the

Guru (teacher) to the *Shishya* (disciple). This tradition emphasized the excellence of *Priyamvada* or felicitous speech. Further, instead of valuing mere possession of cognitive abilities, the application of these abilities in real-life situations is glorified. For example, an intelligent person weighs and evaluates various alternatives before arriving at a decision about what is good and what is bad, in a given context. This indicates the value of reflective thinking. An intelligent person displays "still water runs deep" type of thinking. Likewise, qualities such as planning for the future and learning from past experiences also require transfer and use of abilities in diverse contexts.

The lay people view intelligence situated in the socio-cultural matrices and real-life performances of the people. For example, respect for and service to the elders, parents, and guests, being obedient, and following social norms were reported by all categories of participants irrespective of their background. It may be mentioned that Indian child-rearing practices make a special effort to inculcate in the child a regard for elders (Krishnan, 1998). The economic value of children (e.g. extending the family tree, service to elders, and material contribution received from them) is given primacy by the Indian parents (Srivastava, 1997). In a country where majority of the population is illiterate and lives in the rural area, an individual who helps the needy ones by providing adequate advice/counselling is considered intelligent. Also, in a developing country like India, judicious use of resources (*i.e.*, non-extravagant) is viewed as an attribute of intelligence. The unschooled elderly females at some places saw intelligence localized in activities such as keeping the families united and carrying out family's responsibilities. This probably reflects their concern towards breaking down of the joint family system in recent times.

The third characteristic of an intelligent person that emerged out of this study is the manner in which such an individual approaches and accomplishes a task. Three major categories of entrepreneurial competence have emerged: Systematically and efficiently pursuing a task, hard work, being disciplined, and showing patience. The successful completion of a task demands these characteristics and, if employed, the accomplishment of task becomes easy. Only such persons are characterized intelligent.

The lay people endorsed a score of characteristics related to emotional competence of an intelligent person. These characteristics are related to two broad themes or concerns: Sensitivity to self and sensitivity to others. An intelligent person is self-directed, religious, and health conscious. The characteristics such as empathy, emotional control, honesty, politeness and humility reflect his/her sensitivity to others. Also, speaking of restrained truth is emphasized as an attribute of intelligent persons. Under special circumstances an intelligent person may reject truth and can accept the duty of saving an innocent life. Promise keeping and upholding the truth are, however, not absolute. They are contextually defined and subject to negotiation if lives are saved by partly deviating from them. According to the great Indian epic *Mahabharata*, there is nothing greater than human life. This has also been echoed by Nobel laureate Rabindranath Tagore in his thesis of *Manush Dharma* (duty towards human being).

An interesting feature of this study was the degree of agreement across the participants of different backgrounds. The observed differences were statistically not significant between urban and rural, schooled and unschooled, male and female sub-groups as well as between the various age groups. Also, when asked how intelligent are you, the participants, in general, rated themselves as high or very high on intelligence. This shows that the lay theories as social representations are widely shared.

Despite the fact that about half of the participants considered intelligence as gift of God, they also believed that intelligence is susceptible to diverse influences giving space for training. Factors such as school, family, social, biological, environmental and personal were reported as facilitators of intellectual development. Finally, the present study underlines the relationship between the cognitive and affective domains. To the lay people, though intelligent persons are emotional, they also know how to control their emotions. The concept of *jitendriya* and *nishkama karma* also refer to the Indian indigenous thinking on self-control.

A comparison of ancient (*suktis* and proverbs) and contemporary (lay people) views on intelligence show considerable similarity amongst them. However, in contrast to the ancient views, surprisingly, the contemporary view places greater emphasis on social competence. Though characteristics such as observing norms, service to elders/guests, obedience, helping others and the like have always been stressed in the Indian tradition, it occupied less prominent place in the analysis of *suktis* and proverbs. The cognitive abilities reported by the lay people and in *suktis* and proverbs, by and large, remain the same with a few minor variations. The abilities such as concentration and remaining informed have not been reported in the proverbs. Probably these abilities have been subsumed under comprehension, which has received an important place in the analysis of proverbs but not in the lay people's responses. The speed with which an individual learns has also not been reported in the proverbs. Meta-cognition or the ability to know one's own strengths and weaknesses is mentioned by the lay people. Probably, having cognizance of one's strengths and limitations is essential in the contemporary changing Indian society for effective functioning. Entrepreneurial competence has been stressed in both the traditions. Also, a set of characteristics related to emotional competence almost similar in ancient and contemporary accounts have emerged. Only the lay people have reported few characteristics such as being a good coordinator and remaining health conscious.

In sum, the contemporary Indian view considers an intelligent person as a social being who accomplishes high level of performance on tasks with certain cognitive characteristics. Thus, there are four aspects of intelligence: *Cognitive Competence, Social Competence, Entrepreneurial Competence,* and *Emotional Competence.* These dimensions or facets taken together present an integrated whole. That is, intelligence is not seen as mere possession of any one of these attributes. Rather, in order to be judged intelligent in the Indian context, a person should possess all of these characteristics in proper proportion, and use them according to the demands of situation. The cognitive, social, entrepreneurial, and emotional competencies are interconnected and form a whole. They give direction to the individual for behaviour in a given context. Such a perspective demands rethinking psychological approach towards conceptualization and assessment of intelligence.

8

Epilogue

The study of intelligence in the Western world in the twentieth century has undergone massive transformation. The IQ notion of intelligence with its emphasis on cognitive abilities dominated the first-half of the century. However, because of its limitations, such as equivocality, non-linearity, distance from real life contexts, cultural variations in the structure of the component factors, and dependence on prior experience, multiple perspectives on understanding intelligence have emerged. It has become amply clear that the concept of intelligence is not confined to the cognitive domain alone. Rather, it comprises of several domains that are socio-culturally shaped. There is growing evidence which supports that culture plays crucial role in determining what is to be considered intelligent. The abilities included within 'intelligence' are distributed across groups in different ways. Intelligence may be looked more appropriately in terms of specific contexts in and through which it operates. The present study examines the relationship between culture and intelligence in the Indian context.

The impetus for the present research into the nature of intelligence in relation to culture was two-fold. First, research findings from various cultures have pointed out considerable variety in the emphasis on the socio-cultural practices while conceptualizing intelligence. Second, even within the Western scholarship, the so-called mainstream, investigations in this field document heterogeneity. Taken together, these developments point towards the fact that the entire enquiry and its claims into the nature and assessment of intelligence are the product of a particular theory of mind and it remains intelligible within the given cultural context. Stretching and transporting it to other cultural regions may be problematic and unproductive. However, owing to political, economic, and intellectual imperialism, hegemony of the Western view has been sustained, and the concepts and measures developed and honed there are being proliferated in other parts of the world without realizing the dangers inherent in it. This does not mean that there is no cultural similarity and all cultures are totally distinct. The intercultural communication and acculturation often lead to mutual borrowing and reconfiguration of ideas, practices, and artifacts in any culture at any point of time. Notwithstanding this, there are also possibilities of developing distinct cultural patterns of thought and mind. The cultural psychological perspective, therefore, endorses the view that culture and psyche (or mind) constitute each other (Shweder, 1990). Mind as a physical structure may be one but there are many mentalities (refer Shweder *et al.*, 1997).

A close perusal of research in the field of intelligence in India indicates that these efforts have largely been confined to adaptation and/or development of different types of tests of intelligence following predominantly the psychometric approach employed in the West. An analysis of the contents and psychometric properties of these tests leaves much to be desired. The tests have been adopted/adapted in a haphazard manner and rarely has the procedure of adaptation been followed. Majority of them are characterized by inadequate conceptualization and lack of methodological rigour. The tests have been used for multiple purposes in diverse settings. Also, these tests have been employed to examine the antecedents, correlates and consequences of intelligence in the Indian setting. The results of these studies, in majority of the cases, are not very encouraging. The Indian thought has a long and rich tradition in which little (folk) and great (*shastric*) traditions have grown side by side. Very little attention has been paid towards analyzing this tradition for identifying various indigenous psychological concepts. The present venture makes a beginning in this direction by humbly drawing attention to certain sources.

To discern indigenous perspective on intelligence in the Indian context, a two pronged methodological strategy was adopted in this study. First, efforts were made to analyse the ways Sanskrit *suktis* (selected from more than hundred ancient scriptures) guide behaviours, and the images of intelligent persons as contained in Hindi proverbs. Sanskrit *suktis* and Hindi proverbs were identified after consulting several dictionaries and were content analyzed. Second, a multicentric study empirically analyzed the lay people's understanding and use of intelligence. Participants varying along the dimensions of ecological setting, schooling, sex and age from five different localities, namely Ajmer, Delhi, Gorakhpur, Raipur and Mysore, were included in the study.

The present findings allowed to see continuity and change in the conceptualization of intelligence in the Indian context. In contrast to the Western notion of intelligence, which until recently has championed a decontextualized abstract structure of cognitive abilities, the Indian concept is an all-inclusive, and an integrated one. This view, in addition to giving importance to cognitive abilities, also takes into account the affective and motivational components in a major way. Also, the Indian concept of intelligence is more close to the recently proposed notion of wisdom, which includes procedural knowledge, relativism, and is capable of dealing with uncertainty. In non-western cultures dialectical thinking is observed which considers the individual in his or her total context. To a large extent, it overlaps the characteristics of prudence, social intelligence, emotional intelligence, and practical intelligence.

The analysis of Sanskrit *suktis*, Hindi proverbs and lay person's views revealed four facets of intelligence: *Cognitive Competence, Social Competence, Entrepreneurial Competence, and Emotional Competence*. The emphasis on these dimensions in different sources varied. Sanskrit *suktis* gave the highest weightage to emotional competence which was followed by entrepreneurial competence, cognitive competence and social competence. In contrast, more than half of the proverbs emphasized cognitive competence, followed by entrepreneurial competence, emotional competence and social competence. Lay people assigned greater weightage to cognitive competence, which was followed by social competence. Emotional competence and entrepreneurial competence were given almost equal premium.

It is clear that Indian thinking does recognize the value of cognitive competence. However, the way cognitive competence is taken is quite comprehensive. It places high premium on 'sensitivity to context' stressing thereby the relative and emergent quality of human behaviour. An intelligent person is one who behaves according to *desh, kala,* and *patra,* and maintains a balance. This recongnizes the value of problem oriented contextualized arguments and reasoning. It is reflected in *suktis* where communication and reflective abilities are emphasized. An intelligent person is one who speaks when needed, conveys his/her intentions using minimum words, his/her speech is loaded with hidden meanings, and remains focused on the theme under discussion. Such a person does not say unpleasant things, and his speech is characterized by the term *priyamvada*. Before saying or embarking on any action an intelligent person properly evaluates the advantages and limitations of that action. Among other qualities, it is noticed that an intelligent person is capable of comprehending others' intentions, discriminates between good and bad, and plans suitably for the future. The analysis of Hindi proverbs added few additional cognitive qualities such as readiness to learn, learning from past experiences, and problem solving. According to lay people, an intelligent person, in addition to the above, is attentive, takes decisions, foresighted, resourceful, and knows his/her strengths and weaknesses.

Another feature uncovered in the present work is that Indian thinking does not give significance to mere possession of abstract, decontextualized cognitive abilities, rather it is their application in real life situations that is emphasized. Thus intelligent behaviour is performative and demonstrative. The touchstone of wisdom is held to be problem solving in the real world. It is linked with actions appropriate to the occasion within the *dharmic* order—a principle sustaining the entire cosmos.

The Indian notion of intelligence remains closely tied to the socio-cultural practices and realities. About 15 per cent *suktis* stressed that an intelligent person is one who follows social norms; respects parents, elders, and guests; helps the needy and is friendly with others. However, though an intelligent person follows norms he is not (blindly) led by the masses. Child-rearing practices in India make special efforts to inculcate in the child a regard for norms, practices, and cultural heritage. It is partly also due to the fact that a large majority of Indian parents want children for economic reasons (*e.g.*, extending the family tree, service to elders, and material contribution received from them) than psychological ones. Helping the needy people assumes significance in the Indian context not only because a large chunk of Indian population is illiterate and lives under poverty conditions but also because the ideals of *paropkar, dan,* and *tyag* have been cherished since long. To the average Indian, a person who is sensitive enough and helps in meeting out the emergent needs of the people is intelligent. Also, Indian thinking considers that intelligent persons remain in the company of good people and it is probably this company of right people (*satsangati*) which makes them intelligent (*sarala*) or unintelligent (*kutila*).

Though only a few proverbs were concerned with the social aspect of intelligence, lay people's view did incorporate attributes such as obedience, maintaining unity in the family and carrying out family's responsibilities, participating in group work, and being non-extravagant. In a developing country like India, judicious use of resources is viewed an attribute of intelligent persons. The unschooled elderly females saw intelligence as grounded in the activity of maintaining harmonious relationship within the family. This reflects their concern with breaking down of the traditional joint family system in recent times.

A remarkable feature of intelligence that has emerged from the present work is its emphasis on performance. The analysis of Sanskrit *suktis* revealed that qualities of task performance constituted an important component of intelligence. Such a person remains unaffected by criticism, is practical, patient, vigilant, and is committed. He also maintains secrecy and is hard working. These characteristics refer to a state of informed arousal and dominance of task orientation. The stress on task is not blind, rather it is marked by a realistic appraisal of one's everyday context.

The analysis of proverbs also revealed emphasis on task performance. Here a few more characteristics surfaced such as resourcefulness, goal-directedness, and moderation in behaviour. An intelligent person realizes the intricacies of everyday life problems and responds according to task demands.

Thus the Indian view realizes plasticity in behavioural repertoire. It also emphasizes the fact that excess of anything and everything is bad. The lay people further extended it by including few more attributes such as efficiency, responsibility, discipline, good management, and scientific orientation. These are considered essential for survival in the present day changing scenario where intelligence is being defined in terms of 'output'.

To be considered intelligent, a person must also possess a score of personal and emotional attributes. Control over emotions has been accorded highest priority by both ancient and contemporary views. Since ancient time a person is thought intelligent who achieved full control over his/her impulses and actions. The concepts of *sthitaprajna, jitendriya, nishkama karma, vratas*, etc., are examples of the kind of concern which emphasize control over emotions. There are numerous stories of humans and gods going through austerity, ordeal and tapas to achieve the desired goals.

Also, telling the truth has been considered an essential feature of intelligent persons. At the same time, it is also recommended that one should not tell the truth that is harmful to the society. Thus, the relative nature of truth has been emphasized. The *suktis* also revealed that an intelligent person is kind, stable, polite, lives in the present, and is economically independent. These are perhaps the correlates or the consequences of intelligence. The attributes such as kindness and politeness refer to a person's 'sensitivity to others'. Stability in behaviour, self respect and realistic appraisal of the situation makes him/her dependable in the society. Such a person neither repents for the past, nor indulges in daydreaming, rather focuses on the present. Proverbs have extended this list by including attributes such as self-to-other orientations, open-mindedness, and trustworthiness. Lay people have added few more characteristics to this list. These included empathy, religiosity, health consciousness, adjustment, humanitarian outlook, good conduct and fearlessness. Majority of these characteristics are pro-social in nature.

Analysis of lay people's protocols revealed a belief that intelligence can be increased by enrichment and training. This kind of incremental theory brought into focus factors such as school, family, social context, environmental factors, and personal efforts as facilitators of intellectual development. The study also shows relationship between cognitive and affective domains. To the lay people, though intelligent persons are emotional, they also know how to control their emotions.

In sum, the Indian view places intelligence in the matrix of a practical and social life. It encompasses sociality, emotionality, and task orientation in addition to the cognitive abilities. On the whole, the present findings tend to suggest that 'intelligence' stands for a broad based effective functioning of persons in relation to their multiple contexts. This perspective may be termed as "integral" as it is characterized by and interconnectedness, interdependence, complementarity, and cosmocentricity. It emphasises an integration of multiple aspects of human consciousness (Northrop, 1947; Misra & Srivastava, 2000; Pardue, 1968; Takahasi & Bordia, 2000). It goes beyond merely a unique, rational and logical notion of intelligence. This inclusive view places competencies in context and recognizes the obligations and responsibilities toward self, society, and environment. Integration and adaptation rather than change and innovation are the modes of action normally associated with this tradition. As a process it constantly engages a person in the tasks of achieving excellence in different domains of life. It emphasizes the socio-cultural context and attends to the processes, competencies, and skills which are valued in everyday life. Thus the Indian view is more close to the concept of wholesome knowledge (Assmann, 1994). Interestingly, there appears remarkable resonance in the current moves in intelligence studies and the Indian views. The emerging notion of integral excellence is perhaps a new generation concept that may prove more functional in attending the needs of interdependent persons of the information age.

The present study has certain implications for education. Intelligence as intellectual power is perhaps the greatest source of strength. It is through this human resource that a society gears itself to achieve its goals. This is why education is a priority item on the agenda of any society/country. The system of education tries to strengthen the intellectual potential of the society. Being structured to nurture, stimulate and utilize the intellectual propensities of the people, the education system plays a critical role in shaping the society. The key role of education and learning in societal progress and ensuring quality of life is being widely recognized. It does not need much elaboration that the countries high in human development index invest more into the education sector and their education system is more challenging and more concerned with promoting intellective excellence. It is, therefore, essential that the education system in India be geared towards promotion and utilization of human intellect. This study shows that intelligence has many facets. Educational practitioners need to realize this while planning for education. Like other psychological constructs, intelligence developed and used in the West has been frequently employed in India without realizing the role of cultural context. The present endeavour demonstrates that the Indian notion of intelligence, instead of emphasizing the individual, gives primacy to performance, social harmony, and well-being of the people. Intelligence stands for a broad based adaptive potentiality of a person across different domains of life. Not restricted to cognitive domain alone, it incorporates skills that equip one to overcome life problems, to grow and become what one wants to achieve in personal as well as social domains. These skills are not uniformly distributed in the society and people internalise them, operate with them and in that process move towards increasingly higher level of competence. Thus transcending oneself is a continuous demand on an intellectual being. On the whole, the present findings suggest an integrated and a functional or pragmatic view of intelligence which operates at different levels allowing flexible multifaceted transaction between self and its context. This position broadens our perspective on intelligence and invites further work to identify and assess many of the competencies which have so far been neglected.

In India, tests of intelligence have been extensively used for various purposes such as selection, training, placement, diagnosis and guidance in different settings including educational, clinical, industrial, and defence. In majority of the cases, either tests developed in the West or their so-called adaptations have been used. The present work indicates that we need to revisit the notion of intelligence. It is hoped that the researchers and practitioners shall respond to this challenge in a creative way and enrich the field of intelligence research.

References

Abercombie, J. (1839). *Inquiries concerning the Intellectual Powers and their Investigation of Truth*. Boston: Otis Broaders.

Adhikari, G.S., Adhikari, S., & Tripathi, S.K. (1986). The cognitive properties of human behaviours. *Asian Journal of Psychology and Education, 17*, 26-29.

Alexander, P. (1985). Gifted and non-gifted students' perception of intelligence. *Gifted Child Quarterly, 29*, 137-143.

Ali, M. (1967). A study of behaviour problems among dull and bright children. *Research Bulletin, Department of Psychology, Osmania University, 3*, 27-30.

Amanda, S.M. (1991). *A Study of Intelligence and Achievement of Children in relation to infant feeding Practices and nutrition*. Unpublished doctoral dissertation, Patna University.

Anand, C.L., & Dave, P.N. (1979). Correlates of achievement: A trend report. In M.B. Buch (Ed.), *Second survey of research in education* (pp. 331-363). Baroda: Society for Educational Research and Development.

Anand, C.L., & Padma, M.S. (1987). Correlates of achievement: A trend report. In M.B. Buch (Ed.), *Third survey of research in education* (pp. 648-699). New Delhi: NCERT.

Anandalakshmi, S. (1980). Developmental processes. In U. Pareek (Ed.), *A survey of research in psychology 1971-76* (Vol. 1, pp. 168-207). Bombay: Popular Prakashan.

Anandalakshmi, S. (1994). *The Girl Child and the Family: An Action Research study*. New Delhi: Government of India, Department of Women and Child Development.

Andreasen, N.C. (1977). Reliability and validity of proverb interpretation to assess mental status. *Comprehensive Psychiatry, 18*, 465-472.

Angell, J.R. (1907). The province of functional psychology. *Psychological Review, 14*, 61-91.

Arora, R.K. (1992). Interactional effect of creativity and intelligence on emotional stability, personality adjustment, and academic achievement. *Indian Educational Review, 27*, 86-94.

Aswal, G.S. (2001). Intelligence as a correlate of achievement in mathematics across different levels of SES. *Psycho Lingua, 31*, 127-130.

Azuma, H., & Kashiwagi, K. (1987). Descriptions for an intelligent person: A Japanese study. *Japanese Psychological Research, 29*, 17-26.

Badrinath, C. (1999, February 5). Dharma and governance: Upholding the laws of rule. *The Times of India* (New Delhi), 12.

Balasubramaniyam, P.S. (1997). Correlates of achievement. In *Fifth survey of educational research 1988-92: Trend Reports* (Vol. 1, pp. 723-735). New Delhi: NCERT.

Baldwin, J.M. (1902). Pragmatic and pragmatism. In J.M. Baldwin (Ed.), *Dictionary of philosophy and psychology* (Vol. 2). New York: Peter Smith.

Baltes, P.B., & Smith, J. (1990). Toward a psychology of wisdom and its ontogenesis. In R.J. Sternberg (Ed.), *Wisdom: Its Nature, Origins, and Development* (pp. 87-120). New York: Cambridge University Press.

Baltes, P.B., Dittmann-Kohli, F., & Dixon, R.A. (1984). New perspectives on the development of intelligence in adulthood: Towards a dual process conception and a model of selective optimization with compensation. In P.B. Baltes & O.G. Brim, Jr., (Eds.), *Life-span Development and Behaviour* (Vol. 6). New York: Academic Press.

Banu, N. (1998). Word association as a function of age, intelligence, and mode of association. *Psycho-Lingua, 28*, 103-105.

Baral, B.D., & Das, J.P. (2004). Intelligence: What is indigenous to India and what is shared? In R.J. Sternberg (Ed.), *International Handbook of Intelligence* (pp. 270-301). Cambridge: Cambridge University Press.

Barrett, G.V., Kramen, A.J., & Lucke, S.B. (2003). New concepts of intelligence: Their practical and legal implications for employee selection. In H. Nyborg (Ed.), *The Scientific Study of General Intelligence* (pp. 411-439) Elsevier Science.

Basvanna, M., Rani, M.U. (1984). Differential impact of social and economic factors on intellectual and scholastic abilities. *Journal of Psychological Researches, 28*, 121-128.

Bates, T.C., & Stough, C. (1997). Processing speed, attention, and intelligence: Effects of spatial attention on decision time in high and low IQ subjects. *Personality and Individual Differences, 23*, 861-868.

Baumgarten, F. (1952). A proverb test for attitude measurement. *Personality Psychology, 5*, 249-267.

Bem, D. (1967). Self perception: An alternative interpretation of cognitive dissonance phenomenon. *Psychological Review, 74*, 183-200.

Berliner, D.C. (1988). Meta comments: A discussion of critiques of L.M. Dunn's monograph Bilingual Hispanic Children on the U.S. mainland. *Hispanic Journal of Behavioural Sciences, 10*, 273-299.

Borkowski, J.G. (1994). Contexts and "warm-blooded" cognitions. *Contemporary Psychology, 39*, 156-157.

Berry, J.W. (1974). Radical cultural relativism and the concept of intelligence. In J.W. Berry & P.R. Dasen (Eds.), *Culture and Cognition: Reading in Cross-Cultural Psychology* (pp. 295-329).

Berry, J.W. (1984). Towards a universal psychology of cognitive competence. *International Journal of Psychology, 19,* 335-361.

Berry, J.W., & Irwin, S.H. (1986). Bricolage: Savages do it daily. In R.J. Sternberg & R.K. Wagner (Eds.), *Practical Intelligence: Nature and Origins of Competence in Everyday World* (pp. 271-306). Cambridge: Cambridge University Press.

Bhakoo, O.N., Kaur, S., Narang, A., & Verma, S.K. (1977). A longitudinal study of variations in Developmental Quotients (DQs) in the first thirty months of life. *Indian Journal of Clinical Psychology, 4,* 59-68.

Bhatia, C.M. (1955). *Performance Test of Intelligence.* London: Oxford University Press.

Bhatnagar, A. (1994). Guidance and Counselling in India: Status, development and emerging concerns for research. In *Research Proposals in the Area of Educational Psychology, Guidance and Counselling (1995-96)* (pp. 24-52). New Delhi: NCERT (DEPCG).

Bhattacharya, S.B. (1978). *Interaction of Personality and Creativity.* Unpublished doctoral dissertation, Banaras Hindu University.

Binet, A., & Simon, T. (1911). *A Method of Measuring the Development of Intelligence of Young Children.* London, IL: Courier.

Black, P.W. (1985). Ghosts, gossips, and suicide: Meaning and action in Tobian folk psychology. In G.M. White & J. Kirkpatrick (eds.), *Persons, Self, and Experience: Exploring Pacific Ethnopsychologies* (pp. 245-300). Berkeley: University of California Press.

Bond, M.H., & Cheung, T. (1983). College students' spontaneous self-concept: The effect of culture among students in Hong Kong, Japan, and the United States. *Journal of Cross-Cultural Psychology, 14,* 153-171.

Born, M.P., Bleichrodt, N., & Flier, H.V.D. (1987). Cross-cultural comparison of sex-related differences on intelligence tests: A meta-analysis. *Journal of Cross-Cultural Psychology, 18,* 283-314.

Bowling, A.C., & MacKenzie, B.D. (1996). The relationship between speed of information processing and cognitive ability. *Personality and Individual Differences, 20,* 775-800.

Brescia, W., & Fortune, J.C. (1989). Standardized testing of American Indian students. *College Student Journal, 23,* 98-104.

Brody, N. (1997). Intelligence, schooling, and society. *American Psychologist, 52,* 1046-1050.

Broota, K.D. (1988). Perceptual and cognitive processes. In J. Pandey (Ed.), *Psychology in India: The State-of-the-art* (Vol. 1, pp. 249-288). New Delhi: Sage Publications.

Brown, J. (1992). *The Definition of a Profession: The Authority of Metaphor in the History of Intelligence Testing.* Princeton: Princeton University Press.

Buch, M.B. (Ed.). (1974). *A Survey of Research in Education*. Baroda: The M.S. University of Baroda.

Buch, M.B. (Ed.). (1979). *Second Survey of Research in Education*. Baroda: Society for Educational Research and Development.

Buch, M.B. (Ed.). (1987). *Third Survey of Research in Education 1978-83*. New Delhi: NCERT.

Buch, M.B. (Ed.). (1991). *Fourth Survey of Research in Education 1983-88*. New Delhi: NCERT.

Budoff, M. (1987). Measures for assessing learning potential. In C.S. Lidz (Ed.), *Dynamic Testing* (pp. 173-195). New York: Guilford Press.

Burt, C. (1949). Alternative methods for factor analysis and their relations to Pearson's method of "principal axes". *British Journal of Psychology, 2*, 90-121.

Butterworth, G. (1994). Infant intelligence. In J. Khalfa (Ed.), *What is Intelligence?* (pp. 49-71). Cambridge: Cambridge University Press.

Campbell, F.A., & Ramey, C.T. (1994). Effects of early intervention on intellectual and academic achievement: A follow-up study of children from low income families. *Child Development, 65*, 684-698.

Campione, J.C., & Brown, A.L. (1987). Linking dynamic testing with school achievement. In C.S. Lidz (Ed.), *Dynamic Testing* (pp. 82-115). New York: Guilford Press.

Cantor, N., & Harlow, R. (1994). Social intelligence and personality: Flexible life-task pursuit. In R.J. Sternberg & P. Ruzgis (Eds.), *Personality and Intelligence* (pp. 137-168). Cambridge: Cambridge University Press.

Carroll, J.B. (1993). *Human Cognitive Abilities: A Survey of Factor-Analytic Studies*. Cambridge: Cambridge University Press.

Carugati, F.F. (1990). Everyday ideas, theoretical models and social representations: The case of intelligence and its development. In G.R. Semin & K.J. Gergen (Eds.), *Everyday Understanding: Social and Scientific Explanations* (pp. 130-150). London: Sage Publications.

Caryl, P.G. (1994). Early event-related potentials correlate with inspection time and intelligence. *Intelligence, 18*, 15-46.

Cattell, J.M. (1890). Mental test and measurement. *Mind, 15*, 373-380.

Cattell, R.B. (1971). *Abilities: Their Structure, Growth and Action*. Boston: Houghton-mifflin.

Ceci, S.J. (1990). *On Intelligence... More or Less: A Bioecological Treatise on Intellectual Development*. Englewood Cliffs, NJ: Prentice Hall.

Ceci, S.J., & Williams, W.M. (1997). Schooling, intelligence and income. *American Psychologist, 52*, 1051-1058.

Chan, J. (1991). Are the western type mental tests measuring Chinese mental faculties? *Bulletin of the Hong Kong Psychological Society, 26/27*, 59-70.

Chan, J., & Lynn, R. (1989). The intelligence of six years old in Hong Kong. *Journal of Biosocial Sciences, 21*, 461-464.

Charles, D. (1984). *Aristotle's Philosophy of Action*. London: Duckworth.

Chartesworth, W.R.A. (1979). An ethological approach to studying intelligence. *Human Development, 22*, 212-216.

Chatterjee, P.S. (1983). *A Comparative Study of Personality, Intelligence and Achievement Motivation of Students in Different Academic Groups*. Unpublished doctoral dissertation, Patna University.

Chatterjee, S. Mukherjee, M., & Banerjee, S.N. (1972). Effect of certain socio-economic factors on the scholastic achievement of the school children. *Indian Journal of Psychology, 47*, 133-151.

Chattopadhyaya, P.K., & Bhattacharya, A.K. (1981). Differentiation of the components of intelligence in successive age levels (4-7 years): A factor analytic study. *Child Psychiatry Quarterly, 14*, 38-42.

Chen, M. (1994). Chinese and Australian concepts of intelligence. *Psychology and Developing Societies, 6*, 101-117.

Chen, M.J., & Chen, H.C. (1988). Concept of intelligence: A comparison of Chinese graduates from Chinese and English schools in Hong Kong. *International Journal of Psychology, 23*, 471-487.

Chen, M.J., Braithwaite, V., & Huang, J.T. (1982). Attributes of intelligent behaviour: Perceived relevance and difficulty by Australian and Chinese students. *Journal of Cross-Cultural Psychology, 13*, 139-156.

Choudhury, N., & Gorman, K.S. (1999). The relationship between reaction time and psychometric intelligence in a rural Guatemalan adolescent population. *International Journal of Psychology, 34*, 209-217.

Church, A.T., & Katigback, M.S. (1987). Imposed-etic and emic measures of intelligence as predictors of early school performance of rural Philippine children. *Journal of Cross-Cultural Psychology, 19*, 164-177.

Cole, M., (1990). Cognitive development and formal schooling: The evidence from cross-cultural research. In L.C. Moll (Ed.), *Vygotsky and Education* (pp. 89-110). Cambridge: Cambridge University Press.

Cole, M., & Cole, S.R. (1993). *The Development of Children*. New York: Scientific American Books.

Cole, M. & Scribner, S. (1981). *Comparative Studies of How People Think*. Cambridge: Cambridge University Press.

Cronback, L.J., & Snow, R.E. (1977). *Aptitudes and Instructional Methods*. New York: Irvington.

Cummins, J. (1988). "Teachers are not miracle workers": Lloyd Dunn's call for Hispanic activism. *Hispanic Journal of Behavioural Sciences, 10*, 263-273.

D'Andrade, R. (1987). A folk model of the mind. In D. Holland & N. Quinn (Eds.), *Cultural Models in Language and Thought* (pp. 112-148). Cambridge: Cambridge University Press.

Darwin, C. (1859). *On the Origin of Species*. London: John Murray.

Darwin, C. (1872). *The Expression of Emotions in Man and Animals*. London: John Murray.

Das, I., & Mona, P.K. (1990). The effect of poverty upon intelligence. *Indian Journal of Community Guidance Service, 7*, 34-48.

Das, J.P. (1974). *Caste, Class and Cognitive Competence*. Unpublished manuscript.

Das, J.P. (1994). Eastern views of intelligence. In R.J. Sternberg (Ed.), *Encyclopaedia of Human Intelligence* (pp. 387-391). New York: Macmillan Publishing Company.

Das, J.P. (2001). Reconceptualizing intelligence: Luria's contributions. *Psychological Studies, 46*, 1-6.

Das, J.P., Naglieri, J.A., & Kirby, J.R. (1994). *Assessment of Cognitive Processes: The PASS Theory of Intelligence*. Boston, NY: Allyn & Bacon.

Das, J.P., & Thapa, K. (2000). Intelligence and cognitive processes. In J. Pandey (Ed.), *Psychology in India revisited – Developments in the Discipline*, Vol.1: *Physiological Foundation and Human Cognition* (pp. 151-207). New Delhi: Sage.

Dasen, P. (1984). The cross-cultural study of intelligence: Piaget and the Baoule. *International Journal of Psychology, 19*, 407-434.

Dasen, P.R., Dembele, B., Ettien, K., Kabran, K., Kamagate, D., Koffi, K.A., & N'Guessan, A. (1985). N'glouele, l'intelligence chez les Baoule. *Archives de Psychologie, 53*, 293-324.

Dash, M. (1991). *Analysis of Cognitive and Speech related Processes in relation to Reading Efficiency and IQ*. Unpublished M.Phil. Dissertation, Utkal University.

Dash, U.N., & Das, J.P. (1984). Development of concrete operational thought and information coding in schooled and unschooled children. *British Journal of Developmental Psychology, 2*, 63-72.

Dash, U.N., & Mahapatra, S. (1989). Development and differentiation of simultaneous and successive planning processes. *Psychological Studies, 34*, 75-83.

Dash, U., & Mishra, H.C. (1989). Testing for the effects of schooling on memory in an eco-cultural setting. *Psychology and Developing Societies, 1*, 153-163.

Dash, U., & Mohanty, M.M. (1996). *Schooling and Cognition*. Bhubaneswar: Utkal University, Centre of Advanced Studies in Psychology.

Dash, U.N., Puhan, B.N., & Mahapatra, S. (1985). Information integration modes in concrete operational skills of grade two children. *Psychological Studies, 30*, 20-26.

Dave, P.N. (1974). Correlates of achievement: A trend report. In M.B. Buch (Ed.), *A Survey of Research in Education* (pp. 318-350). Baroda: The M.S. University.

Davis, R. (1993). Biological tests of intelligence as culture fair. *American Psychologist, 48*, 695-696.

Deary, I.J. (1995). Auditory inspection time and intelligence: What is the causal direction? *Developmental Psychology, 31*, 237-250.

Desai, K.G. (1954). *The Construction and Standardization of a Battery of Group Tests of Intelligence in Gujarati for the Age Group 12-16 studying in standards VII to IX of Secondary Schools.* Unpublished doctoral dissertation, Bombay University.

Desai, H.G. (1971). *Effects on Intelligence of Birth Order and Sex.* Unpublished doctoral dissertation, Saurashtra University.

Deshmukh, M.N. (1979). *An Analytical Study of some Scholastic Conditions and Practices and Contributing Factors to Creative Ability.* Unpublished doctoral dissertation, Nagpur University.

Deshpande, M.U. (1971). *An Analytical Study of some Scholastic Conditions and Practices and Contributing Factors to Creative Ability.* Unpublished doctoral dissertation, Nagpur University.

Dixon, R.A., Krammer, D.A., & Baltes, P.B. (1985). Intelligence: A life span developmental perspective. In B.B. Wolmen (Ed.), *Handbook of Intelligence: Theories, Measurement, and Applications* (pp. 301-350). New York: John Willey & Sons.

D'Souza, L., Singh, M., & Basavarajappa (1999). Influence of shyness on performance, personality and intelligence of students of physical education. *Psychological Studies, 44,* 92-94.

Durojaiye, M.O.A. (1993). Indigenous psychology in Africa. In U. Kim & J.W. Berry (Eds.), *Indigenous Psychologies: Research and Experience in Cultural Context* (pp. 211-220). Newbury Park: Sage Publications.

Dweck, C.S., & Elliot, E.S. (1983). Achievement motivation. In P.H. Mussen (Series Ed.) & E.M. Hetherington (Vol. Ed.), *Handbook of Child Psychology*: Vol. 4 (pp. 463-491). New York: Wiley.

Dwivedi, P., & Dubey, B.L. (1989). A longitudinal study of intelligence of rural children (7-11 years) in India. *Child Psychiatry Quarterly, 22,* 51-56.

Erikson, E. (1959). Identity and the life cycle. *Psychological Issues, 1,* 18-164.

Erikson, E.H. (1963). *Childhood and Society.* New York: Norton.

Esquirol, J.E.D. (1838). *Des maladies mentales considerees sousles rapports medical, hygienique, et medico-legal (3* Vols.*).* Paris: Balliere.

Eysenck, H.J., & Barrett, P. (1985). Psychophysiology and the measurement of intelligence. In C.R. Reynolds & C.V. Wilson (Eds.), *Methodological and Statistical Advances in the Study of Individual Differences* (pp. 1-49). New York: Plenum.

Faroqi, M.A. (1974). Some studies on progressive matrices test. In B. Krishnan (Ed.), *Studies in Psychology* (pp. 6-18). Mysore: University of Mysore.

Ferguson, G.A. (1954). On learning and human ability. *Canadian Journal of Psychology, 8,* 95-112.

Feuerstein, R. (1980). *Instrumental Enrichment: An Intervention Programme fcr Cognitive Modifiability.* Baltimore, MD: University Park.

Feurestein, R., Rand, Y., & Hoffman, M.B. (1979). *The Dynamic Testing of Retarded Performers: The Learning Potential Testing Device: Theory Instruments, and Techniques*. Baltimore: University Park Press.

Flugal, G. (1947). An inquiry as to popular views on intelligence and related topics. *British Journal of Educational Psychology, 17,* 140-152.

Flynn, J.R. (1984). The mean IQ of Americans: Massive gains 1932-1978. *Psychological Bulletin, 95,* 29-51.

Flynn, J.R. (1987). Massive IQ gains in 14 nations: What IQ tests really measure. *Psychological Bulletin, 101,* 171-191.

Flynn, J.R. (1994). IQ gains over time. In R.J. Sternberg (Ed.), *Encyclopedia of Human Intelligence* (pp. 617-623). New York: Macmillan.

Flynn, J.R. (1999). Searching for justice: The discovery of IQ gains. *American Psychologist, 54,* 5-20.

Fontes, R., Kellighan, T., Madaus, G., Airasian, P. (1983). Opinions of the Irish public on intelligence. *Irish Journal of Education, 2,* 55-67.

Furnham, A.F. (1987). The proverbial truth: Contextually reconciling the truthfulness of antonymous proverbs. *Journal of Language and Social Psychology, 6,* 49-59.

Furnham, A.F. (1988). *Lay Theories: Everyday Understanding of Problems in Social Sciences*. Oxford: Permagon Press.

Galton, F. (1869). *Hereditary Genius*. London: Macmillan.

Ganguli, H.C. (1971). Psychological research in India. *International Journal of Psychology, 6,* 165-178.

Gardner, H. (1983). *Frames of Mind: The Theory of Multiple Intelligences*. New York: Basic Books.

Gardner, H. (1993). *Frames of Mind: The Theory of Multiple Intelligences*. New York: Basic Books.

Gardner, H. (1997). Fostering diversity through personalized education: Implications of a new understanding of human intelligence. *Prospects, 22,* 347-363.

Gardner, H. (1999). *Intelligence Reframed: Multiple Intelligences in the 21st Century*. New York: Basic Books.

Gaur, J.S., & Mathur, P. (1974). The effect of level of intelligence on the occupational aspirations of the higher secondary school students in Delhi. *Indian Journal of Psychology, 49,* 139-148.

Gautam, R.P. (1971). Relationship between personal and social variables and socio-economic status in the classroom. *Journal of Psychological Researches, 15,* 91-95.

Gauvain, M. (1998). Culture, development, and theory of mind: Comment on Lillard (1998). *Psychological Bulletin, 123,* 37-42.

Geary, D.C., Hamson, C.O., Chen, G., Liu, F., Hoard, M.K., Salthouse, T.A. (1997). Computational and reasoning abilities in arithmetic: Cross-generational change in China and the United States. *Psychonomic Bulletin and Review, 4,* 425-430.

Geertz, C. (1973). *The Interpretation of Cultures.* New York: Basic Books.

Gibbs, R.S., Jr., & Beitel, D. (1995). What proverb understanding reveals about how people think. *Psychological Bulletin, 118,* 133-154.

Gibbs, R.W. (1994). *The Poetics of Mind: Figurative Thought, Language and Understanding.* New York: Cambridge University Press.

Gibbs, R.W., & Beitel, D. (1995). What proverb understanding reveals about how people think. *Psychological Bulletin, 118,* 133-154.

Gill, R., & Keats, D.M. (1980). Elements of intellectual competence: Judgements by Australian and Malay university students. *Journal of Cross-Cultural Psychology, 11,* 233-243.

Goleman, D. (1995). *Emotional Intelligence.* New York: Bantam Books.

Goodnow, J.J. (1976). The nature of intelligent behaviour: Questions raised by cross-cultural studies. In L. Resnick (Ed.), *New Approaches to Intelligence.* Hillsdale, NJ: Erlbaum.

Goodnow, J.J. (1988). Parent's ideas, actions and feelings: Models and methods from developmental and social psychology. *Child Development, 59,* 286-320.

Goodwin, P.D., & Wenzel, J.W. (1981). Proverbs and practical reasoning: A study in sociologic. In W. Meider & A. Dundes (Eds.), *The Wisdom of Many: Essays on the Proverb* (pp. 140-160). New York: Garland.

Great Books of the Western World (1987). Chicago: Encyclopaedia Britanica.

Greenfield, P.M. (1997). You can't take it with you: Why ability assessment don't cross cultures. *American Psychologist, 52,* 1115-1124.

Greenfield, P.M. (1998). The cultural evolution of IQ. In U. Neisser (Ed.), *The Rising Curve: Long Term Gains in IQ and Related Measures* (pp. 81-123). Washington, DC: American Psychological Association.

Gregory, R. (1994). Seeing intelligence. In J. Khalfa (Ed.), *What is Intelligence?* (pp. 13-26). Cambridge: Cambridge University Press.

Grigorenko, E.L., & Sternberg, R.J. (1998). Dynamics testing. *Psychological Bulletin, 124,* 75-111.

Grigorenko, E.L., Geissler, P.W., Prince, R., Okatcha, F., Nokes, C., & Kenny (2001). The organization of Luo Conceptions of intelligence: A study of implict theories in a Kenyan Village. *International Journal of Behavioural Devlopment,* **25**, 367-378.

Grubb, H.J., & Ollendick, T.H. (1986). Cultural-distance perspective: An exploratory analysis of its effect on learning and intelligence. *International Journal of Intercultural Relations, 10,* 399-414.

Guilford, J.P. (1967). *The Nature of Human Intelligence.* New York: McGraw Hill.

Guilford, J.P. (1982). Cognitive psychology's ambiguities: Some suggested remedies. *Psychological Review, 89,* 48-59.

Gulikson, H. (1950). *Theory of Mental Tests.* New York: John Wiley & Sons.

Guo, K., Lei, Q., & Luo, M. (1995). Study of the relationship of reaction time and intelligence in school children. *Psychological Science, 18,* 149-152.

Gupta, A., & Sharma, S. (1991). Interactive effect of trait anxiety and intelligence on an easy task. *Journal of Personality and Clinical Studies, 7*, 9-13.

Gupta, G.C. (1980). Cognitive processes. In U. Pareek (Ed.), *A Survey of Research in Psychology, 1971-1976* (Vol. 1, pp. 208-256). Bombay: Popular Prakashan.

Gupta, R. (2000). Prolonged deprivation and attainment of students. *Psychological Studies, 45*, 96-99.

Gupta, R., Mukherjee, M., & Chatterji, S. (1993). A comparative study of the factors affecting academic achievement among four groups of adolescents. *Indian Journal of Applied Psychology, 30*, 30-38.

Gupta, S. (1991). *A Study of Deprivation in Relation to Certain Cognitive and Noncognitive Variables Among Adolescents.* Unpublished doctoral dissertation, University of Jammu.

Gupta, S. (1991). Effects of time and personality on intelligence test scores. *Personality and Individual Differences, 12*, 1227-1231.

Gupta, S.M., & Chandradash, R. (1994). A study of demographic and cognitive correlates of creativity. *Journal of Educational Research & Extension, 30*, 164-173.

Haier, R.J. (1993). Cerebral glucose metabolism and intelligence. In P.A. Vernon (Ed.), *Biological Approaches to the Study of Human Intelligence* (pp. 317-332). Norwood, NJ: Ablex.

Haksar, A.N.D. (1992). *Tales from the Panchatantra.* New Delhi: National Book Trust.

Haksar, A.N.D. (2000, June 17). The secular face of Sanskrit. *The Times of India* (New Delhi), 14.

Halpern, D.F. (1992). *Sex Differences in Cognitive Abilities*. Hillsdale, NJ: Erlbaum.

Halpern, D.F., & Cess, M. (1994). Laterality, sexual orientation, and immune system functioning: Is there a relationship? *International Journal of Neuroscience, 77*, 167-180.

Harkness, S., Super, C., & Keefer, C. (1992). Culture and ethnicity. In M.D. Levine, W.B. Carey, & A.C. Crocker (Eds.), *Developmental-Behavioral Paediatrics* (pp. 103-108). Philadelphia: Sounders.

Harkness, S., & Super, C.M. (1993). The developmental niche: Implications for children's literacy development. In L. Eldering & P. Leseman (Eds.), *Early Intervention and Culture: Preparation for Literacy. The Interface between Theory and Practice* (pp.115-132). Paris: UNCESCO.

Harper, A.E.J. (1960). Recent advances in psychometry. *Silver Jubilee Volume of Vidya Bhavan Society*, Udaipur.

Haslam, N. (1991). Prudence: Aristotelian perspectives on practical reason. *Journal for the Theory of Social Behaviour, 21*, 151-169.

Haslam, N., & Baron, J. (1994). Intelligence, personality and prudence. In R.J. Sternberg & P. Ruzgis (Eds.), *Personality and Intelligence* (pp. 32-60). Cambridge: Cambridge University Press.

Hayman, R.L., Jr. (1998). *The Smart Culture: Society, Intelligence, and Law.* New York: New York University Press.

Heath, S.B. (1983). *Ways with Words.* Cambridge: Cambridge University Press.

Hebb, D.O. (1949). *The Organization of Behavior.* New York: Wiley.

Herrnstein, R.J., & Murray, C. (1994). *The Bell Curve: Intelligence and Class Structure in American Life.* New York: Free Press.

Hilgard, E.R. (1980). The triology of mind: Cognition, affection, and conation. *Journal of the History of Behavioral sciences, 16,* 107-117.

Hines, M. (1990). Gonadal hormones and human cognitive development. In J. Balthazart (Ed.), *Hormones, Brains, and Behaviors in Vertebrates: I Sexual Differentiation, Neuroanatomical Aspects, Neurotransmitters, and Neuropeptides* (pp. 51-63). Basel, Switzerland: Karger.

Honeck, R.P., Kibler, C.T., & Firmant, M. (1987). Figurative language and psychological view of categorization: Two ships in the night. In R. Haskell (Ed.), *Cognition and Symbolic Structures* (pp.103-120). Norwood, NJ: Ablex.

Honeck, R.P., & Temple, J.G. (1994). Proverbs: The extended conceptual base and great chain metaphor theories. *Metaphor and Symbolic Activity, 9,* 85-112.

Horn, J.L., & Cattell, R.B. (1966). Refinement and test of the theory of fluid and crystallized intelligence. *Journal of Educational Psychology, 57,* 253-270.

Hundal, P.S. (1969). Sex differences in verbal and performance tests of intelligence of different class grades VII, IX, and XI. *Psychologia,* 12, 115-120.

Hunt, E.B. (1980). Intelligence as an information processing concept. *British Journal of Psychology, 71,* 449-474.

Hunt, E. (2001). Multiple views of multiple intelligence. *Contemporary Psychology, 46,* 5-7.

Hunters, J.E. (1983). A causal analysis of cognitive ability, job knowledge, job performance, and supervisor ratings. In F. Landy, S. Zedeck, & J. Cleveland (Eds.), *Performance Measurement and Theory* (pp. 257-266). Hillsdale, NJ: Erlbaum.

Hyde, J., Fennema, E. & Lamon, S.J. (1990). Gender differences in mathematics performance: A meta-analysis. *Psychological Bulletin, 107,* 139-155.

Irvine, J.T. (1978). "Wolof magical thinking": Culture and conservation revisited. *Journal of Cross-Cultural Psychology, 9,* 300-310.

Irvine, S.H. (1969). The factor analysis of African abilities and attainments: Constructs across cultures. *Psychological Bulletin, 71,* 20-32.

Irvine, S.H. (1970). Affect and construct: A cross-cultural check on theories of intelligence. *Journal of Social Psychology, 80,* 23-30.

Jachuck, K. (1984). Level-I and Level-II abilities of socially disadvantaged children: Effects of home environment and caste. *Indian Psychologist, 3,* 42-48.

Jachuck, K. (1993). SES and time-related effects of pre-school education on cognitive abilities. In A.K. Srivastava (Ed.), *Researches in Child and Adolescent Psychology: Seminar Readings* (pp. 24-25). New Delhi: NCERT.

Jachuck, K., & Das, J.P. (1982). Free recall of categorized materials: A cross-cultural examination of Jensen's two level theory. *Indian Psychologist*, 1, 51-56.

Jain, M.C. (1991). *Indian Mental Measurement Handbook: Intelligence and Aptitude Tests.* New Delhi: NCERT.

Jayakar, P. (1988). Some paradigms of the creative process. *Indian Horizon, 37*, 1-4.

Jencks, C. (1979). *Who Gets Ahead? The Determinants of Economic Success in America.* New York: Basic Books.

Jensen, A.R. (1972). *Genetics and Education.* New York: Harper & Row.

Jethwani, P.M. (1986). *An Investigation into the Frustration of School-Going Adolescents of Kutch District in the Context of Cognitive and Non-cognitive Variables.* Unpublished doctoral dissertation, SPU.

Jha, H. (1999). *Man in Indian Tradition: Vidyapati's Discourse on Purush.* Patna:Patna University (Department of Sociology).

Joshi, J.N. (1979). Guidance and counseling: A trend report. In M.B. Buch (Ed.), *Second Survey of Research in Education* (pp. 209-235). Baroda: Centre for Educational Research and Development.

Joshi, J.N., & Gakhar, S. (1987). Guidance and counselling: A trend report. In M.B. Buch (Ed.), *Third Survery of Research in Education* (pp. 440-467). New Delhi: NCERT.

Joshi, J.N., & Passi, B.K. (1968). The role of intelligence and levels of instruction on the development of numerical ability in pupils at the junior secondary stage. *Journal of Psychological Researches, 12*, 57-62.

Joshi, S. (2001). Effect of socialization on cognitive functions. *Social Science International, 17*, 82-94.

Jung, C.G. (1953). *Two Essays on Analytical Psychology*. New York: Pantheon Books.

Kail, R. (2000). Speed of information processing: Developmental change and links to intelligence. *Journal of School Psychology, 38*, 51-61.

Kakar, S. (1978). *The Inner World: A Psychoanalytic Study of Childhood and Society in India*. Delhi: Oxford University Press.

Kakkar, A. (1965). The role of intelligence in adolescent's adjustment. *Indian Journal of Psychology, 40*, 179-184

Kakkar, S.B. (1970). Popularity, intelligence, economic status and academic achievement. *Indian Journal of Psychology, 45*, 233-237.

Kamra, R., & Gakhar, S.C. (1999). A study of scientific creativity as correlates of certain psychological variables. *The Educational Review, 105*, 197-198.

Kar, B.C. (1989). *Studies of Planning as a Cognitive Process: Theoretical and Operational Consideration.* Unpublished doctoral dissertation, Utkal University.

Kar, B.C., & Dash, U.N. (1993). The information integration model: A strategy to study cognitive growth. In A.K. Srivastava (Ed.), *Researches in Child and Adolescent Development: Seminar Readings*. New Delhi: NCERT.

Kaufman, A.S., McLean, J.E., Ishikumo, T., & Moon, S. (1989). Integration of the literature on the intelligence of Japanese children and analysis of the data from a sequential-simultaneous perspective. *School Psychology International, 10*, 173-183.

Kaushik, A., Shastri, G.S., Shastri, S., & Gupta, T. (1990). *Muhawara-Lokokti Kosh*. Delhi: Hindi Pushtak Bhawan.

Kaviraj, M.M. (1966). The doctrine of *pratibha* in Indian philosophy. In G. Kaviraj, *Aspects of Indian Thought* (pp. 1-44). Bardwan: The University of Bardwan.

Kemper, S. (1981). Comprehension and the interpretation of proverbs. *Journal of Psycholinguistic Research, 10*, 179-198.

Khatri, A.A. (1965a). Difference in goals, interests, intelligence, scholastic performance of orphanage reared and family reared children. *Indian Journal of Applied Psychology, 2*.

Khatri, A.A. (1965b). Intellectual deficit of orphanage-reared children. *Indian Journal of Applied Psychology, 53*.

Kishore, G. (1981). *A Developmental Study of Creativity in Relation to Certain Personality Correlates*. Unpublished doctoral dissertation, Aligarh Muslim University.

Kluckhohn, C. (1951). Values and value orientations in the theory of action. In T. Parsons & E.A. Shils (Eds.), *Towards a General Theory of Action*. New York: Harper.

Kohut, H. (1978). Forms and transformations of narcissism. In P. Ornstein (Ed.), *The Search for the Self* (pp.427-460). New York: International Universities Press.

Kranzler, J.H., Whang, P.A., & Jensen, A.R. (1994). Task complexity and the speed and efficiency of elemental information processing: Another look at the nature of intellectual giftedness. *Contemporary Educational Psychology, 19*, 447-459.

Krishnan, B. (1972). Clinical psychology. In S.K. Mitra (Ed.), *A Survey of Research in Psychology* (pp. 1-55). Bombay: Popular Prakashan.

Krishnan, L. (1998). Child rearing: The Indian perspective. In A.K. Srivastava (Ed.), *Child Development: The Indian Perspective* (pp. 25-55). New Delhi: NCERT.

Kulkarni, S.S., & Kumar, K. (1987). Tests and measurement: A trend report. In M.B. Buch (Ed.), *Third Survey of Research in Education* (pp. 468-510). New Delhi: NCERT.

Kulkarni, S.S., & Puhan, B.N. (1988). Psychological assessment: Its present and future trends. In J. Pandey (Ed.), *Psychology in India: The State of the Art* (Vol.1, pp19-92). New Delhi: Sage.

Kumar, K. (1991). Research in tests and measurement: A trend report. In M.B. Buch (Ed.), *Fourth Survey of Research in Education 1983-1988* (Vol. 1, pp. 546-566). New Delhi: NCERT.

Kumar, K., & Mitra, S.K. (1979). Tests and measurements: A trend report. In M.B. Buch (Ed.), *Third Survey of Research in Education* (pp. 236-275). New Delhi: NCERT.

Kumari, D. (1998). *Intellectual Commitment and Educational Interest in Relation to Certain Cognitive and Non-cognitive Variables*. Unpublished doctoral dissertation, University of Jammu.

Laboratory of Comparative Human Cognition (1983). Culture and cognitive development. In P.H. Mussen (Series Ed.) & W. Kessen (Vol. Ed.), *Handbook of Child Psychology*, Vol. 1. *History, Theory and Methods* (pp. 295-356). New York: Wiley.

Lave, J., & Wenger, E. (1991). *Situated Learning: Legitimate Peripheral Participation*. Cambridge: Cambridge University Press.

Lillard, A. (1998). Ethnopsychologies: Cultural variations in theories of mind. *Psychological Bulletin, 123*, 3-32.

Livingston, D.W. (1995). For Whom the Bell Curve tolls. *Alberta Journal of Educational Research, 41*, 335-341.

Long, L., & Mehta, P.H. (1966). *The First Mental Measurement Handbook for India*. New Delhi: NCERT.

Lonner, W.J. (1990). An overview of cross-cultural testing and assessment. In R.W. Brislin (Ed.), *Applied Cross-Cultural Psychology* (pp. 56-76). Newbury Park: Sage Publications.

Lubinski, D., & Humphreys, L.G. (1997). Incorporating general intelligence into epidemology and the social sciences. *Intelligence, 24*, 159-202.

Luria, A.R. (1980). *Higher Cortical Functions in Man*. Yew York: Basic Books.

Lutz, C. (1985). Ethnopsychology compared to what? Explaining behavior and consciousness among the Ifaluk. In G.M. White & J. Kirkpatrick (Eds.), *Person, Self, and Experience: Exploring Pacific Ethonopsychologies* (pp. 35-79). Berkeley: University of California Press.

Lynn, R. (1982). IQ in Japan and the United States shows a growing disparity. *Nature, 297*, 222-223.

Lynn, R. (1997). Intelligence in Taiwan. *Personality and Individual Differences, 22*, 585-586.

Lynn, R., & Hampson, S. (1986). The rise of national intelligence: Evidence from Britain, Japan and USA. *Personality and Individual Differences, 7*, 23-32.

Lynn, R., & Hampson, S. (1987). Further evidence on the cognitive abilities of the Japanese: Data from the WPPSI. *International Journal of Behavioral Development, 10*, 23-36.

Lynn, R., & Shigehisa, T. (1991). Reaction time and intelligence: A comparison of Japanese and British children. *Journal of Biosocial Science, 23*, 409-416.

Lynn, R., & Song, M.J. (1992). General intelligence, visuo-spatial and verbal abilities in Korean children. *Journal of the Indian Academy of Applied Psychology, 18*, 1-3.

Lynn, R., Chan, J.W., & Eysenck, H.J. (1991). Reaction time and intelligence in Chinese and British children. *Perceptual and Motor Skills, 72*, 443-452.

Lynn, R., Cooper, C., & Topping, S. (1990). Reaction Time and Intelligence. *Current Psychology: Research and Reviews*, 9, 264-276.

Lynn, R., Hampson, S., & Bingham, R. (1987). Japanese, British and American adolescents compared for Spearman's g and for the verbal, numerical and visuo-spatial abilities. *Psychologia, 30*, 137-144.

Lynn, R., Pagliari, C., & Chan, J. (1988). Intelligence in Hong Kong measured for Spearman's g and the visospatial and verbal primaries. *Intelligence, 12*, 423-433.

Maciel, A.G., Heckhausen, J., & Baltes, P.B. (1994). A life-span perspective on the interface between personality and intelligence. In R.J. Sternberg & P. Ruzgis (Eds.), *Personality and Intelligence* (pp. 61-103). Cambridge: Cambridge University Press.

Maciel, A.G., Sowarka, D., Smith, J., & Baltes, P.B. (1992, July). *Essential Attributes of Wise People*. Poster presented at the 25th International Congress of Psychology, Brussels, Belgium.

Maciel, A.G., Staudinger, U.M., Smith, J., & Baltes, P.B. (1992, March). *Which factors contribute to wisdom-related knowledge*. Poster presented at the workshop *"Issues in Life-Span Development"*, Germany.

Madhav, B.N.M., & Misra, V. (Eds.) (1965). *Kathawat Kosh*. Patna: Bihar Rashtrabhasha Parishad.

Majumdar, V. (2000, February, 20). Nowhere children. *The Hindustan Times* (New Delhi), 17.

Mamdani, M. (1972). *The Myth of Population Control: Family, Caste and Class in an Indian Village*. New Delhi: Monthly Review Press.

Markus, H.R., & Kitayama, S. (1991). Culture and the self: Implications for cognition, emotion, and motivation. *Psychological Review, 98*, 224-253.

Marzolf, S. (1974). Common sayings and 16PF (Personality factor) traits. *Journal of Clinical Psychology, 30*, 202.

Masters, M.S., & Sanders, B. (1993). Is the gender difference in mental retardation disappearing? *Behavior Genetics, 23*, 337-341.

Mata Prasad, Dwivedi, C.M., Kumar, S., & Rastogi, S.N. (1988). Mental subnormality and social class. *Journal of Personality and Clinical Studies, 4*, 183-186.

Matarazzo, J.D. (1972). *Wechster's Measurement and Appraisal of Adult Intelligence*. Baltimore: Williams and Wilkins.

Mayer, J.D. (1995). A framework for the classification of personality components. *Journal of Personality, 63*, 819-877.

Mayer, J.D., Caruso, D.R., & Salovey, P. (1999). Emotional intelligence meets traditional standard for an intelligence. *Intelligence, 27*, 267-298.

Mayer, J.D., & Geher, G. (1996). Emotional intelligence and the identification of emotion. *Intelligence, 22*, 89-113.

Mayer, J.D., & Salovey, P. (1993). The intelligence of emotional intelligence. *Intelligence, 17*, 433-442.

Mayer, J.D., & Salovey, P. (1997). What is emotional intelligence? In P. Salovey & D. Sluyter (Eds.), *Emotional Development and Emotional Intelligence: Implications for Education* (pp. 3-31). New York: Basic Books.

Mayer, J.D., Salovey, P., & Caruso, D. (1997). *Emotional IQ Test* (CD ROM). Needham, MA: Virtual Knowledge.

Mayer, J.D., Salovey, P., & Caruso, D. (2000). Models of emotional intelligence. In R.J. Sternberg (Ed.), *Handbook of Intelligence* (pp. 396-420). Cambridge: Cambridge University Press.

Mehdi B. (1977). Creativity, intelligence and achievement: A correlational study. *Psychological Studies, 22*, 55-62.

Mehta, P. (1960). Intelligence and family size of secondary school pupils in Rajasthan. *Journal of Psychological Researches, 6*, 59-64.

Menon, S.B., & Ojha, J.M. (1987). Learning, motivation and personality. In M.B. Buch (Ed.), *Third Survey of Research in Education* (pp. 298-439). New Delhi: NCERT.

Menzel, E.W. (1956). *The Use of New Type Tests in India.* London: Oxford University Press.

Mieder, W. (1993). *Proverbs Are Never Out of Season*. New York: Oxford University Press.

Miller, J.G. (1996). A cultural psychology perspective on intelligence. In R.J. Sternberg & E.L. Grigorenko (Eds.), *Intelligence, Heredity, and Environment* (pp. 269-302). Cambridge: Cambridge University Press.

Miller, J.G., Bersoff, D.M., & Harwood, R.L. (1990). Perceptions of social responsibilities in India and the United States: Moral imperatives or personal decisions. *Journal of Personality and Social Psychology, 58*, 33-47.

Miller, P.J., & Goodnow, J.J.(1995). Cultural practices: Toward an integration of development and culture. In J.J. Goodnow, P.J. Miller, & E. Kessel (Eds.), *Cultural Practices as Contexts for Development* (Vol. 67, pp. 5-16). San Francisco: Jossy-Bass.

Misawa, G., Motegi, M., Fujita, K., & Hattori, K. (1984). A comparative study of intellectual abilities of Japanese and American children on the Columbia Mental Maturity Scale. *Personality and Individual Differences, 5*, 173-181.

Mischel, W. (1968). *Personality and Assessment.* New York: Wiley.

Mishra, P. (1991). *Decoding Competence and Speech-Related Cognitive Process: Developmental Changes.* Unpublished M.Phil. Dissertation, Utkal University.

Misra, G. (1983). Deprivation and development: A review of Indian studies. *Indian Educational Review, 18,* 12-32

Misra, G. (1990). Psychology of deprivation. In G. Misra (Ed.), *Applied Social Psychology in India* (pp. 119-140). New Delhi: Concept.

Misra, G. (1994). Psychology of control: Cross-cultural considerations. *Journal of Indian Psychology,* 12, 8-45.

Misra, G. (1999). Toward an indigenous psychology of cognition: Knowing in the Indian tradition. *Journal of Indian Psychology, 17,* 1-22.

Misra, G., & Mohanty, A.K. (2000). Poverty and disadvantage: Issues in retrospect. In A.K. Mohanty & G. Misra (Eds.), *Psychology of Poverty and Disadvanatage* (pp. 261-284).New Delhi: Concept.

Misra, G. & Srivastava, A.K. (2002). *Towards Integral Intelligence.* In P. Boski, F.J.R. van de Vijver, & A.M. Chodynicka (Eds.), *New Directions in Cross-Cultural Psychology* (pp. 193-208).

Misra, G., & Tripathi, K.N. (1998). Cognitive development. In A.K. Srivastava (Ed.), *Child Development: The Indian Perspective* (pp. 75-111). New Delhi: National Council of Educational Research and Training.

Misra, G., Sahoo, F.M., & Puhan, B.N. (1997). Cultural bias in testing: India. *European Review of Applied Psychology, 47,* 309-316.

Mishra, R.C. (1997). Cognitive processes. *In Fifth survey of Educational Research 1988_92: Trend Reports* Vol. 1 (pp. 128-146). New Delhi: National Council of Educational Research and Training.

Mitra, S.K. (1968). Review of tests and measurement. In S.B. Adaval (Ed.), *The Third Indian Yearbook of Education.* New Delhi: NCERT.

Mitra, S.K. (Ed.) (1972). Psychological research in India. In S.K. Mitra (Ed.), *A Survey of Research in Psychology* (pp. XVII-XXXIII). Bombay: Popular Prakashan.

Mitra, S.K., & Kumar, K. (1974). Tests and measurement: A trend report. In M.B. Buch (Ed.), *A Survey of Research in Education* (pp. 212-263). Baroda: The M.S. University.

Moffitt, T.E., Gabrielli, W.F., Mednick, S.A., & Schulsinger, F. (1981). Socio-economic status, IQ, and delinquency. *Journal of Abnormal Psychology, 90,* 152-156.

Mohanty, A.K., & Puhan, B.N. (1980). Strategy in cross-cultural testing and personnel selection in developing countries. *ISPT Journal of Research, 90,* 152-156.

Mohanty, B. (1980). Effects of socio-cultural disadvantage on intelligence and short term memory. *Indian Psychological Review, 19,* 17-24.

Moniar-Williams, M. (1964). *A Dictionary: English and Sanskrit.* Delhi: Motilal Banarasidas.

Moscovici, S. (1984). The phenomenon of social representations. In R.M. Farr & S. Moscovici (Eds.), *Social Representations.* Cambridge: Cambridge University Press.

Moulik, T.K. (1980). Psychology of Poverty in India. In U. Pareek (Ed.), *A Survey of Research in Psychology, 1971-1978* (Vol. 2, pp. 655-681). Bombay: Popular Prakashan.

Muddu, V. (1980). *A Study of Some Personality Correlates of Intelligence and Creative Abilities Among High School Students in Andhra Pradesh.* Unpublished doctoral dissertation, Osmania University.

Mukherjee, B.N. (1980). Psychological theory and research methods. In U. Pareek (Ed.), *A Survey of Research in Psychology, 1971-76* (Vol. 1, pp. 1-35).

Mukherjee, B.N. (1993). Needed research in psycho-educational assessment in India. *Psychological Studies, 38,* 85-100.

Mukherjee, B.N. (1997). Educational assessment and evaluation. *In Fifth Survey of Educational Research, 1988-92: Trend Reports* Vol. 1. New Delhi: NCERT.

Mukherjee, M., Chatterjee, S., & Gupta, R. (1992). Effects of prolonged deprivation upon intelligence level of school going adolescents. *Journal of Psychometry, 5,* 1-9.

Mulia, R.D. (1991). A comparative study of social maturity of higher secondary school students in the context of their streams, sex, and DIQs. *Journal of Education and Psychology, 48,* 145-155.

Mundy-Castle, A.C. (1974). Social and technological intelligence in western and non-western cultures. *Universitas, 4,* 46-52.

Muralidharan, R. (1974). Home stimulation and child development. *Indian Educational Review, 5,* 43-51.

Muralidharan, R. (1991). Introduction. In M.C. Jain (Ed.), *Indian Mental Measurement Handbook: Intelligence and Aptitude Tests.* New Delhi: NCERT.

Muralidharan, R., & Srivastava, A.K. (1995). Temple ecology and cognitive development: A report from south India. *Psychology and Developing Societies, 7,* 47-64.

Murthy, C.V., & Panda, S.C. (1987). A study of intelligence, SES and birth order among children belonging to SC, ST and non SC, ST groups. *Indian Journal of Behaviour, 11,* 25-30.

Murthy, H.N. (1966). Relation of intelligence and emotional stability. *Journal of Education and Psychology, 23,* 243-247.

Naglieri, J.A., & Bardos, A.N. (1983). Canadian children's performance on the Matrix Analogies Test. *School Psychology International, 9,* 309-313.

Nathawat, S.S. (1974). The intellectual and temperamental performance of delinquent boys on the Bhatia battery and Porteus mazes. *Journal of Clinical Psychiatry, 2,* 99-105.

Nayar, P.R. (1997). Psychology of education. In *Fifth Survey of Educational Research 1988-92: Trend Reports* Vol. I (pp. 76-105). New Delhi: NCERT.

National Council of Educational Research and Training (1997). *Fifth Survey of Educational Research 1988-92: Trend Reports* Vol. I. New Delhi: NECRT.

Neisser, U. (1976). General. Academic, and artificial intelligence. In L. Resnick (Ed.), *Human Intelligence: Perspectives on Its Theory and Measurement* (pp. 179-190). Norwood, NJ: Ablex.

Neisser, U. (1979). The concept of intelligence. In R.J. Sternberg & D.K. Detterman (Eds.), *Human Intelligence Perspectives in its Theory and Measurement* (pp. 179-190). Norwood, NJ: Ablex.

Neisser, U., Boodoo, G., Bouchard, T.J., Jr., Boykin, A.W., Brody, N., Ceci, S.J., Halpern, D.F., Loehlin, J.C., Perloff, R., Sternberg, R.J., & Urbina, S. (1996). Intelligence: Knowns and unknowns. *American Psychologist, 51*, 77-101.

Nigam, V., & Sharma, R. (2001). Cognitive development in children in relation to socioeconomic status. *Psycho Lingua, 31*, 69-72.

Nippold, M.A., Martin, S.A., & Erskinne, B.J. (1988). Proverb comprehension in context: A developmental study with children and adolescents. *Journal of Speech and Hearing Research, 31*, 19-28.

Nisbett, R. (2003). *The geography of thought.* New York: Free Press.

Northrop, F.S.C. (1947). *The Meeting of East and West.* New York: Macmillan.

Ochs, E. (1988). *Culture and Language Development: Language Acquisition and Language Specialization in a Samoon Village.* Cambridge: Cambridge University Press.

Ogbu, J.U. (1986). Castelike stratification as a risk factor for mental retardation in the United States. In D.C. Farram & J.D. McKinney (Eds.), *Risk in Intellectual and Psychological Development* (pp. 83-120). London: Academic Press.

Padaki, V., & Vyasulu, V. (1980). Towards environmental psychology. In U. Pareek (Ed.), *A Survey of Research in Psychology 1971-76* (Vol. II, pp. 618-654). Bombay: Popular Prakashan.

Padma, M.S. (1991). Research in correlates of achievement: A trend report. In M.B. Buch (Ed.), *Fourth survey of research in education* (pp. 807-870). New Delhi: NCERT.

Padmavati, K.R., Devdas, R.P., & Indira, B. (1968). Nutritional status and mental ability of 5 to 7 years old children. *Adolescents from Home Science Research Series* (Avinashlingam Science College), 7, 18.

Pal, S.K., & Misra, K.S. (1992). A study of cognitive processes, academic motivation, social behaviour patterns and moral judgements of adolescents from deprived ecologies. *Researcher and Studies, 43*, 1-7.

Panda, K.C. (1991). Research in psychology of education: A trend report. In M.B. Buch (Ed.), *Fourth Survey of Research in Education 1983-88* (Vol. I, pp. 309-465).

Panda, K.C. (1997). Social process. In *Fifth Survey of Educational Research 1988-92: Trend Report* Vol. I (pp. 147-165). New Delhi: NCERT.

Panda, S. (1991). *Effect of Certain Organismic Variables on Cognitive Style Among Preschool Children and an Analysis of Its Correlates.* Unpublished doctoral dissertation, Utkal University.

Pandey, J. (Ed.). (1988). *Psychology in India: The state-of-the-art* (3 Vols.). New Delhi: Sage.

Parameswaran, E.G. (1972). Developmental psychology. In S.K. Mitra (Ed.), *A Survey of Research in Psychology* (pp. 56-79). Bombay: Popular Prakashan.

Pardue, P.A. (1968). *Buddhism*. New York: Macmillan.

Pareek, U. (Ed.) (1980). *A Survey of Research in Psychology*, 1971-1976 (2 vols). Bombay: Popualar Prakashan.

Passi, B.K. (1997). Creativity and innovations. In *Fifth Survey of Educational Research 1988-1992: Trend Reports* Vol. I (pp. 170-215). New Delhi: NCERT.

Patel, B.V. (1983). *Construction and Standardization of Silent Reading Comprehension Tests in Gujarati for Pupils of Classes IV, VI, and VII.* Unpublished manuscript, Sardar Patel University.

Patel, C.B., & Kapadia, S.T. (1985). A study of anxiety among the school-going children. *Asian Journal of Psychology and Education, 16*, 1-12.

Pathak, M.P., Saxena, N.K., & Mishra, L.S. (1983). Some psychological factors associated with mental retardation. *Child Psychiatry Quarterly, 16*, 116-122.

Pathak, P. (1962). Exploratory study of creativity and intelligence and scholastic achievement. *Psychological Studies, 7*, 1-9.

Patil, I. (1982). *A Psychological Study of Intellectually Superior*. Unpublished doctoral dissertation, Karnataka University.

Pea, R.D. (1993). Practices of distributed intelligence and designs for education. In G. Solomon (Ed.), *Distributed Cognitions* (pp. 47-87). New York: Cambridge University Press.

Peng, K. & Nisbett, R.E. (1999). Culture, dialectics, and reasoning about contradiction. *American Psychologist, 54*, 741-754.

Pestonjee, D.M. (1997). *Handbook of Psychological and Social Instruments*, New Delhi: Concept.

Pestonjee, D.M. (1997) *Third Handbook of Psychological and Social Instruments.*

Phatak, P. (1970). *Mental and Motor Growth of Indian Babies (1 Month-30 months), Longitudinal Growth of Indian Children*. Baroda: M.S. University.

Piaget, J. (1969). *Language and Thought in Child*. New York: Basic Books.

Piaget, J. (1972). *The Psychology of Intelligence*. Totowa, NJ: Littlefield Adams.

Poole, F.J.P. (1985). Coming into social being: Cultural images of infants in Bimin-Kuskusmin folk psychology. In G.M. White & J. Kirkpatrick (Eds.), *Person, Self, and Experience: Exploring Pacific Ethnopsychologies* (pp. 183-244). Berkeley: University of California Press.

Porter, N. (1891). *The Human Intellect with an Introduction upon Psychology and the Soul*. New York: Charles Scribner's Sons.

Prabhu, G.G. (1972). Deviance and pathology. In U. Pareek (Ed.), *A Survey of Research in Psychology 1971-1976* (Vol. I, pp. 207-232). Bombay: Popular Prakashan.

Puhan, B.N. (1982). *Issues in Psychological Measurement*. Agra: National Psychological Corporation.

Putnam, D.B., & Kilbride, P.L. (1980). *A relativistic understanding of social intelligence among the Sanghay of Mali and Samia of Kenya*. Paper presented at the meeting of the Society for Cross-Cultural Research, Philadelphia.

Puttabuddi, R.C. (1983). *A comparative study of general intelligence of IX and X grade students of Karnataka as measured by Cattell's Culture Fair test of intelligence scale-3 in relation to their sub-culture, socio-economic status, and caste affiliation*. Unpublished doctoral dissertation, Gujrat University.

Quetelet, A. (1842). *A Treatise on Man and the Development of his Faculties*. Edinburg: William and Robert Chambers.

Rai, R.N., & Pandey, R.C. (1994). Intellectual ability in rejected and non-rejected Mizo students. *Disabilities and Impairments, 8*, 94-97.

Raina, M.K., & Srivastava, A.K. (2000). India's search for excellence: A clash of ancient, colonial, and contemporary influences. *Roeper Review, 22*, 102-108.

Raj, H.S.S. (1978). *The Overlap of Creativity with Certain Cognitive and Affective Variables*. Unpublished doctoral dissertation, University of Kerala.

Ramanujan, A.K. (1990). Is there an Indian way of thinking? An informal essay. In M. Marriott (Ed.), *India through Hindu Categories* (pp. 41-58). New Delhi: Sage.

Rangari, A. (1987). Caste affiliation, sex, area of residence and SES as a source of variation in intelligence of students. *Indian Psychological Review, 32*, 43-47.

Rangari, A., & Palsane, M.N. (1982). Relative intelligence of schedule and non-schedule caste students. *Bombay Psychologist, 34*, 112-119.

Rao, S.N. (1971). A prognostic study of achievement in relation to academic adjustment. *Indian Educational Review, 6*, 196-213.

Rao, N. (1978). *A study of socio-psychological correlates of social development of high school children in grades VIII, IX, and X in some high schools of Bangalore city*. Unpublished doctoral dissertation, Bangalore University.

Rao, T.V. (1980). Psychology of work: Individual in organization. In U. Pareek (Ed.), *A Survey of Research in Psychology 1971-1976* (Vol. 2 pp. 476-576). Bombay: Popular Prakashan.

Rao, T.V., Mehta, P., & Rao, M.L. (1979). Personality, learning and motivation: A trend report. In M.B. Buch (Ed.), *Second Survey of Research in Education* (pp. 163-208). Baroda: Centre for Educational Research and Development.

Rastogi, K.G. (1974).Intelligence, achievement, and value system of students in different professional courses. *Teacher Education, 9*, 29-36.

Rath, R. (1972). Social psychology: A trend report. In S.K. Mitra (Ed.), *First Survey of Research in Psychology* (pp. 362-413). Bombay: Popular Prakashan.

Rath, R. (1974). *Teaching and Learning Problems of the Disadvantaged Tribal Children.* Presidential address, 12th Annual Conference of the Indian Academy of Applied Psychology, Utkal University, Bhubaneswar.

Rath, R., Dash, A.S., & Dash, U.N. (1979). *Cognitive Abilities and School Achievement of the Socially Disadvantaged Children in Primary Schools.* Bombay: Allied Publishers.

Reed, T.E., & Jensen, A.R. (1992). Conduction velocity in a brain nerve pathway of normal adults correlates with intelligence level. *Intelligence, 16,* 259-272.

Rehberg, R.A., & Rosenthal, E.R. (1978). *Class and Merit in the American High School.* New York: Longman.

Rogers, T. (1990). Proverbs as psychological theories...or is it the other way around? *Canadian Psychology, 31,* 195-207.

Rogoff, B., & Chavajay, P. (1995). What's become of research on the cultural basis of cognitive development? *American Psychologist, 50,* 859-877.

Roid, G. H. (2003). *Stanford-Binet Intelligence Scales, Fifth Edition.* Itasca, IL: Riverside.

Roid, G. H. & Pomplum, M. (2005). Interpreting the Stanford-Binet Intelligence Scales, Fifth Edition. In D. P. Flanagan & P. L. Harrisson (Eds.), *Contemporary Intellectual Assessment: Theories, Tests, and Issues* (pp. 325-343). New York : The Guilford Press.

Rushton, J.P. (1997). Cranial size and IQ in Asian Americans from birth to age seven. *Intelligence, 25,* 7-20.

Ruzgis, P., & Grigorenko, E.L. (1994). Cultural meaning systems, intelligence and personality. In R.J. Sternberg & P. Ruzgis (Eds.), *Personality and Intelligence* (pp. 248-270). Cambridge: Cambridge University Press.

Sagar, L. (Ed.), (1990). *Vishwa Sanskrit Sukti Kosh* (3 Vols.). Jodhpur: Ramanand Garg & Co.

Sahu, S. & Devi, G. (1984). Reading ability and information processing strategies. *Journal of Reading Research, 7,* 33-40.

Salovey, P., Mayer, J.D. (1990). Emotional intelligence. *Imagination, Cognition, and Personality, 9,* 185-211.

Sangwan, S. (2001). Ecological factors as related to IQ of the children. *Psycho Lingua, 31,* 89-92.

Saraswathi, T.S., & Dutta, R. (1988). Current trends in developmental psychology: A life-span perspective. In J. Pandey (Ed.), *Psychology in India: The State-of-the-art* (Vol. I, pp. 93-152). New Delhi: Sage.

Sarbin, T., Taft, R., & Bailey, D. (1960). *Clinical Inference and Cognitive Theory.* New York: Holt, Rinehart & Winston.

Sansanwal, D.N., & Sharma, D. (1993). Scientific creativity as a function of intelligence, self-confidence, sex, and standard. *Indian Journal of Psychometry and Education, 24*, 37-44.

Scheibel, A. (1996). *Introduction to Symposium on the Evolution of Intelligence.* Centre for the study of Evolution and the Origin of Life, University of California, Los Angeles.

Schiele, J.H. (1991). An epistemological perspective on intelligence assessment among African-American children. *Journal of Black Psychology, 17*, 23-36.

Schooler, C. (1998). Environmental complexity and the Flynn Effect. In U. Neisser (Ed.), *The Rising Curve: Long Term Gains in IQ and Related Measures* (pp.67-79). Washington, DC: American Psychological Association.

Sengupta, M. (1979). *Intellective and Non-intellective Factors Associated with Engineering Creativity*. Unpublished Doctoral Dissertation, Meerut University.

Serpell, R. (1974). Aspects of intelligence in a developing country. *African Social Research, 17*, 578-598.

Serpell, R. (1977). Strategies for investigating in its cultural context. *The Quarterly Newsletter of the Institute of Comparative Human Development, 1*, 11-15.

Serpell, R. (1979). How specific are perceptual skills? A cross-cultural study of pattern reproduction. *British Journal of Psychology, 70*, 365-380.

Serpell, R. (1982). Measures of perception, skills, and intelligence. In W.W. Hartup (Ed.), *Review of Child Development Research*: Vol. 6 (pp. 392-440). Chicago: University of Chicago Press.

Shanbhag, V. (1988). Effect of nutrition on development of intelligence with special reference to Ayurveda. In G.S. Koshe, U. Khire, B. Kulkarni, & c. Damle (Eds.), *National Seminar on IQ Controversy: Proceedings* (pp. 316-323). Pune: Jnana Prabodhini's Institute of Psychology.

Shanwal, V.K. (2002). *A Study of Correlates and Nurturance of Emotional Intelligence in Primary School Children*. Unpublished doctoral dissertation, Jamia Millia Islamia, (Education Department.), New Delhi.

Sharma, K. (1981). *Some Socio-Economic Characteristics and Intellectual Abilities of High School Students*. Unpublished doctoral dissertation, Magadh University.

Sharma, R., & Bansal, I. (1991-92). A study of academic achievement and intelligence of extrovert and introvert adolescent girls. *Indian Psychological Review, 37*, 11-14.

Sharma, S. (1990). *Effect of Socio-Cultural Disadvantage on Cognitive and Non-cognitive Variables: A Study of Secondary High School Students of Haryana*. Unpublished doctoral dissertation, Kurukshetra University.

Sharma, S.R. (1983). *Vargikrit Hindi Lokokti Kosh*. New Delhi: Takshashila Prakashan.

Sharma, E., & Jaswal, S. (1999). Personality as a determinant of academic stress among adolescents. *Indian Journal of Psychological Issues, 7*, 16-23.

Shukla, H.L., & Sharma, R.N. (1986). *Hindi Lokokti Kosh*. Delhi: Rajesh Prakashan.

Shukla, S.N. (1991). *Learning and Memory Among Socially Deprived Groups: A Developmental Study*. Unpublished doctoral dissertation, Avadh University, Faizabad.

Shweder, R.A. (1990). Cultural psychology – what is it? In J.W. Stigler, R.A. Shweder. & G. Herdt (Eds.), *Cultural Psychology: Essays on Comparative Human Development* (pp. 1-43). New York: Cambridge University Press.

Shweder, R.A., & Bourne, E. (1982). Does the concept of the person vary cross-culturally? In A.J. Marshella & G. White (Eds.), *Cultural Conception of Mental Health and Therapy* (pp. 97-137). Boston: Reidel.

Shweder, R.A., Goodnow. J., Levine, R.A., Hatano, G., Markus, H., & Miller, P. (1997). The cultural psychology of development: One mind, many mentalities. In W. Damon (Ed.), *Handbook of Child Psychology* (pp. 865-893). New York: John Wiley.

Sibia, A., Misra, G., & Srivastava, A.K. G. (2004). Towards understanding emotional intelligence in the Indian Context: Perspectives of Parents, teachers and children. *Psychological Studies*, **49**, 114-123.

Sibia, A., Srivastava, A.K., & Misra, G. (2003). The notion of emotional intelligence: Western and Indian perspectives. *Indian Psychological Abstracts and Reviews*.

Sibia, A., Srivastava, A.K., & Misra, G. (2005). *Identification and Nurturance of Emotional Intelligence in Primary School Children : An Exploration*. New Delhi: NCERT.

Sigel, *I.E.* (Ed.) (1995). *Parental Belief Systems*. Hillsdale, NJ: Erlbaum.

Singh, A.K. (2000). Are the poor less intelligent? Or, much ado about nothing. IN A.K. Mohanty & G. Misra (Eds.), *Psychology of Poverty and Disadvantage* (pp. 157-167). New Delhi: Concept.

Singh, O.P. (2001). Developmental quality analysis of the whole response (W) among the Rorschach protocols of institutionalized children. *Journal of Personality and Clinical Studies, 17*, 45-49.

Singh, L.B., & Sinha, B. (1983). The Santal students: Their intelligence and achievement motivation. *Indian Journal of Social Work, 44*, 167-173.

Singh, R. (2001). *Learning Style of High School Students as Related to Some Learner's Characteristics*. Unpublished doctoral dissertation, Kurukshetra University.

Singh, T., & Dwivedi, C.B. (1993). Deprivation, context, and processing of textual materials. *Journal of Genetic Psychology, 154*, 73-83.

Singh, Y., Bhargava, M., & Kumar, B. (1981). The value of children. *Indian Psychological Review, 20*, 47-54.

Singh, T., Siddiqui, A., & Srivastava, A.K. (1995). An exploration of children's conception of intelligence. *Journal of Indian Psychology, 13*, 47-55.

Smirnov, S.D. (1994). Intelligence and personality in the psychological theory of activity. In R.J. Sternberg & P. Ruzgis (Eds.), *Personality and Intelligence* (pp. 221-247). Cambridge: Cambridge University Press.

Sinha, D. (1970). *Academic Achievers and Non-achievers*. Allahabad: United Publishers.

Sinha, D. (1977). Some social disadvantages and development of certain perceptual skills. *Indian Journal of Psychology, 52*, 115-132.

Sinha, D. (1980). Some cognitive and motivational concomitants of poverty. *Social Change, 10*, 3-8.

Sinha, D. (1983). Human assessment in the Indian context. In S.H. Irvine & J.W. Berry (Eds.), *Human assessment and cultural factors* (pp. 17-34). New York: Plenum Press.

Sinha, D., & Shukla, P. (1974). Deprivation and development of skill for pictorial depth perception. *Journal of Cross-Cultural Psychology*, 434-450.

Sinha, D., Tripathi, R.C., & Misra, G. (1988). *Deprivation: Its Social Roots and Psychological Consequences*. New Delhi: Concept.

Sinha, J.B.P., & Kanungo, R.N. (1997). Context sensitivity and balancing in Indian organizational behaviour. *International Journal of Psychology, 32*, 93-105.

Sivandam, C. (1974). A comparative study of intelligence of normal delinquent and criminal female subjects. *Indian Journal of Criminology, 2*, 52-55.

Spearman, C. (1927). *The Abilities of Man*. New York: Macmillan.

Springer, S.P., & Deutsch, G. (1985). *Left Brain, Right Brain*. New York: Freeman.

Srikantaiah, S.C., & Sastry, C.Y. (1969). *Observations on Malnutrition and Mental Development*. Abstracts of paper, Nutrition Society of India.

Srivastava, A. K. (1995). Extent of acculturation of the Indian society. *Social Change*, 25, 121-131.

Srivastava, A.K. (1997). The changing place of child in Indian families: A cross-generational study. *Trends in Social Science Research, 4*, 191-200.

Srivastava, A.K., & Misra, G. (1996). Changing perspectives on understanding intelligence: An appraisal. *Indian Psychological Abstracts and Reviews, 3*, 3-34.

Srivastava, A.K., & Misra, G. (1999a). An Indian perspective on understanding intelligence. In W.J. Lonner, D.L. Dinnel, D.K. Forgays, & S.A. Hayes (Eds.), *Merging past, present, and future: Selected proceedings of the 14th international congress of the international association for cross-cultural psychology* (pp. 159-172). Lisse, The Netherlands: Swets and Zeitlinger.

Srivastava, A.K., & Misra, G. (1999b). Social representation of intelligence in the Indian folk tradition: An analysis of Hindi proverbs. *Journal of Indian Psychology, 17*, 23-38.

Srivastava, A.K., & Misra, G. (1999 c). What it means to be an intelligent person? Views of the lay people. *Indian Psychological Review, 52*, 123-133.

Srivastava, A.K., & Misra, G. (2000). *Culture and Conceptualization of Intelligence*. New Delhi : NCERT.

Srivastava, A.K., & Misra, G. (2001). Lay People's understanding and use of intelligence: An Indian perspective. *Psychology and Developing Societies*, 13, 25-49.

Srivastava, A.K., Sibia, A. & Misra, G. (in press). Research on emotional intelligence: The Indian experience. In R. Emmerling, V.K. Shanwal, & M.K. Mandal (Eds.), *Emotional intelligence: Theoritical and Cultural Perspectives*. New York : Nova Science Publishing.

Srivastava, A.K., Tripathi, A.M., & Misra, G. (1995). Western and Indian perspectives on intelligence: Some reflections. *Indian Educational Review, 30*, 30-45.

Srivastava, A.K., Tripathi, A.M., & Misra, G. (1996). The status of intelligence testing in India: A preliminary analysis. *Indian Educational Review, 31*, 1-11.

Stanley, J.C., Benbow, C.P., Brody, L.E., Dauber, S., & Lupkowski, A. (1992). Gender differences on eighty-six nationally standardized aptitude and achievement tests. In N. Colangelo, S.G. Aussoline, & D.L. Ambroson (Eds.), *Talent Development*. NY: Trillium Press.

Stern, W. (1912). *Die psychologischen methoden der intelligenzpsufung*. Leipzig: Barth.

Sternberg, R.J. (1977). *Intelligence, information processing and analogical reasoning: The componential analysis of human abilities*. Hillsdale, NJ: Erlbaum.

Sternberg, R.J. (1982). Who's intelligent? *Psychology Today, 4*, 30-39.

Sternberg, R.J. (1985). *A Triarchic Theory of Human Intelligence*. New York: Cambridge University Press.

Sternberg, R.J. (1988). *The Triarchic Mind: A New Theory of Human Intelligence*. New York: Viking Press.

Sternberg, R.J. (1990a). *Metaphors of Mind: Conceptions of the Nature of Intelligence*. New York: Cambridge University Press.

Sternberg, R.J. (1990b). *Wisdom: Its Nature, Origins and Development*. Cambridge: Cambridge University Press.

Sternberg, R.J. (1993). *Sternberg Triarchic Abilities Test*. Unpublished test.

Sternberg, R.J. (1997). The concept of intelligence and its role in life long learning and success. *American Psychologist, 52*, 1030-1037.

Sternberg, R.J. (1999). A triarchic approach to the understanding and assessment of intelligence in multicultural population. *Journal of School Psychology, 37*, 145-159.

Sternberg, R.J. (2003). "My house is a very very very fine house"—but it is not the only house. in H. Nyborg (Ed.), *The Scientific Study of General Intelligence* (pp. 373-395). Elsevier Science.

Sternberg, R.J. (2004). Culture and intelligence. *American Psychologist*, 59, 325-338.

Sternberg, R.J., Conway, B.E., Ketron, J.L., & Bernstein, M. (1981). People's conceptions of intelligence. *Journal of Personality and Social Psychology, 41*, 37-55.

Sternberg, R.J., Dennis, M., & Beatty, P. (1996). *Cognitive Assessment Survey*. Unpublished test.

Sternberg, R. J., & Grigorenko, E. L. (2005). Intelligence and culture: How culture shapes what intelligence means, and the implications for a science of well-being. In F. A. Huppert, N. Baylis, & B. Keverne (Eds.), *The science of well-being* (pp. 361-378). New York: Oxford University Press.

Sternberg, R.J., Torff, B., & Grigorenko, E.L. (1998). Teaching triarchically improves school achievement. *Journal of Educational Psychology, 90*, 374-384.

Sternberg, R.J., & Wagner, R.K. (Eds.) (1986). *Practical Intelligence: Nature and Origins of Competence in the Everyday World*. New York: Cambridge University Press.

Sternberg, R.J., Wagner, R.K., Williams, W.M., & Horvath, J.A. (1995). Testing common sense. *American Psychologist, 50*, 912-927.

Stout, G.F., & Baldwin, J.M. (1901). Intellect (or intelligence). In J.M. Baldwin (Ed.), *Dictionary of Philosophy and Psychology* (Vol. I). New York: Macmillan.

Sudhir, M.A., & Muraleedharan-Pillai, P.G. (1987). Science achievement in relation to intelligence and socio-economic status: A study of secondary school students in Aizawl. *Indian Journal of Psychometry and Education, 18*, 37-44.

Super, C.M., & Harkness, S. (1983). *Looking Across at Growing Up: The Cultural Expression of Cognitive Development in Middle Childhood*. Unpublished manuscript, Harvard University.

Takahasi, M., & Bordia, P. (2000). The concept of wisdom: A cross-cultural comparison. *International Journal of Psychology, 35*, 1-9.

Tewari, P.S.N., & Srivastava, S. (1998). *Study of Environmental Needs, Family Atmosphere and Competence among Children*. National Seminar on Environment and Cognition, DDU Gorakhpur University, 24-25 April.

Tharp, R.G., & Gallimore, R. (1988). *Rousing Minds to Life*. Cambridge: Cambridge University Press (*http://www.ncrel.org/sdrs/areas/issues/students/learning/lr l zpd.htm*).

Thompson, G.H. (1939). *The Factorial Analysis of Human Ability*. London: University of London Press.

Tikhomirov, D.K., & Znakov, V.V. (1989). Current problems in the psychology of understanding and the creation of "understanding systems". *Soviet Psychology, 27*, 70-85.

Thorndike, E.L., Bregman, E.D., Cobb, M.V., & Woodyard, E.I. (1926). *The Measurement of Intelligence*. New York: Teachers College.

Thurstone, L.L. (1938). *Primary Mental Abilities*. Chicago: University of Chicago Press.

Tripathi, L.B., & Misra, G. (1974). Cognitive activities as a function of prolonged deprivation. *Psychological Studies, 20*, 54-61.

Tripathi, N.M. (1991). *Family experiences and cultural background as factors in the development of pattern reproduction skill.* Unpublished doctoral dissertation, Banaras Hindu University, Varanasi.

Tripathi, R.C. (1988). Applied social psychology. In J. Pandey (Ed.), *Psychology in India: The state-of-the-art* (Vol. II, pp.95-158). New Delhi: Sage.

Trueba, H.T. (1988). Comments on L.M. Dunn's Bilingual Hispanic Children on the U.S. mainland: A review of research on their cognitive, linguistic and scholastic development. *Hispanic Journal of Behavioral Sciences, 10*, 253-262.

Tyagi, M. (1999). Altruism as a function of sex and intelligence. *Praachi Journal of Psycho-Cultural Dimensions, 15*, 95-98.

Valsiner, J. (1989). *Human Development and Culture: The Social Nature of Personality and its Study.* Massachusetts: Lexington Books.

Valsiner, J. (1994). *Comparative-Cultural and Constructivist Perspectives.* Norwood, NJ: Ablex.

Van Lancker, D.R. (1990). The neurology of proverbs. *Behavioral Neurology, 3*, 169-187.

Vaughan, F. (2002). What is spiritual intelligence? *Journal of Humanistic Psychology, 42*, 16-33.

Verma, S.B., & Verma, M. (Ed.), (1985). *Vishwa Sukti Kosh* (3 Vols.). Delhi: Prabhat Prakashan.

Vernon, P.A. (1971). *The Structure of Human Abilities.* London: Methuen.

Vernon, P.A. (1987). *Speed of Information Processing and Intelligence.* Norwood, NJ: Ablex.

Vernon, P.A. (1993). *Biological Approaches to the Study of Human Intelligence.* Norwood, NJ: Ablex.

Vidhu, M. (1968).*The relationship of neuroticism and extraversion to intelligence and educational achievement of different age levels.* Unpublished doctoral dissertation, Punjab University.

Vygotsky, L.S. (1976). *Mind in Society: The Development of Higher Psychological Processes.* Cambridge, MA: Harvard University Press.

Wechsler, D. (1958). *The Measurement and Appraisal of Adult Intelligence.* Baltimore: Williams & Wilkins.

Wechsler, D. (1974). *Manual for the Wechsler Intelligence Scale for Children* (Rev.). New York: Psychological Corporation.

Weiner, M. (1990). *The Child and the State in India: Child Labour and Education Policy in Comparative Perspective.* Princeton, New Jersey: Princeton University Press.

Werner, G.E., & Muralidharan, R. (1970). Nutrition, cognitive status, and achievement motivation of New Delhi nursery school children. *Journal of Cross-Cultural Psychology, 1*, 271-281.

Wertsch, J.V. (1991). *Voices of the Mind.* Cambridge: Harvard University Press.

Wertsch, J.V., Rio, P.D., & Alvarez, A. (1995). Sociocultural studies: History, action and mediation. In J.V. Wertsch, P.D. Rio, & A. Alvarez (Eds.), *Sociocultural Studies of Mind* (pp.1-34). Cambridge: Cambridge University Press.

White, G.M. (1985). Premises and purposes in a Solomon Islands ethnopsychology. In G.M. White & J. Kirkpatrick (Eds.), *Person, Self, and Experience: Exploring Pacific Ethnopsychologies* (pp. 328-366). Berkeley: University of California Press.

White, K.R. (1982). The relation between socio-economic status and academic achievement. *Psychological Bulletin, 91,* 461-481.

Whiteman, M., & Deutsch, M. (1968). Social disadvantage as related to intellectual and language development. In M. Deutsch, I. Katz, & A.R. Jensen (Eds.), *Social Class, Race and Psychological Development* (pp. 86-114). New York: Holt, Rinehart & Winston.

Wober, M. (1974). Towards an understanding of the Kinganda concept of intelligence. In J.W. Berry & P.R. Dasen (Eds.), *Culture and Cognition* (pp. 261-280). London: Methuen.

Wober, M. (1975). *Psychology in Africa.* London: International African Institute.

Yairi, E., & Ambrose, N. (1992). Onset of stuttering in preschool children: Selected factors. *Journal of Speech and Hearing Research, 35,* 782-788.

Yang, S., & Sternberg, R.J. (1997). Conception of intelligence in ancient Chinese philosophy. *Journal of Theoretical and Philosophical Psychology, 17,* 101-119.

Yussen, S.R., & Kane, P.T. (1983). Children's idea about intellectual ability. In R. Leahy (Ed.), *The Child's Construction of Social Inequality* (pp. 109-133). New York: Academic Press.

Zohar, D., & Marshall, I. (2001). *Spiritual Intelligence: The Ultimate Intelligence.*

Zhu, J., & Weiss, L. (2005). The Wechsler scales. In D. P. Flanagan & P. L. Harrison (Eds.), *Contemporary intellectual assessment : Theories, tests, and issues* (pp. 297-324). New York : The Guilford Press.

Index

Author Index